The EXTREME SEARCHER'S
Internet Handbook
4th Edition

Raves for *The Extreme Searcher's Internet Handbook*

"A treasure trove of tips and tricks for finding information online. ... Despite being aimed at serious searchers, this is an excellent book for people of any skill level."

—Chris Sherman, SearchDay

"A phenomenal resource for both extreme and not-so-extreme researchers. Great tips, clear explanations, and years of expertise distilled into 250 pages of clear, engaging text. This book should be on every searcher's desk."

—Mary Ellen Bates, author,
Building & Running a Successful Research Business,
and co-author, *Researching Online for Dummies*

"A highly useful guide for librarians, teachers, researchers, students, and anyone else wanting to use the internet for more serious search purposes. ... easy to read ... succeeds in giving in-depth advice ... while avoiding technical jargon."

—Sarah McNicol, *New Library World*

"A wonderful volume ... has extreme quantities of new and useful information ... highly recommended for librarians, researchers, students, teachers, and extreme searchers everywhere."

—Melissa Aho, *Public Services Quarterly*

"Hock has provided a superb reference book of use to a wide range of people with all sorts of online needs."

—Donna Carroll, *Reference Reviews*

"This book ... and its supplemental website are an excellent resource for those of us who don't have the time to keep up with all the new and changing resources on the internet outside of our area of expertise."

—Margaret Henderson, *Issues in Science and Technology Librarianship*

"Clearly laid out and easy to read. Screenshots supplement the written information and a full index ensures that readers will be able to find content quickly and easily. ... a very useful book to have."

—Phil Bradley, *Program: Electronic Library and Information Systems*

"Buying this book has to be the quickest way you can access years of hard-won web searching experience. Invaluable."

—William Hann, FreePint

"Should be required reading for librarians, online professionals, and anyone else who wants to get the most out of the internet. Recommended."

—*CHOICE*

"[Hock's] clear and useful guide will help anyone interested in going beyond Google, explaining when, why, and how best to use various search tools and other web resources."

—*Library Journal*

"A great how-to guide by one of the world's foremost search trainers."

—Greg Notess, Search Engine Showdown

The EXTREME SEARCHER'S Internet Handbook
4th Edition

A Guide for the Serious Searcher

Randolph Hock

Foreword by Gary Price

CyberAge Books
Medford, New Jersey

First printing, 2013

The Extreme Searcher's Internet Handbook:
***A Guide for the Serious Searcher*, Fourth Edition**

Library of Congress Cataloging-in-Publication Data

Hock, Randolph, 1944- author.
  The Extreme Searcher's Internet Handbook : A Guide for the Serious Searcher / By Randolph Hock. -- Fourth Edition.
        pages cm
    Includes index.
    ISBN 978-1-937290-02-3
    1. Web search engines. I. Title. II. Title: Web search engines.
    ZA4226H63 2012
    025.04252--dc23

                                                                    2012039960

Printed and bound in the United States of America.

President and CEO: Thomas H. Hogan, Sr.
Editor-in-Chief and Publisher: John B. Bryans
VP Graphics and Production: M. Heide Dengler
Managing Editor: Amy M. Reeve
Editorial Assistant: Brandi Scardilli
Cover Design: Lisa Conroy
Indexer: Candace Hyatt

www.infotoday.com

To Pamela

Contents

Foreword, by Gary Price xi

Acknowledgments xiii

Introduction xv

About The Extreme Searcher's Web Page xxi

Chapter 1 Basics for the Serious Searcher 1

The Pieces of the Internet 1

A Very Brief History 2

Searching the Internet: Web "Finding Tools" 8

General Strategies 13

Content on the Internet 18

Content—The Deep Web 23

Copyright 26

Citing Internet Resources 27

Keeping Up-to-Date on Internet Resources and Tools 28

Chapter 2 Directories and Portals 31

General Web Directories 32

Classification of Sites in General Web Directories 33

Searchability of General Web Directories 34

When to Use a General Web Directory 34

The Major General Web Directories 35

Other General Web Directories 40

Specialized Directories 42

How to Find Specialized Directories 43

What to Look for in Specialized Directories and How They Differ 45

Some Prominent Examples of Specialized Directories 45

General Web Portals 54

Summary 59

Chapter 3   Search Engines: The Basics 61
How Search Engines Are Put Together 61
How Search Options Are Presented 63
Typical Search Options 64
Search Engine Overlap 69
Results Pages 70
Search Engine Accounts 71
Specialty Search Engines 71
Metasearch Engines 72
Search Engine Shortcuts 73
Keeping Up-to-Date on Web Search Engines 73

Chapter 4   Search Engines: The Specifics 75
Google 75
Bing 100
Yahoo! 107
Ask.com 118
Additional General Web Search Engines 122
Visualization Search Engines 126
Search Engine Comparison Searches 128

Chapter 5   Discussion Groups, Forums, Newsgroups, and Their Relatives 131
Groups of Groups and Individual Groups 133
Groups Search Engines 135
Mailing Lists 143
Instant Messaging 147
Netiquette Points Relating to Groups and Mailing Lists 147

Chapter 6   An Internet Reference Shelf 149
Thinking of the Internet as a Reference Collection 149
Criteria Used for Selecting the Tools Covered 150
Traditional Tools Online 150
Encyclopedias 151
Dictionaries 153
Combined Reference Tools and Almanacs 155
Addresses and Phone Numbers 156

Quotations.. 157

Foreign Exchange Rates/Currency Converters.. 160

Weather... 160

Maps.. 161

Gazetteers... 162

ZIP Codes.. 162

Stock Quotes 162

Statistics.. 163

Books... 165

Historical Documents 170

Government and Country Guides.. 170

Company Information.. 173

Associations 176

Professional Directories... 177

Other Information About People 177

Literature Databases.. 180

Colleges and Universities... 182

Fact-Checking Sites.. 183

Travel 184

Film 185

Reference Resource Guides 186

Chapter 7   Sights and Sounds: Finding Images, Audio, and Video

Chapter 7   **Sights and Sounds: Finding Images, Audio, and Video**............................ 187

The Copyright Issue... 187

Images... 188

Audio and Video.. 201

Chapter 8   News Resources

Chapter 8   **News Resources**.. 213

Types of News Sites on the Internet 213

Finding News—A General Strategy... 214

News Resource Guides.. 215

Major News Networks and Newswires.. 218

Newspapers 221

Radio and TV 222

Aggregation Sites... 223

Specialized News Services.. 227

Blogs.. 228

RSS 230

Alert Services 231

Chapter 9 Finding Products Online 233

Categories of Shopping Sites on the Internet 233

Looking for Products—A General Strategy 234

Company/Product Catalogs 234

Shopping Malls 236

Price Comparison Sites 238

Auctions 243

Classifieds 243

Product and Merchant Evaluations 244

Buying Safely 246

Chapter 10 Your Own Place on the Web:
Participating and Publishing 249

A "Place" on the Web 249

Web-Based Software 250

Social Networking Sites 251

Sharing Sites 252

Microblogs 253

Blogs 254

Podcasts 257

Crowdsourcing 257

Your Own Full-Fledged Website 258

Websites 259

Conclusion 267

Glossary 269

URL List 279

About the Author 297

Index 299

FOREWORD

When Ran asked me to write the foreword to this fourth edition of *The Extreme Searcher's Internet Handbook*, I thanked him for the honor and immediately began to think about how things have changed since he asked me to write the foreword to the first edition some 12 years ago.

The past 12 years seem nothing short of a century, if not a millennium, when it comes to web search and online information retrieval.

Back then, there were many more players in the web search business, and things we now routinely expect a search engine to offer—such as the ability to search PDF files—were not available from any well-known search tool.

It's actually a fun exercise (at least for a search geek like me, and perhaps you) to think about all that we've seen in the past 12 years.

Here are some of the changes that immediately come to mind:

- The growth of one dominant web search company, Google
- The expansion in mobile access and retrieval of data
- The growth of social media and all of the material it makes available and searchable
- The birth of the "cloud" and the ability to access and search your data from any web browser
- The digitization and ability to search millions of books, magazines, and other print publications
- Non-text formats becoming "more" searchable and accessible
- The growing volume of information as governments make their data more open and searchable

It would be easy to go on and list many more. However, one thing has not changed. In fact, it's likely more important today than ever before.

What is it?

Serious searchers still have a need for practical web search and online information retrieval *knowledge*, clearly presented by an expert and available to quickly refer back to at any time.

Allow me to explain why this knowledge is so important.

First, as the databases from Google, Bing, and other web search tools grow larger, it becomes ever more challenging to find what you want when you want it. In other words, the haystack is growing and finding the needles takes more time and requires greater skill.

Of course, search engines will always give you *something*, but a small amount of education will make your search experience more productive and, most importantly, ensure you are getting the best answers possible. You'll get better results in less time and very likely with a reduced amount of aggravation. That's a good thing.

With the acquisition of *The Extreme Searcher's Internet Handbook*, that education and knowledge is at your fingertips. (And don't forget that many of the concepts and some of the techniques Ran explains can be applied to search resources well beyond the many he covers in the book.)

Second, issues that arise along with the growth of the internet and the amount of material you can access are credibility, currency, and accuracy. It's both a blessing that the internet allows anyone to say just about anything (everyone has a voice) but it's also a challenge (and becoming more so each day) to make sure that the information you're finding is not only accurate but comes from a credible source.

To put it another way, you don't want to be the person who turns in a school research paper based on out-of-date statistics or who includes inaccurate data when preparing an important report for the boss.

Finally, I think knowledge about how and *when* to use specialty search tools and resources is more important today than ever. This runs the gamut from little-known features on Bing or Google to search tools devoted solely to news, shopping, or just about any other imaginable topic. An understanding that these tools are available and can make your searching easier and more productive is essential for any serious searcher.

For these and many other reasons, you are to be congratulated. You've not only made an effort to learn, you've entrusted your education to Ran Hock—an experienced, world-renowned teacher who clearly explains how to effectively search the web and how to put the power of that knowledge to work for you.

—Gary D. Price, MLIS
Co-Founder and Editor, *Library Journal*'s INFOdocket.com
Co-Founder and Editor, FullTextReports.com
Information Industry Analyst

Acknowledgments

As this book now goes into its fourth edition, I continue to be grateful to the readers who have passed on so many kind comments, to all who have bought the book, and to the instructors who have chosen to use the book as a text in their courses.

As with my other books, I extend my thanks and appreciation to the wonderful group of people at Information Today, Inc. I particularly thank Amy Reeve, Managing Editor (who continues to extend more kindness to this author than he deserves); the always supportive and enthusiastic John Bryans, Editor-in-Chief and Publisher; Heide Dengler, VP of Graphics and Production; Brandi Scardilli, Editorial Assistant; Kara Jalkowski, Book Designer; Lisa Conroy, Cover Designer; and Rob Colding, Marketing Coordinator. I continue to be immensely grateful to their leader, Information Today President and CEO, Tom Hogan, Sr., for the extraordinary things that he has done and continues to do for all of us in the information community.

On the home front, I again thank my wonderful wife, Pamela, who deals lovingly and well with the vicissitudes of having a writer in the house.

INTRODUCTION

For many years, Thomas's English Muffins has had a slogan proclaiming that the tastiness of its muffins was due to the presence of myriad "nooks and crannies." The same may be said of the internet. It is in the internet's nooks and crannies that the true "tastiness" often lies. Almost every internet user has used Google and probably Yahoo!, and any group of experienced searchers could probably come up with a dozen or so sites that every one of them has used. But even for experienced searchers, time and task constraints have meant that some nooks and crannies have not been explored and exploited. These unexplored areas may be broad internet resources (discussion groups), specific types of resources (multimedia), or the nooks and crannies of a specific site (even Google). This book is intended to be an aid in that exploration.

Back on the culinary scene, I am told that some people don't take the few extra seconds to maximize tastiness by splitting their English muffins with a fork, but, driven by their busy schedules, just grab a knife and slice them. This book is written for those seeking to savor the extra tastiness from the internet. It will hopefully tempt you to discover what the nooks and crannies have to offer and how to split the internet muffin with a fork almost as quickly as you can slice it with a knife.

Less metaphorically, this book is written as a guide for researchers, students, writers, librarians, teachers, and others, covering what serious users need to know to take full advantage of internet tools and resources. It focuses on what the serious searcher "has to know" but, for flavor, a dash of the "nice-to-know" is occasionally thrown in. It assumes that you already know the basics, frequently use the internet, and know how to use your browser. For those who are less experienced online searchers, my aim is to provide a lot that is new and useful. For those of you with more experience, I hope to reinforce what you know while introducing some new perspectives and new content.

If you are among those who find themselves not just using the internet but *teaching* it, this book should help you address an extensive range of questions. Much of what is included is based on my experience training thousands of internet users from a wide range of professions, across a broad age range, and from more than 40 countries.

BRIEF OVERVIEW OF CHAPTERS

The chapter topics reflect congruence between the types of things that experienced internet users most frequently inquire about and a categorization of the kinds of resources available on the internet. An argument could certainly be made that the content should have been divided differently. While there is a chapter on finding products online, for example, you may wonder why there is not one specifically on "company information." This is because company information pervades almost every chapter. Not every chapter will be of utmost interest to every reader, but it's worth giving each chapter at least a quick glimpse. You may be surprised what some nooks (and crannies, of course) contain.

Although the nature of each chapter means that each has its own organization, they all share some common elements. Typically, each chapter includes these aspects:

- Useful background information, along with suggestions, tips, and strategies for finding and making the most effective use of sites in that area.

- Resource guides that will lead you to collections of links to major sites on the topic.

- Selected sites, which were chosen because 1) they are *valuable* resources that many, if not most, readers should be aware of, and 2) they are *representative* of types of sites that are useful for the topic. Deciding which sites to include was often difficult. Many of the sites included in this book are considered to be the best in their area, but space limitation meant that hundreds of great sites had to be excluded. These difficult decisions were made more palatable, however, because the resource guides included in the chapters will lead you quickly to those other great sites—you're only one or two clicks away.

Following is a quick rundown of what each chapter covers.

Chapter 1: Basics for the Serious Searcher

This chapter covers background information that serious searchers need to know in order to be conversant with internet content and issues. The background it includes helps users understand more fully the characteristics, content, and searchability of the internet. For those who teach others how to use the internet, it provides answers to some of the more frequently asked questions. Among the things included in Chapter 1 are a brief history of the internet, a look at the kinds of available "finding tools," issues such as retrospective coverage and copyright, resources regarding citing internet sources, and others for keeping up-to-date.

Chapter 2: Directories and Portals

For finding precisely what we need on the web, there are a variety of tools, including search engines, general directories, specialized directories, and portal sites. This chapter discusses the two categories of directories (general and specialized) and general, but customizable, portals. The directories provide a good look at what kinds of resources are available while providing insight and help in focusing on a topic and identifying the most valuable resources. Portals pull together selected news, weather, and other frequently needed information and can add greatly to the efficiency of getting what you need.

Chapter 3: Search Engines: The Basics

This chapter provides background and details about search engines that the serious searcher needs to know in order to get the best results. It also presents a case for not getting too excited about metasearch engines.

Chapter 4: Search Engines: The Specifics

This chapter examines the leading engines in detail, identifying their strengths, weaknesses, and special features, and it includes an overview of other engines. It also describes "visualization" engines (for a very different and fruitful "look" at search engine results).

Chapter 5: Discussion Groups, Forums, Newsgroups, and Their Relatives

Newsgroups, discussion groups, mailing lists, and other interactive forums form a class of internet resources that too few researchers take advantage of. These tools, which can be useful for a broad range of applications from solving a software problem to competitive intelligence, can be gold mines. This chapter outlines what they are, why they are useful, and how to locate the ones you need.

Chapter 6: An Internet Reference Shelf

All serious searchers have a collection of tools they use for quick answers—the web equivalent of a personal reference shelf. This chapter emphasizes the variety of resources that are available for finding quick facts, offers some direction on finding the right site for a specific need, and suggests several dozen sites of which most serious searchers should be aware.

Chapter 7: Sights and Sounds: Finding Images, Audio, and Video

Not only are there billions of images, audio files, and video files available on the web, but they are searchable (and, even better, they are findable). Whether you are looking for photos of world leaders or rare birds, a famous speech, the sound of an elephant seal, or your favorite song, this chapter provides a look at what resources and tools are available for finding a needed file, and it discusses techniques for doing so effectively.

Chapter 8: News Resources

This chapter covers the range of news resources available on the internet—news services and newswires, newspapers, news aggregation services, and more—and explains how to find what you are looking for effectively and efficiently. The chapter not only emphasizes the searchability of these resources, but it also calls attention to the limitations the researcher faces, particularly in regard to archival and exhaustivity issues.

Chapter 9: Finding Products Online

Whether for their own purchase, an organization's purchase, or competitive analysis purposes, some searchers find themselves tracking and comparing products online. This chapter shows where to look and how to do it efficiently and effectively.

Chapter 10: Your Own Place on the Web: Participating and Publishing

The web has become a much more interactive, participatory, collaborative, and sharing place than it was a few years ago. Millions of people are "publishing" on the web, perhaps without even realizing it. This chapter discusses the general options that are available for becoming a part of the web, ranging from tweeting to having a full-blown website.

SOME INTRODUCTORY ODDS AND ENDS

Most of the sites I discuss in the book do not charge for access. Occasionally, reference is made to sites that require a paid subscription or offer information for a fee; these are included here in part as a reminder that (as the serious searcher is already aware) not all of the good stuff is available for free on the internet. Commercial services such as LexisNexis, Factiva, and Dialog contain proprietary information that is critical for many kinds of research and is not available on the free web.

All sites included here were chosen because they have useful content. Except for association, government, and academic sites, most of the sites mentioned are supported by ads. On the internet, just as with television and radio, if the ratio of advertisements to useful content is too high, we can switch to another channel or another website. Some of us have come to appreciate the ads to some extent, aware as we are that advertising makes many valuable sites possible.

A Word on "Usage"

Although *internet* and *web* are not synonymous, most users do not distinguish between them. When it makes a difference, I use the most appropriate term. Where I refer to resources that are generally on the web part of the internet, web is used. Where the terms are interchangeable, either term may be used.

About the Fourth Edition

I continue to be very gratified by the warm reception the first three editions of this book have received, which is the major impetus for the fourth edition. I have been particularly pleased that in addition to its use by individuals interested in becoming more capable internet users, the book has also gained increased use as a textbook and is now being used for both graduate courses and at the undergraduate level for research and information literacy courses. Since the third edition, much of the content of the book has changed, but much has also stayed the same. Almost all of the "old standby" websites are still there, though they are often enhanced and occasionally their names have changed. The descriptions of practically all of the sites that were in the third edition required at least some updating, and many sites, especially the search engines and social networking sites, required very substantial updating to reflect changes in content and changes in the interfaces. Some new topics have been introduced or significantly expanded. For example, in Chapter 1, a discussion of the concepts of *recall* and *precision* has been added, and in Chapter 10, a look at fact-checking sites is now included. A few sites (very few) from the third edition have gone away completely and several new sites have been added for this edition.

Some Final Basic Advice Before You Proceed

As we have encountered the internet over the last decade or so, most of us have learned much of what we know about it in a rather piecemeal fashion, for instance, having been told about a great site, having bumped into it, or having read about it. Although this is, in many ways, an effective approach to exploring the internet, it can leave gaps in our knowledge. Because each user has individual needs, no single book can fill all of the gaps, but this one attempts to help by providing a better understanding of what is out there—as well as some starting points and suggestions for getting what you need—to help you find your way to the most useful nooks and crannies.

As you explore, keep in mind the following three guidelines to help you get the most value from the internet:

One: "Click everywhere."
Two: "Click where you have never clicked before."
Three: "Split your muffins with a fork."

About the Extreme Searcher's Web Page

As a supplement to this book (and his other books), the author maintains The Extreme Searcher's Web Page at www.extremesearcher.com. There you will find information about the author's books and links to sites included in this and his other books. A list of links for all of the websites included in this book can be found at that site. URLs for sites covered in this book occasionally change, and once in a while (we hope not very often), a website covered may just disappear. The Extreme Searcher's Web Page is updated on a continuing basis to account for those changes, and you will sometimes also find new sites added there. (If you should find a "dead link" on the site before the author does, you are encouraged to report it to him at the email address below.)

Since links to all websites in the book are on The Extreme Searcher's Web Page, if you bookmark that site (and use it), you will not have to type in any of the URLs included in the book. You should find the site particularly helpful for browsing through the sites covered here.

Enjoy your visit and please send any feedback to ran@extremesearcher.com.

Disclaimer

Neither the publisher nor the author makes any claim as to the results that may be obtained through the use of The Extreme Searcher's Web Page or of any of the internet resources it references or links to. Neither publisher nor author will be held liable for any results, or lack thereof, obtained by the use of this page or any of its links; for any third-party charges; or for any hardware, software, or other problems that may occur as the result of using it. The Extreme Searcher's Web Page is subject to change or discontinuation without notice at the discretion of the publisher and author.

CHAPTER 1

BASICS FOR THE SERIOUS SEARCHER

In writing this book, I have made the assumption that the reader knows the internet basics—what it is, how to get connected, most common terminology, and so forth. The "basics" covered in this chapter involve background information that serious searchers need to know to be fully conversant with internet content and issues, as well as general ways of approaching internet resources to find just what you need. I go over some details already familiar to many readers, but I include this background material 1) to allow readers to understand more fully the characteristics, content, utility, and nuances of the internet in order to use it more effectively, and 2) to help those who find themselves teaching others how to use the internet, by providing answers to some of the more frequently asked questions.

As for general approaches to finding the right resources, this chapter provides an overview and comparison of the kinds of "finding tools" available and a set of strategies that can be applied. The coverage of strategies goes into some detail on topics (such as Boolean logic) that will also be encountered elsewhere in the book. Integral to all of this are some aspects and issues regarding the *content* that is found on the internet. These aspects include the questions of retrospective coverage, *quality* of content, and general accessibility of content, particularly the issue of the Deep Web (aka, the Invisible Web, the Hidden Web). Woven into this content fabric are issues, such as copyright, that affect how information found on the internet can be used. Although only lightly touched upon, it is important that every serious user have an awareness of these issues. Lastly, the chapter provides some useful resources for keeping up with the latest internet tools, content, and issues.

THE PIECES OF THE INTERNET

First, the *internet* and the *web* are not synonymous, although the terms are frequently used interchangeably. As late as the mid-1990s, the internet had some clearly distinguishable parts, as defined by their functions. Much internet usage could be thought of as internet *sans* content. It was simply a communications channel that allowed easy transfer of information. Typically, a user at one university could use the internet to send or request a file from someone at another university using FTP (File Transfer Protocol). Sending email via the internet was becoming tremendously popular. A user of a commercial search service such as Dialog or LexisNexis could harness the internet as an alternative to proprietary telecommunications networks, basically sending and receiving proprietary information. "Content" parts of the internet could indeed be found, such as Usenet newsgroups, where anyone with a connection could access a body of publicly available information. Gophers (menu-based directories allowing access to files, mainly at universities) were also beginning to provide access to content.

The world changed, and content was destined to become king, when Tim Berners-Lee at CERN (Conseil Européen pour la Recherche Nucléaire) in Geneva created the World Wide Web in 1991. The web provided an easy-to-use interface for both potential content providers and users, with a GUI (Graphical User Interface) incorporating hypertext point-and-click navigation of text, graphics, and sounds, and created what was for most of us at that time an unimaginable potential for access to information.

Within less than five years, the web had overtaken email and FTP in terms of internet traffic. By 2000, usage of the other parts of the internet was becoming fused into the web. Usenet newsgroups were being accessed through a web interface, and web-based email was becoming the main—or only—form of email for millions. FTP was typically being managed through a web interface. Gophers were replaced by web directories and search engines, and gophers are now extinct, except for the furry kind.

A VERY BRIEF HISTORY

The following selection of historical highlights provides a perspective for better understanding the nature of the internet. It should be emphasized that the internet is the result of many technologies (computing, time-sharing of computers, packet-switching, etc.) and many visionaries and great technical thinkers coming together over a period of a few decades. In addition, what they were able to accomplish was dependent upon minds and technologies of preceding decades. This selection of highlights is merely a sampling and leaves out many essential technical achievements and notable contributors. The points here are drawn primarily from the resources listed at the end of this timeline.

1957   The USSR launches *Sputnik*.

1958   Largely as a result of the *Sputnik* launch, ARPA (Advanced Research Projects Agency) is established to push the U.S. ahead in science and technology. High among its interests is computer technology.

1962   J. C. R. Licklider writes about his vision of a globally interconnected group of computers providing widespread access to data and programs; the RAND Corporation begins research on distributed communications networks for military purposes.

Early 1960s   Packet-switching moves from theory to practice.

Mid- to Late-1960s   ARPA develops ARPANET to promote the "cooperative networking of time-sharing computers" with four host computers connected by the end of 1969 (Stanford Research Institute, UCLA, UC Santa Barbara, and University of Utah).

1965   The term *hypertext* is coined by Ted Nelson.

1968   The Tymnet nationwide time-sharing network is built.

1971   ARPANET grows to 23 hosts, including universities and government research centers.

1972   The International Network Working Group (INWG) is established to advance and set standards for networking technologies; the first chairman is Vinton (Vint) Cerf, who is later often referred to as the "Father of the Internet."

1972–1974   Commercial database services—Dialog, SDC Orbit, Lexis, the New York Times DataBank, and others—begin making their subscription services available through dial-up networks.

1973   ARPANET makes its first international connections at the University College of London (England) and the Royal Radar Establishment (Norway).

1974   "A Protocol for Packet Network Interconnection," which specifies the details of TCP (Transmission Control Protocol), is published by Vint Cerf and Bob Kahn.

1974   Bolt, Beranek & Newman, contractor for ARPANET, opens a commercial version of the ARPANET called Telenet, the first public packet-data service.

1977   There are 111 hosts on the internet.

1978   TCP is split into TCP and IP (Internet Protocol).

1979   The first Usenet discussion groups are created by Tom Truscott, Jim Ellis, and Steve Bellovin, graduate students at Duke University and the University of North Carolina, and Usenet quickly spreads worldwide.

The first emoticons (smileys) are suggested by Kevin McKenzie.

1980s   The personal computer becomes a part of millions of people's lives.

There are 213 hosts on ARPANET.

BITNET (Because It's Time Network) is started, providing email, electronic mailing lists, and FTP service.

CSNET (Computer Science Network) is created by computer scientists at Purdue University, University of Washington, RAND Corporation, and BBN, with National Science Foundation (NSF) support. It provides email and other networking services to researchers without access to ARPANET.

1982 The term *internet* is first used.

TCP/IP is adopted as the universal protocol for the internet.

Name servers are developed, allowing a user to get to a computer without specifying the exact path.

There are 562 hosts on the internet.

France Telecom begins distributing Minitel terminals to subscribers free of charge, providing videotext access to the Teletel system. Initially providing telephone directory lookups, then chat and other services, Teletel is the first widespread home implementation of these types of network services.

1984 Orwell's vision, fortunately, is not fulfilled, but computers are soon to be in almost every home.

There are more than 1,000 hosts on the internet.

1985 The WELL (Whole Earth 'Lectronic Link) is started. Individual users, outside universities, can now easily participate on the internet.

There are more than 5,000 hosts on the internet.

1986 NSFNET (National Science Foundation Network) is created. The backbone speed is 56K. (Yes, as in the total transmission capability of a single 56K dial-up modem.)

1987 There are more than 10,000 hosts on the internet.

1988 The NSFNET backbone is upgraded to a T1 at 1.544 Mbps (megabits per second).

1989 There are more than 100,000 hosts on the internet.

ARPANET fades away.

There are more than 300,000 hosts on the internet.

1991 Tim Berners-Lee at CERN (Conseil Européen pour la Recherche Nucléaire) in Geneva introduces the World Wide Web.

NSF removes the restriction on commercial use of the internet.

The University of Minnesota releases the first gopher, which allows point-and-click access to files on remote computers.

The NSFNET backbone is upgraded to a T3 (44.736 Mbps).

1992   There are more than 1,000,000 hosts on the internet.

Jean Armour Polly coins the phrase "surfing the internet."

1994   The first graphics-based browser, Mosaic, is released.

Internet talk radio begins.

WebCrawler, the first successful web search engine, is introduced.

A law firm introduces internet "spam."

Netscape Navigator, the commercial version of Mosaic, is shipped.

1995   NSFNET reverts to being a research network; internet infrastructure is now primarily provided by commercial firms.

RealAudio is introduced, meaning that you no longer have to wait for sound files to download completely before you begin hearing them, allowing for continued ("streaming") downloads.

Consumer services such as CompuServe, America Online, and Prodigy begin to provide access through the internet instead of only through their private dial-up networks.

1996   There are more than 10,000,000 hosts on the internet.

1997   Google comes into existence.

1999   Microsoft's Internet Explorer overtakes Netscape as the most popular browser.

1999   Testing of the registration of domain names in Chinese, Japanese, and Korean languages begins, reflecting the internationalization of internet usage.

2001   Mysterious monolith does not emerge from the Earth and no evil computers take over any spaceships (as far as we know).

2002   Google is indexing more than 3 billion webpages.

2003   There are more than 200,000,000 IP hosts on the internet.

2004   Weblogs (blogs), which started in the mid-1990s, gain widespread popularity and attention.

Facebook is launched.

2005   More than 50 percent of Americans who access the internet at home have a high-speed connection.

Google begins "personalizing" search results.

2006   Developmental focus is on a more interactive, personalized web, with collaboration, sharing, desktop-type programs, social networking, and use of APIs (Application Program Interfaces) to integrate data from multiple sources over the web. This shift is tagged "Web 2.0."

Twitter is created.

2009 Worldwide, there are more than 1.5 billion internet users, with the largest number of users in Asia (more than 650 million users).

2011 Twitter and Facebook play a significant role in the "Arab Spring."
Of the estimated 2.1 billion internet users in the world, 44 percent are in Asia, 23 percent in Europe, 13 percent in North America, 10 percent from Latin America/Caribbean, 6 percent in Africa, 3 percent in the Middle East, and 1 percent in Oceania/Australia (www.internetworldstats.com/stats.htm).

Internet History Resources

Anyone interested in information on the history of the internet beyond this selective list is encouraged to consult the following resources.

On the Internet: A Brief History of the Internet, Part I

www.isoc.org/oti/articles/0597/leiner.html

Compiled by Barry M. Leiner, Vinton G. Cerf, David D. Clark, Robert E. Kahn, Leonard Kleinrock, Daniel C. Lynch, Jon Postel, Larry G. Roberts, and Stephen Wolff, this site provides historical commentary from many of the people who were actually involved in the internet's creation.

Internet History and Growth

www.isoc.org/internet/history/2002_0918_Internet_History_and_Growth.ppt

This PowerPoint presentation by William F. Slater III provides an informative look at the internet's pioneers and provides an excellent collection of statistics on internet growth.

Hobbes' Internet Timeline

www.zakon.org/robert/internet/timeline

This detailed timeline emphasizes technical developments and who was behind them, plus a variety of statistical charts.

Internet World Stats

www.internetworldstats.com/stats.htm

This website provides a compilation of current statistics, with graphs, for internet usage worldwide.

The "New" Web:
Web 2.0 and Social Networking

By 2006, most heavy-duty internet users had begun to hear the term *Web 2.0* fairly frequently—a term coined (and trademarked) in conjunction with a series of web development conferences that began in 2004. Web 2.0 refers to a "second generation" of the web that provides a much greater focus on user-produced content, collaboration and sharing by users, and desktop applications made available on the web. Forerunners of this include wikis, blogs, RSS, folksonomies (tagging), and podcasts. Though Web 2.0 has no precise definition, some people also define this generation of the web in terms of the kinds of programs and techniques used, including APIs, social software, and Ajax (Asynchronous JavaScript And XML). The glossary of this book has brief definitions of those terms. From one perspective, what Web 2.0 is really about is the *user*, with a focus on areas of user interaction such as communication, participation, publication, social software, sharing, and "the web as platform."

Though individual websites are not usually labeled as Web 2.0, if you look closely, you will have seen these elements in a significant portion of the websites you use, particularly Facebook and Twitter. You are seeing manifestations of it 1) when you encounter sites that allow for user-applied "tags" (such as Flickr), in the way a search engine might "suggest" search phrases as you type in your terms, 2) in the ability to zoom and drag maps, and 3) in new content appearing instantly as you move your cursor. This flexible interactivity with webpages and with the web carries over into increased interactivity with other people on the web and can make web-based software (such as Google Drive) flow as smoothly as similar programs on your desktop.

Although most people believe that Web 2.0 has been an overwhelming positive development, there is at least one downside for the serious searcher and researcher: a corollary development that might be dubbed the "narcissistic web"—a version of the web that, inadvertently perhaps, causes users to narrow their world, see only what they want to see, and bias their results, without necessarily even realizing it. With sites like Facebook, we very knowingly pull ourselves into circles of friends and acquaintances we have designated. However, particularly with the personalization of results from Google, Amazon, and other sites, users need to be aware that more and more they may be exposed to a less objective view of the world.

By 2011, the characteristics identified with Web 2.0 had become so commonplace that the term itself was much less frequently encountered. The "new" thrust getting the most attention was a phenomenon closely related to Web 2.0, social networking. Social networking particularly and emphatically builds on certain aspects of Web 2.0, especially user-produced content, collaboration and sharing by users, and of course, social software.

The concept of social networking on the internet is not new. Indeed, pre-web user groups, such as those found on Usenet, could conceivably be classed as social networking. Take the same general idea and add in Web 2.0 technologies, and we get a quite different animal. One major defining characteristic of what we currently think of as social networking is that the anticipated audience for the user-produced content is usually the user's "friends," as well as acquaintances, friends of friends, colleagues, people we wish we knew, etc. Content is usually much more "personal."

For the typical internet user, the prevalence of social networking can have some very beneficial aspects, aspects that extend beyond social to cultural. For most people, there was an expectation not very long ago that we wouldn't be able to keep in touch with more than a small handful of acquaintances. Now, using sites such as Facebook and Twitter, we can. There are, of course, concomitant downsides, particularly involving privacy and one of our most precious personal commodities, our time. Old social and cultural rules such as "Don't take candy from strangers" and "Be careful to whom you give you phone number" have been supplanted with new rules such as "Be careful who you friend" and "Don't give anyone, including your mother, your password."

For the more-than-casual internet user, including researchers and investigators, social networking presents other benefits, opportunities, challenges, and issues. If we want to know details about people's lives, there is—and you know this already—far more publicly available information out there than there was four or five years ago. At the same time, some information that was out there a few years ago may no longer be accessible, as people become more sensitive to and careful about what information they share on social networking sites. (More about using social networking for research can be found in Chapter 6.)

Social networking as a core internet activity is here to stay. Who the players are and how to best take advantage of it are likely to change rather frequently.

Searching the Internet: Web "Finding Tools"

Whether your hobby or profession is cooking, carpentry, chemistry, or anything in between, the right tools can make all the difference. The same is true for searching the web. A variety of tools are available to help you find what you need, and each tool does things a little differently, sometimes with a different purpose or different emphasis, as well as different coverage and different search features.

To understand the variety of tools, it can be helpful to think of most finding tools as falling into one of three categories (although many tools will be hybrids): 1) general directories, 2) search engines, and 3) specialized directories. The third category could indeed be lumped in with the first because both are directories, but for a couple of reasons discussed later, it is worthwhile to treat them separately.

All three categories may also incorporate another function, that of a "portal," which is a website that provides a gateway not only to links but also to a number of other information resources that go beyond just the searching or browsing function. These resources may include news headlines, weather, stock market information, alerts, yellow pages, and other kinds of handy information. A portal can be general, as in the case of My Yahoo!, or it can be specific for a particular discipline, region, or country. General portals are usually personalizable, allowing users to select their own content.

Other finding tools provide identification of other kinds of internet content, such as discussion groups (forums), images, and audio. These tools may exist either as their own sites, or they may be incorporated into any of the three main categories of tools. These specialized tools will be covered in later chapters.

General Web Directories

The general web directories, such as the Yahoo! Directory and Open Directory, are websites that provide a large collection of links arranged in categories to enable browsing by subject area (see Figure 1.1). Interestingly, general directories, though once the major web finding tool, are now almost an historical artifact, displaced very largely by search engines.

The advantages of general directories had been the categorization and the selectivity of content. The categories provide easy browsing of topics, and the selectivity provides a focus on sites that are generally highly regarded for their content and usefulness. However, with the greatly improved relevance ranking provided by search engines (particularly with respect to the much greater role in ranking that "popularity" of sites plays), the selectivity provided by directories has become much less needed and much less used. The prominence of the Yahoo! Directory on Yahoo!'s main page has rapidly diminished—as late as 2002, the directory was Yahoo!'s most prominent feature, whereas today it doesn't even merit a link on Yahoo!'s main page.

The Role of General Directories

General web directories can be a good starting place when you have a very general question (*museums in Paris*, *dyslexia*), when you don't quite know where to go with a broad

Figure 1.1 Open Directory main page

topic and would like to browse down through a category to get some guidance, or when you want to get a general feel for the variety of content available for a particular topic.

General web directories are discussed in detail in Chapter 2.

TIP:

If your question contains just one or two concepts and you only want a small handful of results, you may want to consider using a directory. If your question contains three or more concepts, definitely start with a search engine.

Web Search Engines

Whereas a directory may be a good start when you want to be directed to just a few selected items on a fairly general topic, search engines are the place to go when you want something on a fairly specific topic (*ethics of human cloning*, *Italian paintings of William Stanley Haseltine*). Instead of searching brief descriptions of, at most, a few million web-sites, as with directories, search engine services allow you to search virtually every word from several billion webpages. In addition, web search engines allow you to use much more sophisticated techniques, so you can focus on your topic more effectively (Figure 1.2). The pages included in web search engines are not placed in categories (hence, you cannot browse a hierarchy), and usually no direct human selectivity was involved in determining whether a webpage is included in the search engine's database. As the searcher, *you* provide the selectivity by the search terms you choose and by the further narrowing techniques you apply.

The Role of Search Engines

If your topic is very specific or if you expect that very little is written on it, a search engine will be a much better starting place than a directory. If your search needs to be exhaustive, use a search engine. If your topic is a combination of three or more concepts (e.g., *Italian, paintings, Haseltine*), use a search engine. Search engines are covered in detail in Chapters 3 and 4.

Specialized Directories (Resource Guides, Research Guides, and Metasites)

Specialized web directories are collections of selected internet resources (collections of links) on a particular topic. The topic could range from something as broad as medicine to something as specific as biomechanics. These sites go by a variety of names such as resource guides, research guides, metasites, cyberguides, and webliographies. Although their main function is to provide links to resources, they may also incorporate some additional portal features such as news headlines.

Indeed, this category could have been lumped in with the general web directories, but it is kept separate for two main reasons. First, the large general directories, such as the Yahoo! Directory and Open Directory, have several things in common besides being general: They provide categories you can browse, they have a search feature, and when you get to know them, they tend to have the same look and feel in other ways as well. The second main reason for keeping the specialized directories as a separate category is that

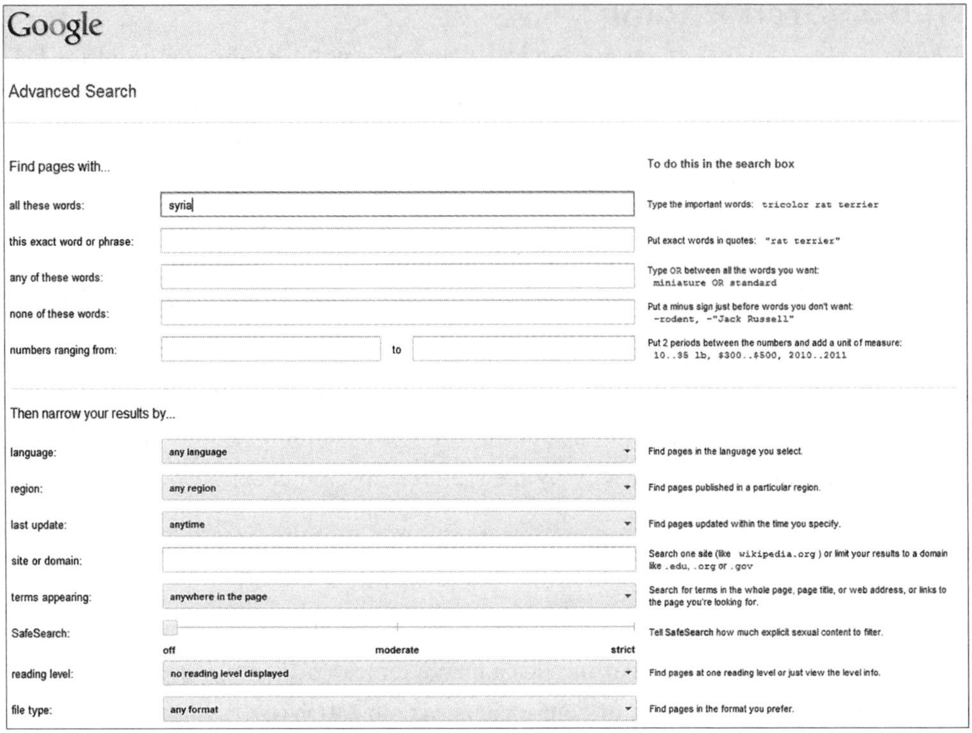

Figure 1.2 Google's advanced search page

they deserve greater attention than they often get. More searchers need to tap into their extensive utility.

The Role of Specialized Directories

Use specialized directories when you need to get to know the web literature on a topic, in other words, when you need a general familiarity with the major resources for a particular discipline or area of study. These sites can be thought of as providing some immediate expertise in using web resources in an area of interest. When you are not sure how to narrow your topic and would like to browse, these sites can also often be better starting places than a general directory because they reflect a greater expertise in the choice of resources for a particular area than a general directory, and they often include more sites on the specific topic than are found in the corresponding section of a general directory.

Specialized directories are discussed in detail in Chapter 2.

General Strategies

For starters, there is no right or wrong way to search the internet. If you find what you need and find it quickly, your strategy is good. Keep in mind, though, that finding what you need involves other issues: Was it really the correct answer? Was it the best answer? Was it the complete answer?

At the broadest level, assuming that your question is one for which the internet is the best starting place, one approach to finding what you need on the internet is to start by answering the following three questions:

1. Exactly what is my question? (Identify what you need to know and how exhaustive or precise your answer needs to be.)
2. What is the most appropriate tool to start with? (See the previous sections on the categories of finding tools.) Often your knowledge of specific websites will lead you directly to one of those sites, rather than going though a search engine or directory.
3. What search strategy should I start with?

Answering these questions often takes place without much conscious effort and may take a matter of seconds. For instance, if you wanted to find out who General Carl Schurz was, you could go to a search engine and type in those three words. The quick-and-easy, keep-it-simple approach is often the best.

Even with a more complicated question, it is often worthwhile to start with a very simple approach to get a sense of what is out there, then develop a more sophisticated strategy based on an analysis of your topic into concepts.

Organizing Your Search by Concepts

Organizing your search in terms of concepts is an effective way of addressing the first question just mentioned: "Exactly what is my question?" Thinking in terms of concepts is both a natural way of organizing the world around us and a way of organizing your thoughts about a search. Thinking in concepts allows you to identify your most critical search criteria and is a central part of most searches. Concepts are the ideas that must be present for a resultant answer (the retrieved item) to be relevant, each concept corresponding to one required criterion. Sometimes a search is so specific that only a single concept may be involved, but most searches involve a combination of two, three, or four concepts. For instance, if our search is for *hotels in Albuquerque*, our two concepts are *hotels* and *Albuquerque*. If we are trying to identify webpages on this topic, any webpage that includes both concepts possibly contains what we are looking for, and any page that is missing either of those concepts is not going to be relevant.

The experienced searcher knows that for any concept, there will often be more than one term (*cars* as well as *automobiles*) that may indicate the presence of the concept, and these alternate terms also need to be considered. Alternate terms may include the following, among other things, 1) grammatical variations (e.g., *electricity*, *electrical*); 2) synonyms, near-synonyms, or closely related terms (e.g., *culture*, *traditions*); and 3) a term and its narrower terms. For an exhaustive search on the concept *Baltic states*, you may also want to search for *Latvia*, *Lithuania*, and *Estonia*. In an exhaustive search for information on the production of electricity in the Baltic states, you would not want to miss the webpage that dealt specifically with "Production of Electricity in Latvia."

When the idea of thinking in concepts is expanded further, it naturally leads to a discussion of Boolean logic, which will be covered in Chapter 4. In the meantime, the major point here is that, in preparing your search strategy, you need to think about what concepts are involved, and remember that, for most concepts, looking for alternate terms may be important.

How Much Information Do I Need?

As well as the content criteria (concepts) just mentioned, for an effective search, you must have a feel for how much information you need and, related to that, how tolerant you need to be in regard to the relevance of each individual answer returned by the search. In technical terms, we are talking about *recall* and *precision*, two terms that have long been used in the world of information retrieval to measure the effectiveness of search techniques, algorithms, and engines. Here we are looking at recall and precision as factors to consider as we plan a search in order to optimize our search effectiveness.

In the search context, recall can be defined as what proportion is retrieved of the total number of things in the database that are relevant to your search topic—or more simply, how much was found out of all the good stuff out there. For example, if the search engine database actually contains 10 records that are relevant to our topic and the search statement you use retrieves six of those, your recall is 60 percent.

Search precision is the other end of the spectrum. It can be defined as how many of the total number of things retrieved are actually relevant (to the topic for which you searched)—in other words, of what was found, how much of it was good? If your search retrieved 10 items and three of those are relevant (useful), your precision is 30 percent.

For some searches, we need high recall, and for others, we need high precision. We can achieve those goals by using the appropriate features provided by search tools. If you want to find someone's address, all that is required is one simple, quick answer. You don't care if that answer is in a hundred places on the web. Recall can be extremely low, yet you will still be satisfied with the result. At the same time, precision is very important in that search. You don't want to dig through 20 records to find one correct address. On the other hand, suppose that your organization is considering investing $20 million in the development of a new medical device, and you are charged with finding out if similar devices are already out there on the market. In this case, it is critical that you miss absolutely nothing, so recall is extremely important. Because of the risk involved, you might be willing to read through hundreds of records, even if it turns out that none of them are relevant. Very low precision is quite acceptable in this situation. In planning a strategy for a search, we should know which direction we need to take. How important for our search is recall, and how important is precision?

How easily and effectively we achieve necessary levels of recall and precision can be controlled by the search engine techniques and features we choose to use. Some features provide high precision; some provide high recall. As one brief example, suppose you are looking for biographical material on a political candidate. You want multiple perspectives, but you don't have time to read through dozens and dozens of sources. You need high precision but recall is only moderately important because you don't want to look at hundreds of relevant pages that might be out there. In this case, you might want to take advantage of title searching (a feature discussed in some detail a bit later). With this technique, you can limit your retrieval to only those records (e.g., webpages) in which the person's name is in the title (e.g., of the page, article). This technique would assure rather high precision (relevance). The right combination of search features can provide the appropriate balance of recall and precision. As search features are discussed in this chapter and in Chapters 3 and 4, consider how each can be used to fine-tune your recall and precision, and hence improve the quality of your searching.

A Basic Collection of Strategies

Just as there is no one right or wrong way to search the internet, there can be no list of definitive steps or one specific strategy to follow in preparing and performing every search. Rather, it is useful to think in terms of a toolbox of strategies and select whichever tool or combination of tools seems most appropriate for the search at hand. Among the more common strategies, strategic tools, or approaches for searching the internet are the following:

1. Identify your basic ideas (concepts) and *rely on the built-in relevance ranking* provided by search engines. When you enter terms in the major search engines and many other search sites, only those records (webpages) that contain all those terms

will be retrieved, and the engine will automatically rank the order of output based on various criteria (Figure 1.3).

2. Use simple *narrowing techniques* if your results need refining:

   • Add another concept to narrow your search (instead of *hotels Albuquerque*, try *inexpensive hotels Albuquerque*).

   • Use quotation marks to indicate phrases when a phrase defines your concept(s) more exactly than if the words occur in different places on the page, for example, "*foreign policy.*" Most websites that have a search function allow you to specify a phrase (a combination of two or more adjacent words in the order written) by the use of quotation marks.

   • Use a more specific term for one or more of your concepts (i.e., instead of *intelligence*, try *military intelligence*).

   • Narrow your results to include only those pages that contain your most important terms in the title of the page. (These kinds of techniques will be discussed in Chapter 4.)

3. *Examine your first results* and look for, and then use, relevant terms you might not have thought of at first. As appropriate, look particularly for more specific terms or broader terms.

4. *If you do not seem to be getting enough relevant items, use the Boolean OR* operation to allow for alternate terms; for example, *electrical OR electricity* would find all items that have either the term *electrical* or the term *electricity*. How you express the OR operation may vary a bit with the finding tool, but in most cases, it is the word OR, in capital letters.

5. *Use a combination of Boolean operations* (AND, OR, NOT, or their equivalents) to identify those pages that contain a specific combination of concepts and alternate terms for those concepts (e.g., to get all pages that contain either the term *cloth* or the term *fabric* and also contain the words *flax* and *shrinkage*). As will be discussed later, Boolean is not necessarily complicated and is often implied without you doing anything; it can be as simple as choosing between "all of these words" or "any of these words" options.

6. *Look at what else the finding tools (particularly search engines) can do* to allow you to get as much as you need—and only what you need—and which techniques/

features aid you in achieving the necessary levels of recall and precision. Advanced search pages are one place you can look if you do not recall options available to you.

Ask five different experienced searchers and you will get five different lists of strategies. The most important thing is to have an awareness of the kinds of techniques that are available to you for getting everything you need and, at the same time, only what you need.

TIP:

If you don't immediately see a link to get back to the homepage of a site, try clicking on the site's logo. It usually works.

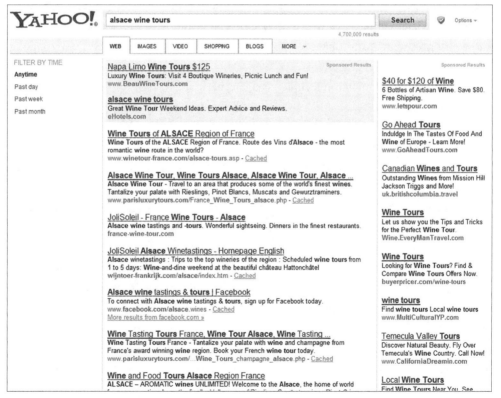

Figure 1.3   Ranked output from Yahoo! (note "Sponsored Results")

Content on the Internet

Not only the amount of information but also the kinds of information available and searchable on the internet has continued to increase rapidly. In understanding what you are getting—and not getting—as a result of a search of the internet requires consideration of a number of factors. These factors include the quality of content, time frames covered, and a recognition that various kinds of material exist on the internet that are not readily accessible by search engines. In *using* the content found on the internet, other issues must also be considered, such as copyright.

Assessing Quality of Content

A favorite complaint of those remaining people who are still a bit shy of the internet is that the quality of information they find is often low. The same could be said about information available from a lot of other resources. A newsstand may have both the *Economist* and the *National Enquirer* on its shelves. On television, you will find both The History Channel and infomercials. Experience has taught us how, in most cases, to make a quick determination of the relative quality of the information we encounter in our daily lives. In using the internet, many of the same criteria can be successfully applied, particularly those criteria we are accustomed to applying to traditional print resources, both popular and academic.

These traditional evaluation techniques and criteria that can be applied in the internet context include:

1. Consider the source.

From what organization does the content originate? Look for the name of the organization both on the webpage and in the URL. Is the content identified as coming from a known source such as a news organization, a government, an academic journal, a professional association, or a major investment firm? Just because the information does not come from such a source is certainly not cause enough to reject it outright. On the other hand, even if it does come from such a source, don't bet the farm on this criterion alone.

Look at the URL. Often you will immediately be able to identify the owner. Peel back the URL to the domain name. If that does not adequately identify its origins, you can check details of the domain ownership on sites that provide access to a Whois database, such as Network Solutions' Whois Search (www.networksolutions.com/whois) or DomainTools (www.domaintools.com). For most countries, Whois-type sites are available. The Internet Assigned Numbers Authority provides a list of Whois sites by country (www.iana.org/domains/root/db).

Be aware that some look-alike domain names are intended to fool the reader as to the origin of the site. The top-level domain (.edu, .com, etc.) may provide some clues about the source of the information, but do not make too many assumptions here. An .edu or .ac domain does not necessarily assure scholarly content, given that students as well as faculty can often easily get a space on the university server.

A tilde [~] in a directory name is sometimes an indication of a personal page. Again, don't reject something on such a criterion alone. There are some very valuable personal pages out there.

Is the actual author identified? Is there an indication of the author's credentials? The author's organization? Search for other things by the same author. Does she or he publish a lot on spontaneous human combustion or extraterrestrial origins of life on Earth? If you recognize an author's name and the work does not seem consistent with other works from the same author, question it. It is easy to impersonate someone on the internet.

2. Consider the motivation.

What seems to be the purpose of the site—academic, political, consumer protection, sales, entertainment (don't be taken in by a spoof!)? There is nothing inherently bad (or for that matter necessarily inherently good) in any of those purposes, of course, but identifying the motivation can help assess the degree of objectivity. Is any advertising on the page clearly identified, or is advertising disguised as something else?

3. Look at the quality of the writing.

If there are spelling and grammatical errors, assume that the same level of attention to detail probably went into the gathering and reporting of the "facts" given on the site.

4. Look at the quality of the documentation of sources cited.

First, remember that even in academic circles, the number of footnotes is not a true measure of a work's quality. On the other hand, and more importantly, if facts are cited, does the page identify the origin of the facts? If a lot rests on the information you are gathering, check out a few of the cited sources to be sure they really do give the facts that were quoted.

5. Is the site and its contents as current as they should be?

If a site is reporting on current events, the need for currency and the answer to the question of currency will be apparent. If the content is something that should be up-to-date, look for indications of timeliness, such as a "last updated" date on the page or telling examples of outdated material. For example, if it is a site that recommends which search engines to use, and AltaVista is still listed, don't trust the currency (or for that matter, accuracy) of other things on the page. What is the most recent material that is referred to? If you find a number of dead links, assume the author of the page is not giving it much attention.

6. Are you covering the appropriate range of sources necessary for your topic?

The scope criterion applies not so much to evaluating the quality of individual sites but to the quality of the overall results of your search for a particular topic. To whatever degree your topic requires, make sure that you have searched far enough back in time and covered, as appropriate, material from various languages and countries, different types of documents (e.g., news, academic, technical reports, books, forums), and different perspectives (e.g., political, cultural, geographic). To address these criteria, take advantage of language tools available on the web, search engines that specifically cover special sources such as news and forums, and specialized directories relating to your topic. Also, never forget that part or all of your answer may lie not in the web but in more traditional tools such as indexing services and databases found in libraries.

7. For facts you are going to use, verify using multiple sources or choose the most authoritative source.

Unfortunately, many "facts" given on webpages are simply wrong, whether from carelessness, exaggeration, guessing, or other reasons. Often facts are wrong because the person creating that page's content did not bother to check the facts. If you need a specific fact, such as the date of a historic event, look for more than one webpage that gives the date and see if they agree. Also remember that some websites are more authoritative than others. If you have a quotation in hand and want to find who said it, you might want to go to a source such as Bartleby.com (which includes very respected quotations sources), instead of taking the answer from a webpage of lesser-known origins. Also see the fact-checking sites included in Chapter 6.

For more details and other ideas about evaluating quality of information found on the internet, the following two resources will be useful.

Virtual Chase: Information Quality

www.virtualchase.justia.com/other-resources/information-quality

Created by law librarian Genie Tyburski and now maintained by Justia.com, this site provides an excellent overview of the factors and issues to consider when evaluating the quality of information found on a website. The site provides checklists and examples of sites that demonstrate both good and bad qualities.

Evaluating the Quality of WWW Resources
library.valpo.edu/user/evaluation.html
   This site from Valparaiso University provides a detailed set of criteria and checklists that address the topic of evaluating web resources.

Retrospective Coverage of Content

It is tempting to say that a major weakness of internet content is the lack of retrospective coverage. This is certainly an issue for which the serious user should have a high level of awareness. It is also an issue that should be put into perspective. The importance and amount of relevant retrospective coverage available depends on the kind of information you are seeking at any particular moment and on your particular question. It is safe to say that no webpages on the internet were created before 1991.

Books, Ancient Writings, and Historical Documents

The lack of pre-1991 webpages does not mean that earlier *content* is not available. Indeed, if a published work is moderately well-known and was written before 1922 or so, you are at least as likely to find it on the internet as in a small local public library. Take a look at what can be found in Google Books and Gallica, and at the list of works included in the Project Gutenberg site and The Online Books Page (see Chapter 6). Among these sites, you will find works by almost every published author, or in some cases, just bibliographic information, but for authors whose works are no longer in copyright, you will find usually the full text of works.

Scholarly and Technical Journals and Popular Magazines

If you are looking for full-text articles from journals or magazines written several years ago, you are not likely to find them free on the internet (and, for most journal articles, you are not even likely to find the ones written this week, last month, or last year). This lack of content is more a function of copyright and requirements for paid subscriptions than a matter of the retrospective aspect. The distinction also needs to be made here between free material and "for fee" material on the internet. On a number of internet sources (such as ingentaconnect and Google Scholar), you can find references to scholarly and other material going back several years. Most likely, you will need to pay to see the full text, but fees tend to be very reasonable. Whatever source you use for serious research, whether it's the internet or another, examine the source to see how far back it goes.

Newspapers and Other News Sources

If, when you speak of news, you think of "new news," retrospective coverage is not an issue. But if you are looking for newspaper articles or other news reports dating back more than a few days, the time span of available content on any particular site is crucial. In 2000, many newspaper websites contained only the current day's stories, with a few having up to a year or two of stories. Fortunately, more and more newspaper and other news sites are now archiving their material, and you may find several years of content on the site. Look closely at the site to see exactly how far back articles are available.

Old Webpages

A different aspect of the retrospective issue centers on the fact that many webpages change frequently and many simply disappear altogether. Pages that existed in the early 1990s are likely to be either gone or to have different content than they did then. This becomes a significant problem when trying to track down early content or citing early content. Fortunately, there are at least partial solutions to the problem. For very recent pages that may have disappeared or changed in the last few days or weeks, a search engine's "cache" option may help. For webpages in their databases, major search engines have stored a copy. If you find the reference to the page in search results, but when you try to go to it, either the page is completely gone or the content that you expected to find on the page is no longer there, click on the cached option and you will get to a copy of the page as it was when the search engine last indexed it. Even if you found the page elsewhere initially, search for it using a search engine, and if you find it there, try the cache.

For locating earlier pages and their content, try the Wayback Machine.

Wayback Machine—Internet Archive
www.archive.org

The Wayback Machine provides access to the Internet Archive, which has the purpose of "offering permanent access for researchers, historians, and scholars to historical collections that exist in digital format." It allows you to search more than 150 billion pages and see what a particular page looked like at various periods in internet time. A search yields a list of what pages are available for specific dates as far back as 1996 (Figure 1.4). As well as webpages, it archives moving images, texts, music (including more than 100,000 concert recordings from more than 5,200 bands), and other audio. It contains over 2 petabytes of data.

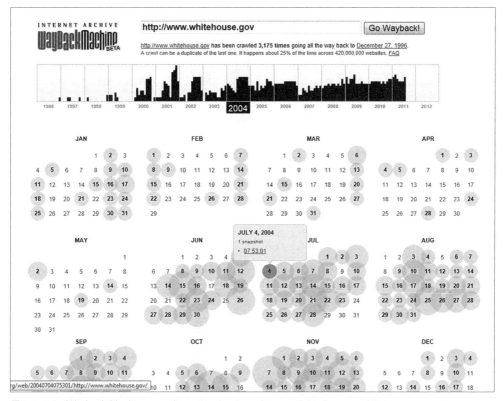

Figure 1.4   Wayback Machine search results showing pages available for www.whitehouse.gov

CONTENT—THE DEEP WEB

No matter how good you are at using web search engines, there are valuable resources on the web that search engines will not find for you. You can get to most of them if you know the URL, but a search engine search will probably not find them for you. These resources, often referred to as the Deep Web, the Hidden Web, or the Invisible Web, contain a variety of content, including—and most importantly—databases of articles, data, statistics, and government documents. The term *invisible* here refers to "invisible to search engines." There is nothing mysterious or mystical involved.

Knowing about the Deep Web is important because the Deep Web contains a lot of tremendously useful information—and it is large. Various estimates put the size of the Deep Web at from 200 to 500 times the content of the visible web. Before that number sinks in and alarms you, keep in mind the following:

1. The Deep Web contains very important material.

2. For the information there that you are likely to have a need for and have the right to access, there are ways of finding out about it and getting to it.

3. While the sheer volume seems overwhelming, most of the material may be meaningless except to those who already know about it, or to the producer's immediate relatives. Much of the material that can't be found is probably not worth finding.

To adequately understand what the Deep Web is all about, users must know why certain kinds of content are not visible to search engine searches. Note the use of the word *content* instead of the word *sites*. The main page of a Deep Web site is usually easy to find and is covered by search engines. It is the rest of the site (webpages and other content within the site) that may be hidden. Search engines do not index certain web content mainly for the following reasons:

1. The search engine *does not know about the page*. No one has submitted the URL to the search engine, and no pages currently covered by the search engine have linked to it. (This falls in the category, "Hardly anyone cares about this page, you probably don't need to, either.")

2. The search engines have *decided not to index* the content because it is too deep in the site (and probably less useful), the page changes so frequently that indexing the content would be somewhat meaningless to index (e.g., as in the case of some news pages), or the page is generated dynamically and likewise is not amenable to indexing. (Think in terms of "Even if you searched and found the page, the content you searched for would probably be gone.")

3. The search engine has been *asked not to index* the content by the presence of a robots.txt file on the site that asks engines not to index the site or not to index specific pages or particular parts of the site. (A lot of this content could be placed in the "It's nobody else's business" category.)

4. The search engine *does not have or use the technology required to index some non-HTML content*. This applies to files such as images and a few other file types. Until 2001, this category included file types such as PDF (Portable Document Format) files, Excel files, Word files, and others that began to be indexed by the major search engines in 2001 and 2002. Audio and video content, such as "flash" movies, have been difficult to index, but with an increased amount of readable data attached to such files, the files are much more searchable and retrievable than they were just a few years ago. Because of this increased coverage, the Deep Web may actually be shrinking in proportion to the size of the total web.

5. The search engine cannot get to the pages to index them because *it encounters a request for a password or the site has a search box* that must be filled out in order to get to the content.

It is the last part of the last category that holds the most interest for searchers—sites that hold their information in databases. Prime examples of such sites would be phone directories, literature databases (such as Medline), newspaper archives, and patents databases. As you can see, if you can find out that the site exists, then you can search its contents (without going through a search engine). This leads to the obvious question of where a searcher can find out about sites that contain unindexed (Deep Web) content.

The best way to find out about these sites is to find a good specialized directory (resource guide) that covers your area of interest. In such a directory, you will find reference to the major websites in that subject area, including websites that contain databases (see Chapter 2 for the discussion of specialized directories).

In the past, there were multiple sites that contained collections of links to major Deep Web websites. Some of the best known have now been discontinued or have not been updated because of the difficulty of adequately keeping up. The following site, however, is a directory of searchable databases that provides another way of finding Deep Web websites for a broad variety of subject areas. For more information on what the Deep Web is, why things are invisible to search engines, and so on, you may also want to check out the excellent (even though rather dated) book by Chris Sherman and Gary Price, *The Invisible Web: Uncovering Information Sources Search Engines Can't See* (CyberAge Books, Medford, NJ, 2001).

 TIP:

On virtually every site, look for a site index and a search box. They are often more useful for navigating a site than the graphics and links on its homepage.

CompletePlanet

www.completeplanet.com

The site claims to cover "70,000 searchable databases and specialty search engines," but a significant number of the sites are such things as company website searches, university catalogs, and art gallery catalogs, many of which are not necessarily "invisible."

It does list a lot of useful resources, but the content on the CompletePlanet site also brings home the point of how trivial much of the Deep Web material can be.

COPYRIGHT

Because of the serious implications of this topic, this section could extend for thousands of words. Because this chapter is about basics, however, a few general points will be made here, and the reader is encouraged to go for more detail to the sources listed next, which are much more authoritative and extensive on the copyright issue. For those in large organizations, particularly an educational institution, you may want to check your organization's website for local guidelines regarding copyright.

Here are some basic points about copyright:

1. For the U.S., "Copyright is a form of protection provided by the laws of the United States (title 17, U.S. Code) to the authors of 'original works of authorship,' including literary, dramatic, musical, artistic, and certain other intellectual works" (www.copyright.gov/circs/circ01.pdf). As stated on the official U.K. Intellectual Property site, "Copyright gives the creators of a wide range of material, such as literature, art, music, sound recordings, films and broadcasts, economic rights enabling them to control use of their material in a number of ways, such as by making copies, issuing copies to the public, performing in public, broadcasting and use online. It also gives moral rights to be identified as the creator of certain kinds of material, and to object to distortion or mutilation of it" (www.ipo.gov.uk/types/copy/c-about/c-about-faq/c-about-faq-whatis.htm). Other countries will have similar definitions and descriptions according to their own legal definition of copyright. Regardless of the country, copyright (and any failure to acknowledge it appropriately) has legal, moral, and economic implications and repercussions.

2. Assume that what you find on a website is copyrighted, unless the site states otherwise or you know otherwise, based, for example, on the age of the item. See the site for the copyright office in your own country for details about the time frames for copyrights. (In the U.S., of considerable use for webpage creators is the fact that "Works by the U.S. Government are not eligible for U.S. copyright protection" (www.copyright.gov/circs/circ01.pdf). You should still identify the source when quoting something from a site, even if the material is not under copyright.

3. The same basic rules that apply to using printed material also apply to using material you get from the internet. Among the most important things to remember: For
anything you write for someone else to read, cite the sources you use.

For more information on copyright and the internet, see the following sources.

U.S. Copyright Office
www.copyright.gov

The official U.S. Copyright Office site has copyright information (for the U.S.) directly
from the horse's mouth.

[U.K.] Intellectual Property Office—Copyright
www.ipo.gov.uk/copy

The copyright section of the U.K. Patent Office site describes in detail, but also in
a very readable fashion, what both the creators and users of copyrighted material need
to know.

Canadian Intellectual Property Office—A Guide to Copyrights
www.cipo.ic.gc.ca/eic/site/cipointernet-internetopic.nsf/eng/h_wr02281.html

This is, as the site has said, a "guide," not a legal document. Look particularly at the FAQ
(Frequently Asked Questions) page. (For other countries, do a search for analogous sites.)

Copyright Website
www.benedict.com

This site is particularly good for addressing, in a layperson's language, the issues
involved in the copyright of digital materials. It also provides background and discussion
on some well-known legal cases on the topic.

Copyright and Fair Use in the UMUC Online or Face-to-Face Classroom
www.umuc.edu/library/libhow/copyright.cfm

This page, from the University of Maryland, is an example of an institutional site that
provides practical guidelines—in this case, in the educational context—for use of copyrighted material on websites and elsewhere.

CITING INTERNET RESOURCES

The biggest problem with citing a source you find on the internet is identifying the author,
the publication date, and so forth. In many cases, the information just isn't there, or you

have to really dig to find it. Basically, when citing internet sources, you need to give as much of the typical citation information as you would for a printed source (author, title, publication, date, etc.), add the URL, and include a comment such as "Retrieved from the World Wide Web, November 15, 2012" or "Internet, accessed November 15, 2012." If your reader isn't particularly picky, you can just give the information about who wrote it, the title (of the webpage), a date of publication if you can find it, the URL, and when you found the material on the internet. If you are submitting a paper to a journal for publication, to a professor, or including it in a book, you need to be more careful and follow whatever style guide is recommended.

Since the details of exactly how you will write the latter kind of citation will vary both with the particular style (MLA, APA, Chicago, etc.) and with the type of publication (articles, books, newsletters, stand-alone website page, etc.), it is not feasible to provide examples here. Fortunately, many style guides are available online. The following two sites provide links to popular style guides online.

Know Which Style to Use: Citation Styles
subjectguides.library.american.edu/citation

From the library at American University, this site offers not just multiple links to well over a dozen style guides online but also to guides for citing particular kinds of sources (film, government documents, etc.) and to software that can help manage and write citations.

Citation Styles, Style Guides, and Avoiding Plagiarism: Citing Your Sources
www.lib.berkeley.edu/instruct/guides/citations.html

This site provides a compilation of guidelines based on the following well-known style guides: MLA, APA, Chicago, and Turabian.

KEEPING UP-TO-DATE ON INTERNET RESOURCES AND TOOLS

For those who want to be alerted to the more valuable resources that become available online, the following sites will be useful. Also, numerous specialized sites that cover specific areas (such as science) or tools (such as search engines) will be mentioned throughout the following chapters. All the sites listed here provide free email alert services and provide archives of past content.

ResourceShelf by FreePint

www.resourceshelf.com

This site, published by FreePint (see next entry), provides extensive updates and commentary on new resources on the web and changes to existing resources. The site also provides the weekly ResourceShelf Newsletter, which includes a sampling of new posts and featured sites.

FreePint

www.freepint.com

This U.K.-based site has been publishing articles and reports to support information work since 1997. The FreePint Newsletter highlights the latest articles and reports, as well as editorial commentary on tools and resources in the evolving world of information practice, content, and strategy.

ResearchBuzz

www.researchbuzz.me

This site, maintained by Tara Calishain, covers news on a broad spectrum of internet research tools and provides articles, archives, and an email newsletter.

Internet Scout Project

www.scout.wisc.edu

The Internet Scout Project produces the Scout Report, published since 1994, which provides well-annotated reviews of new sites, with a weekly report on websites for research, education, general interest, and network tools.

CHAPTER 2

DIRECTORIES AND PORTALS

Though we may seldom consciously think about it, when we are on a quest for anything (*quest* as in *quest*ion), we usually take one of two routes: browsing or asking. Using a department store analogy, if I am looking for men's suits, I can *browse* the store directory, find that menswear is on the third floor, go there, and browse there for the signs that lead to men's suits, then follow other signs that lead to the right style, price, and size. Along the way, I may gain information about what else is available. If I am looking for digital picture frames, I could take the same approach, but I might not be sure whether to look in the home furnishings department with other frames or in the electronics section. In either case, I also have the option of just asking a sales associate, who, with a little bit of luck, will tell me precisely where to go. There are benefits to both approaches, which present the temptation here to go into a long (perhaps risky) soliloquy on hunters versus gatherers, gender differences (men's archetypal antipathy toward asking directions), etc.

Finding things on the internet is similar. We can browse through labels (categories), or we can ask directly, using a search engine. Even for individual websites, we often have the choice of just asking, using a search box, or browsing categories. Each approach has its advantages and disadvantages, bringing up issues such as terminology, serendipity, efficiency, reliability, and so on. In this chapter, we look at tools for browsing: directories and portals. General directories try to organize selected sites from across all subject areas, specialized directories focus more precisely on a specific subject or content type, and portals bring together (usually on a single page) a collection of selected content (links or actual information) relevant to a specific subject area or an individual's needs. The common themes of all of these tools are *selectivity* and *organization* of information.

GENERAL WEB DIRECTORIES

General web directories are websites that selectively catalog and categorize the broad range of sites available on the web and usually include only sites that are likely to be of interest to a large number of users. Although general web directories, such as the Yahoo! Directory, have quite a bit in common with web search engines, they also differ tremendously from search engines, particularly in size, purpose, and, of course, selectivity and organization.

General web directories serve unique research purposes and in some cases may be the best starting point, even though their databases include far less than 1 percent of what search engine databases cover.

The content of general directories is (usually) handpicked by people who ask, "Is this site of enough interest to enough people that it should be included in the directory?" If the answer is yes (and in some cases, if the owner of the site has paid a fee), the site is added to the directory's database (catalog) and is listed in one or more of the subject categories. The result is a collection of sites that is selective (sites have to meet the selection criteria) and categorized (all sites are arranged in categories; see Figure 1.1 in the previous chapter). Because of the selectivity, the directory user is working, theoretically, with higher quality sites—the wheat and not the chaff. Because the sites are arranged in categories, the user has the option of starting at the top of the category hierarchy and browsing down until the appropriate level of specificity is reached. In further contrast to search engines, directories (both general and specialized) usually have only one entry for each site, instead of including many pages from the same site. For search purposes, the directories may index a site only under the words in the category, the name of the site, and a brief description, in contrast to search engines, which may index every word on a page.

The databases of general web directories are far smaller than those created and used by web search engines, the former containing at most a few million sites and the latter billions of pages. Web directories are designed primarily for browsing and for answering general questions. Sites on very specific topics, such as "UV-enhanced dry stripping of silicon nitride films" or "social security retirement program reform in Croatia," are generally not included. As a result, directories are most successfully used for general rather than specific questions, for example, *types of chemical reactions* or *social security*. Although browsing through the categories is the major idea behind the design of general web directories, directories do provide a search box to allow you to bypass the browsing and go directly to the sites in the database.

As stated in Chapter 1, though they were once (circa early 1990s) the major web "finding tool," general web directories are now almost an historical artifact, having been largely replaced by search engines. The advantages of general directories had been their categorization and selectivity. They still provide categories for easy browsing of topics, but the selectivity function has become much less relevant. The greatly improved ranking of results now offered by search engines has resulted in "high quality" sites that are now much more likely to appear near the top of the list of search engine results. Interest in general directories has plummeted, reflected in the fact that the prominence of the Yahoo! Directory on Yahoo!'s main page has diminished: As late as 2002, the directory was Yahoo!'s most prominent feature, while today it does not even have a link on Yahoo!'s main page. Yahoo! seems to have been quietly marginalizing its directory, although it does continue to add sites. The other major general directory, Open Directory, is still alive, but it receives little attention from the general web user.

Strengths and Weaknesses of General Web Directories

Strengths

✔ Selective

✔ Classified (categorized)

✔ Easily browsed

✔ Good for general questions

✔ Most have some searchability

Weaknesses

✔ Very small database compared to web search engines

✔ May not have sites addressing very specific topics

✔ Typically less search functionality than most search engines

✔ Paid inclusion may affect quality

✔ Tend to index only the main pages of sites

CLASSIFICATION OF SITES IN GENERAL WEB DIRECTORIES

General web directories typically organize sites into about a dozen broad categories, with each of those categories broken down into additional levels of hierarchy. This categorization can be the most important reason to go to a directory. It allows browsing down through the levels of the classification hierarchy and can provide valuable direction for a searcher who is not quite sure how to narrow down a broad topic.

Different directories use different classification schemes, which may influence a user to choose one over another. Some directories use cross-references (indicated by an @

sign), which means that you do not have to rely entirely on choosing exactly the correct category in which to begin your browsing.

SEARCHABILITY OF GENERAL WEB DIRECTORIES

Most general web directories have a search box on their main page, which can cause confusion with web search engines. (Technically, almost any website that has a search box does indeed have a search engine behind it, but that's not what is generally meant by *web search engine*.) By entering a term in a directory's search box, you will usually be searching the directory's database. Both the Yahoo! Directory and Open Directory automatically AND all of the terms you enter, and they will allow you to use quotation marks to search for phrases and a minus sign to exclude a term. Open Directory has an advanced search page, and the Yahoo! Directory provides filter options on its results pages. By those means, you can narrow search results to sites falling within a particular category and also apply other criteria.

Size of Web Directory Databases

Whereas major web search engines can contain as many as several *billion* records (webpages), directories typically have a few *million* or a few thousand records (sites). This is good news and bad news: good because it is reflective of the high degree of selectivity, bad because you are sidestepping the vast majority of web content that is out there.

WHEN TO USE A GENERAL WEB DIRECTORY

When all of these factors are combined, they point to some fairly obvious situations where starting with a directory may be your best bet:

1. For a general question—in other words, when you don't have something very specific in mind—a general web directory can be the place to go. What defines general versus specific? As a rule of thumb, you might think in terms of the number of concepts involved. Let's say you're headed to Poland for the first time, and you just want to look around on the web to see what information is available about the country. One or two concepts such as *Poland* or *Poland museums* is fairly general, so you might want to head for a directory rather than a search engine. A search involving three concepts is getting more specific than a general directory may be

able to support, for example, *Poland art museums*. Similarly, if a single term is very specific, such as *cyclopentanecarbaldehyde*, don't count on a directory.

2. This is basically a corollary of the previous point: Start with a general web directory when you know you need to get more specific than what you have in mind at the moment, and you need to browse to help narrow your search.

THE MAJOR GENERAL WEB DIRECTORIES

Two very large general web directories and a few directories that are smaller and more selective but not subject-specific make up the major general web directories category. We'll look here at the two largest and some additional representative, well-known, more selective sites. Following that is a discussion of specialized directories that focus on particular subject areas.

Yahoo! Directory

dir.yahoo.com

The Yahoo! Directory is the best-known general web directory, although it is probably smaller than Open Directory. For Yahoo! users, it is important to clearly distinguish the Yahoo! Directory from the Yahoo! web search. Yahoo! started as a directory rather than as a search engine, and in its first years, Yahoo!'s main page was primarily a directory, with the list of categories dominating the page. By 2001, the emphasis on the main page had moved in the direction of a web portal, with a lot more resources besides just the directory. In 2004, Yahoo!'s marketing emphasis moved to the search function, as Yahoo! began offering its own general web search databases in order to compete with Google. By mid-2006, the directory function was, to say the least, "downplayed," with the directory categories not shown at all on the main page or even directly linked to it. (Hopefully, Yahoo! will continue to at least maintain the directory, but as with many other internet companies, the user's fate rests in the hands of whichever Silicon Valley marketing whiz is currently in charge.) To get to the Yahoo! Directory, the easiest way is to go directly to dir.yahoo.com.

With regard to selectivity in the Yahoo! Directory, companies can pay Yahoo! to "examine" their sites for possible inclusion. A look at many of the company listings included in the directory leads one to strongly suspect that many sites are included not because of the quality and usefulness of their content but because payment was possibly involved.

Browsing Yahoo!

Yahoo! has categorized the sites in its directory into more than a dozen major categories on the Directory homepage, each typically with three to six sublevels, for example:

Home > Science > Mathematics > Geometry >
Computational Geometry > Trigonometry

You can get a fairly full understanding of the capabilities Yahoo! provides for browsing through a close examination of a directory page. Figure 2.1 shows a page that resulted from clicking on the Social Science category, and from there, on Anthropology and Archaeology.

Note the following points:

1. There is a search box that allows you to search the web, the Directory, or just within the current category. The Categories choice is a very powerful tool. If you

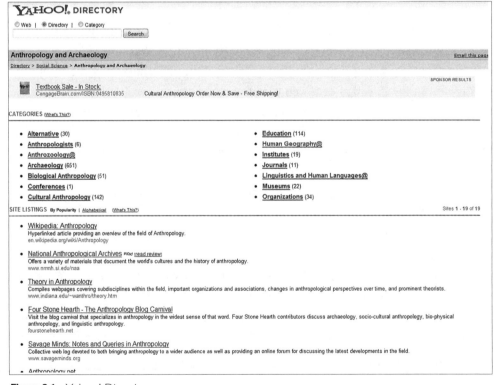

Figure 2.1 Yahoo! Directory page

are looking for graphics sites (from the "graphic arts" side rather than from the computer and web side), you might start by browsing from Arts and Humanities to Design Arts to Graphic Design. At that point, because more than 1,000 Yahoo! listings are available from the various subcategories shown there, you might use the search box to search just in the current category to avoid encountering many irrelevant sites.

2. Near the top of each page, Yahoo! reminds you where you are in the directory (Directory > Social Science > Anthropology and Archaeology). (In the web design world, these kinds of links are known as "breadcrumbs.") The preceding levels are clickable here, allowing you to go back up the hierarchy one or more steps.

3. The Categories section of each page shows what additional subcategories are available and how many listings are in each. The @ sign indicates that this is a cross-reference to a category primarily found elsewhere in the hierarchy. In this example, on the Anthropology and Archaeology page, if you click on Human Geography, you will be taken to a page from the Geography category.

4. Site Listings lists the sites classified at this current level of specificity. Clicking on an entry will take you to the actual site. In some cases, the list can be broken down by popularity or in alphabetical order. The Sponsor Results found on directory pages are ads.

Yahoo!'s Search Filters

When you use the search boxes found in the Yahoo! Directory, you will see a number of filters on the left side of search results pages. These allow you to filter results by the categories in which your search results were found, by time frame, and by concepts related to your topic.

Yahoo! Directory RSS Feeds

If you would like to be alerted to new entries in Yahoo! Directory categories, you can take advantage of the Subscribe via RSS section on the Directory's main page. With this feature, you can have Yahoo! automatically notify you, through your personalized My Yahoo! portal or other RSS reader, of new additions in any of more than 30 directory categories/subcategories. (RSS feeds are discussed in detail in Chapter 8, but briefly, RSS [Really Simple Syndication] is an HTML format by which news providers, websites, blogs, and others can easily distribute their content to users.)

Yahoo! Kids

Yahoo! Kids (kids.yahoo.com) is the version of Yahoo! built for kids ages 6 to 12. The directory portion of the site contains age- and content-appropriate sites, along with a number of other references and other features to use at home and in the classroom.

Open Directory Project

www.dmoz.org

Open Directory Project (Open Directory) is the largest of the general web directories (with about 5 million sites) and differs from Yahoo!'s directory in at least two significant ways: 1) Instead of paid editors, Open Directory uses volunteers (more than 90,000 of them); and 2) there are no paid listings. The Open Directory database is used as a directory on almost 90 other sites.

 TIP:

Browsing a general web directory can be a great way to get ideas for term papers.

Browsing Open Directory

Open Directory divides its site into 16 top-level categories, and each is further categorized into several additional levels, such as:

Top: Society: Government: Finance: Central Banks: Supranational

The World category is unique in that it provides directory access to websites in more than 80 languages. The subcategories found there will differ.

A look at a sample directory page (as with Yahoo!) can identify some of Open Directory's most important aspects (Figure 2.2). The most significant features include the following:

1. A search box gives the option of searching the entire directory or just the current category.

2. A reminder, under the search box, is given of where you are in the subject hierarchy. Each level is clickable, allowing you to move back up the hierarchy easily.

3. The subject hierarchy is followed by a list of the subcategories and usually a "See also" list of additional categories. The latter points to other sections in the Open Directory, as does the @ sign that occurs after some of the subcategories.

4. Following the subcategories will be the listings of the sites themselves, with brief annotations.

5. If the directory database contains articles on this topic in languages other than English, you will see a listing for "This category in other languages."

6. Unique to Open Directory is the Descriptions link in the upper right-hand corner of the page. Clicking on this will take you to a "scope note" defining what kinds of things are placed in this category.

7. At the bottom of the pages are links to several search engines. Clicking the links will execute a search on the name of the current category using these tools.

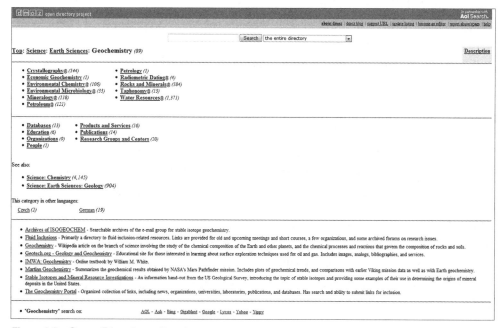

Figure 2.2 Open Directory directory page

Searching Open Directory

The Open Directory database can be searched using the search box found on the main page, at the top of directory pages, and at the bottom of search results pages. Search syntax is a bit more sophisticated than that offered by Yahoo!:

- Multiple terms are automatically ANDed. Eastern Europe will get only those items containing both terms (capitalization is ignored).
- The automatic AND can be overridden by use of an OR (capitalization not required), for example, *cycling OR bicycling*.
- You can specify a phrase by using quotation marks (e.g., *"Native American"*).
- Prefixes can be used to limit results to records that have a particular term in the title, URL, or description (e.g., *t:austria, u:cam, u:cam.ac.uk* or *d:gardening*).
- These functions can be used in combination. However, if you are looking for that degree of specificity, consider using a search engine instead of a directory.

There are other search features described on the Help on Search screen; unfortunately (at least as of this writing), they do not seem to actually work.

Open Directory search results pages contain the following details (Figure 2.3):
- Category headings containing the term you searched for or headings that were identified through the websites identified by the search. The number of sites in the category is also shown.
- Sites where the title of the site or the annotation contained your term(s). The category in which the term occurred is also shown and is clickable so it can take you to that category.
- As when browsing through categories, links to search engines are given at the bottom of search results pages. Clicking on any of these links will cause you to be switched to that engine, and your search will be executed there. Another Open Directory search box will also be found at the bottom of search results pages.

Open Directory's Advanced Search Page

The link to the advanced search page, found on Open Directory's main page beside the search box, takes you to a page where you can limit your search to a particular category, to Categories Only or Sites Only, or to sites that fall in the categories of Kids, Teens, or Mature Teens.

OTHER GENERAL WEB DIRECTORIES

Other general web directories are available, although none as large as the two just discussed. Most of the others specialize in some way, and the dividing line between general and specialized is a bit hazy. Some directories are general with regard to subjects covered but specialized with regard to geographic coverage, such as the numerous country-specific directories. Those directories that are specialized by subject are covered later in this chapter.

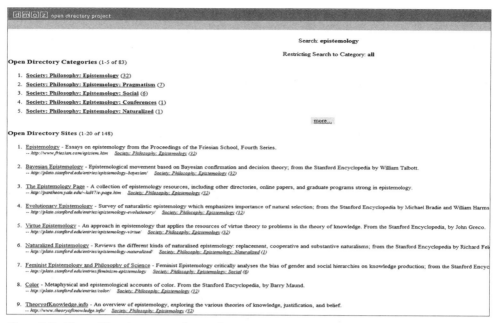

Figure 2.3   Open Directory search results page

Here, though, we will look at one more directory that is general concerning subject coverage but is much more selective and, hence, much smaller. Others fall in this category, but this one is certainly among the best and is representative of the genre. One additional directory that is general in terms of subject area but specialized in that it focuses on academic material, INFOMINE, is discussed later in this chapter.

ipl^2: Information You Can Trust

www.ipl.org

ipl^2 is the result of a 2009 merger of two highly respected directories, Librarians' Internet Index and Internet Public Library, resulting in a collection of more than 46,000 well-organized, annotated, "librarian-approved resources," including ready reference resources, books, magazines, newspapers, and other special collections (for topics such as blogs, mobile apps, and Native American authors). There is also a special emphasis on resources for children, teens, and teachers. ipl^2 offers a free "ask a question" reference service and a free regular newsletter that provides email updates on new sites added.

Browsing ipl^2

The ipl^2 main page provides links for Resources by Subject; Newspapers and Magazines; Special Collections Created by ipl2; For Kids; and For Teens. Click on Resources by Subject to access 12 subject areas for browsing (each with numerous subcategories).

Searching ipl^2

A search box appears on most pages. You can use the Boolean operators AND, OR, and NOT (see Chapter 3 for more on Boolean), as well as question marks to allow for one or more variable characters (*br??d*) and an asterisk for an unlimited number of characters (*german**). These can be used within or at the end of terms. See ipl's Search Help page for even more options.

Where to Find Other General Directories

Unfortunately, most lists of searching tools do not adequately distinguish between search engines and directories; they simply lump the two species together. Keeping that in mind, one place to go for a list of regional (continent- or country-specific) tools is Search Engine Colossus (www.searchenginecolossus.com).

Most Important Things to Remember About Directories

1. Web directories are most useful when you have a general rather than a specific question.
2. The content of directories is selected by humans who evaluate the usefulness and appropriateness of sites considered for inclusion.
3. Directories tend to have one listing per website and do not index individual pages.

SPECIALIZED DIRECTORIES

For some immediate expertise in web resources on a specific topic, there is no better starting point than the right specialized directory. Also known as resource guides, meta-sites, cyberguides, webliographies, or just plain "collections of links," these sites bring together selected internet resources on specific topics. They provide not only a good starting place for effectively utilizing internet resources in a particular area, but also, very importantly, they instill a confidence in knowing that no really important tools in that area are being missed. The variety of these sites is endless. They can be discipline-oriented or industry-oriented; they may focus on a specific kind of document (e.g., newspapers or historical documents) or take virtually any other slant toward identifying a useful category of resources.

If the producer of the site adds some valuable content to the collection of links, such as news headlines or lists of events, you not only have a specialized directory, but a specialized portal or gateway, making it even more useful as a starting point.

Strengths and Weaknesses vs. Other Kinds of Finding Tools

Strengths | **Weaknesses**

✔ Specialized

✔ Very selective

✔ Provides some immediate "web expertise"

✔ Relatively small

✔ Variable quality and consistency

✔ Most are browsable but not searchable

HOW TO FIND SPECIALIZED DIRECTORIES

There are at least a couple of ways to identify systematically a specialized directory for a particular area of interest. Some easy and reasonably effective ways include using Yahoo!'s Web Directories subcategory, searching for them in search engines, keeping an eye out for them in professional journal articles and books, and using directories of directories.

Using Yahoo!

Yahoo! lists thousands of specialized directories. In fact, it lists one or more specialized directories for almost 800 categories, ranging from semiconductors to storytelling to sumo. The trick to finding them in Yahoo! is simple: Just look for the Web Directories subcategory, either by browsing through the Yahoo! categories list or by putting your subject and the phrase *"web directories"* in Yahoo!'s Directory's search box. You may actually get more complete results by doing a regular search engine search and searching for something like *sumo "web directories" site:dir.yahoo.com.* (This syntax will be explained in Chapter 3.)

Using Professional Publications

Keep an eye out for articles that discuss internet resources for specific areas in professional publications (printed and online): journals such as *Online Searcher* and websites for searchers such as FreePint (www.freepint.com).

Using Directories of Directories

Directories of directories are valuable resources for locating topic-specific information. The following two sites contain collections of specialized directories (and may contain other content as well).

The WWW Virtual Library

www.vlib.org

Perhaps the best-known catalog of web directories, The WWW Virtual Library, was started by none other than Tim Berners-Lee, founder of the web. It contains an excellent selection of specialized directories arranged by category. In essence, it is one large directory with individual sections maintained by a large number of volunteers, but because the format of each section is also very independently done, The WWW Virtual Library is indeed a collection of individual directories. The quality of the individual directories tends to be quite high.

Search Engine Guide—Search Engines Directory

www.searchengineguide.com/searchengines.html

Although this site does not adequately distinguish between search engines and directories, if you use the search box or browse the categories listed there, you will find a useful collection of specialized directories.

Using Search Engines to Find Specialized Directories

You may be successful in finding a specialized directory in your subject area by searching a term for your area AND the word *resources*, for example, *biology resources*. You may want to be more specific by using the phrase *"internet resources,"* for example, *biology "internet resources."* You can also try using *metasite* in addition to or instead of *resources*. For industry portals, search for the industry plus the word *portal*, for example, *"electronics industry" portal*. If you would like to get a site that provides a list of printed resources for a subject as well as internet resources, use the word *pathfinder*. Many libraries provide pathfinders that are guides to both the literature and internet resources in their libraries. Even if you don't have access to the library that produced it, the guide can provide reminders of print sources you might want to track down.

WHAT TO LOOK FOR IN SPECIALIZED DIRECTORIES AND HOW THEY DIFFER

Many areas have a variety of directories. If you want to find the best, several factors must be considered. An excellent specialized directory does not have to be strong in all of these facets, but, depending on your needs, you might want to focus on a few particular aspects. Directories tend to differ mainly in these ways:

- Size: Sometimes large is good; sometimes having fewer sites to focus on is good.
- Categorization/Classification: Especially if the number of sites included is large, it is helpful to have them divided into useful categories.
- Annotations: A large portion of specialized directories (including many very good ones) do not have annotations describing the sites they list. Annotations, however, can be very useful, as they provide a quick overview of what the sites cover and any special characteristics of the sites.
- Searchability: A fairly small portion of specialized directories provide a search box to save users from having to browse. If the directory is large, this can be quite useful.
- Origin: Who (or what organization) produced the site is sometimes a good indication of the quality you can expect from the site. Unfortunately, many sites do not give a clear indication of who produced them, and you may have to rely on the URL for a clue.
- Portal features: If, in addition to the collection of links, other features are included, the site can be especially powerful. Look for such features as news headlines, lists of events (conferences, etc.), professional directories (e.g., a list of members if it is a site produced by an association), directories of companies in that area, and so on.

SOME PROMINENT EXAMPLES OF SPECIALIZED DIRECTORIES

The examples of specialized directories included here are mentioned for a variety of reasons: Some were chosen simply because they are sites that most serious searchers should be aware of, some demonstrate particularly good or unique characteristics of a specialized directory, and some are very wide ranging (as well as having other values as a specialized directory). In some categories, such as Government, more than one example is listed to show contrasts between sites. (Sometimes multiple directories are listed for an area because I just could not make up my mind which one to choose.)

Don't forget that effective use of a directory approach for identifying relevant sites can mean using a combination of the general web directories covered in the previous chapter and the specialized directories covered here. In one sense, each section of a general directory such as Yahoo! Directory or Open Directory is itself a specialized directory.

General, Academic, and Reference Tools

The first site that follows provides an extensive collection of links to reference tools such as encyclopedias, dictionaries, and so forth. The next two sites focus on a broad range of subjects, but their coverage is limited primarily to those of interest in the academic/research setting. The last one included in this section, the Library of Congress Gateway, provides links to library catalogs available online.

Refdesk

www.refdesk.com

This fairly extensive collection is actually arranged more as a portal, with news headlines and other features, as well as links to valuable reference resources. (It had achieved a well-deserved status on its own but got a boost when then-U.S. Secretary of State Colin Powell said something to the effect that it should be on the screen of every State Department employee.) Most of the reference tools are found toward the bottom of the page.

INFOMINE

infomine.ucr.edu

A well-organized, categorized, and searchable collection of more than 100,000 links (some chosen by librarians and some identified by robots/crawlers), this directory is specialized in that it focuses on "scholarly" internet resources. Look here for sources that will be useful at the university level. The advanced search page has quite extensive searching capabilities for a specialized directory. INFOMINE comes from the University of California, with contributions from librarians at a number of other universities.

The advanced search page (Figure 2.4) has extensive searching capabilities. You can specify the fields you wish to search (author, subject, title words, etc.) and the category (BioAgMed, BusEcon, PhysSciEngr, GovInfo, SocSciHum, etc.). You can also limit your search to records created by experts (vs. experts and robots) and to either those that are free or fee-based. There is a Resource Options selection with which you can limit to one of 10 categories, such as article databases and digital libraries.

Library of Congress Gateway to Library Catalogs

lcweb.loc.gov/z3950/gateway.html

Going beyond just a "collection of links," this site uses a consistent interface to bring together the capability of searching (one at a time) the contents of the online catalogs for about 1,000 libraries in the U.S. and elsewhere. All of these are catalogs that use the Z39.50 standard for online library catalogs.

Social Sciences and Humanities

Best of History Web Sites

www.besthistorysites.net

Best of History Web Sites furnishes annotated and rated links to more than 1,200 history-related websites in categories such as Prehistory, Ancient/Biblical, Medieval,

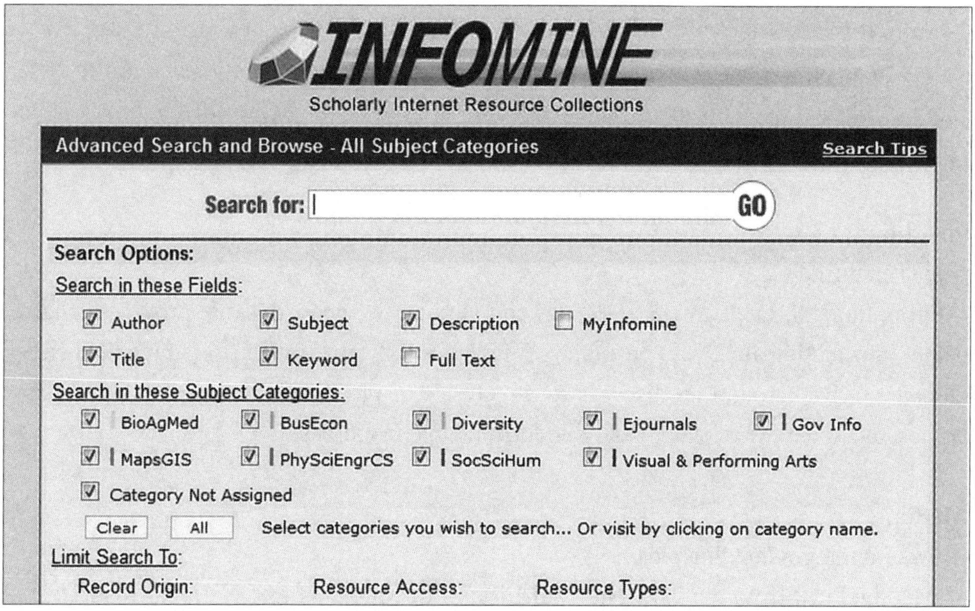

Figure 2.4 INFOMINE advanced search page

U.S. History, Early Modern European, World War II, Art History, Oral History, General Resources, and Maps. There are also categories for Lesson Plans/Activities, Maps, and Research.

Virtual Religion Index

www.virtualreligion.net/vri

With a focus on scholarly sites, this directory site contains extensive links on the world's major (and minor) religions and on the academic study of religion and religious issues.

Physical and Life Sciences and Technology

Besides the examples that follow, your best bet for focusing on a specific science may be to try the techniques for finding specialized directories mentioned earlier or to browse the appropriate section on sites such as INFOMINE. The first site that follows covers sciences and technology at a general level, while the others are some notable examples of science sites in specific areas.

Selected Internet Resources in Science and Technology

www.loc.gov/rr/scitech/resources.html

From the U.S. Library of Congress, this resource guide arranges resources in over a dozen areas of science and technology, and it also has an interesting selection of other categories, such as Women in Science, Technology and Medicine, Inventions, Meteor Showers, and Ice Cream.

healthfinder

www.healthfinder.gov

From the U.S. Department of Health and Human Services, this site provides reliable health information aimed at consumers. It includes links that range from a medical encyclopedia to background on diseases to directories of physicians, hospitals, and nursing homes, and a variety of other easily understandable resources.

MedlinePlus

www.nlm.nih.gov/medlineplus

MedlinePlus, from the U.S. National Library of Medicine and National Institutes of Health, is a portal that offers a combination of information provided directly on the site and an extensive collection of links. The Health Topics section contains more than 900 topics related to medical conditions, diseases, and wellness. Other parts of the MedlinePlus site include Drug Information, Medical Encyclopedia, Dictionaries, News (health news from the past 90 days), and Directories (doctors, dentists, and hospitals). Take advantage of the collection of videos and interactive tutorials.

Business and Economics

In addition to the specialized directories listed here for business-related information, be sure to look at the sites listed in Chapter 6 for company information. Some of the sites listed there, such as CorporateInformation, can also be considered specialized directories.

New York Times > Business > A Web Guide: Business Navigator

www.nytimes.com/ref/business/business-navigator.html

This highly selective collection of business-related links includes categories for Markets (exchanges, etc.), Investing, Company Information (directories, news, etc.), Banking & Finance, Government and Public Organizations (Federal Reserve, IRS, BLS, etc.), Business and Financial News, Business Directories, and Miscellany. Only about half of the 150 or so sites listed are annotated (and just briefly), but the clarity, selectivity, and categories into which they are divided make it an easy and quick guide to critical business resources.

CEOExpress

www.ceoexpress.com

CEOExpress is a cluttered-looking but rich site with a strong emphasis on business news sites (Figure 2.5). For a good understanding of what it can provide, spend three or four minutes browsing the unique arrangement of category links. The main site is free, but a paid subscription provides customization of the homepage, email, and other tools and benefits.

globalEDGE: Global Resource Directory

globaledge.msu.edu/Global-Resources

From Michigan State University, globalEDGE includes well-organized, annotated links to thousands of sites on global business activities.

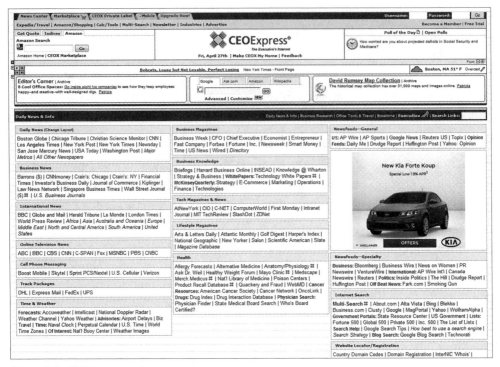

Figure 2.5 CEOExpress main page

Resources for Economists on the Internet

www.rfe.org

Edited by Bill Goff and sponsored by the American Economic Association, this site lists more than 2,000 resources categorized into 97 sections. These sections range from the obvious things of interest to economists, such as data, to less obvious but very useful categories, such as software and mailing lists. (If you need a break, check out the Neat Stuff section.)

Government and Governments

Although some countries have a single site that provides links to sites for individual government departments or ministries, many do not, and it is not always easy to identify the particular agency site you need. The first two sites that follow are directories that make this task much easier by bringing together large collections of government sites, organized by country or other category. The next three sites are examples of portals for specific countries, and the final site in this section is a resource guide for political parties worldwide.

Governments on the WWW

www.gksoft.com/govt

Although rather tardy in updating, this site contains links to more than 17,000 websites from governments and multinational organizations around the world, including parliaments, law courts, embassies, cities, public broadcasting corporations, central banks, political parties, and the like. There are no annotations, but the names of the sites are translated into English.

eRepublic.org

www.erepublic.org

If a national government has a central website portal, you should find a link to it at eRepublic.org. Depending upon the country, you may find additional links to ministries, embassies, and so on.

USA.gov

www.usa.gov

This site is the official portal to U.S. government sites. From the main tabs on the homepage, look particularly under Explore Topics (Figure 2.6) for categories by topic (Defense and International Relations, Health and Nutrition, etc.) and under Find Government Agencies for branches of the federal government plus state, local, and tribal government links. The A–Z Index of Government Agencies is especially helpful for locating links to specific agencies, commissions, offices, etc.

Directgov: Website of the U.K. Government

www.direct.gov.uk

The official U.K. government portal site provides links to U.K. public sector information. The main portions on the site are arranged by subject (e.g., Education and Learning, Home and Community) and by resources for specific groups of people (Young People, Britons Living Abroad, Caring for Someone, Disabled People, Parents). The A–Z of Central Government link leads to an alphabetic list of government ministries, agencies, and other public bodies.

Government of Canada Official Website

www.canada.gc.ca

The homepage of the Government of Canada Official Website offers sections on Governance and Services, a Resource Centre (with contact information and links to

Figure 2.6 USA.gov Explore Topics page

departments and agencies), and links to specific services for citizens, plus a variety of news and special features.

Political Resources on the Net

www.politicalresources.net

This site is an excellent resource for quickly identifying the sites of political parties for any country. On the map on the homepage, click on a continent and then the country. Links for international parties and other related resources are also provided.

Legal

FindLaw

www.findlaw.com

This very rich portal contains links to a broad range of legal subjects, from lawyers and law firms to cases and codes. Don't expect it to turn you into an expert legal researcher, but if you are one, you are probably already making good use of this site. If you aren't one, it will point you in the right direction for many of the best legal resources on the internet. FindLaw's main page is aimed at consumers, but on that page, you will find a link that takes you to the legal professionals' site (lp.findlaw.com). Legal resources are primarily focused on the U.S. (federal, state, and territories).

GlobaLex

www.nyulawglobal.org/globalex

GlobaLex is much more than a specialized directory—it is also a "research guide" that includes articles about the legal systems of more than 100 countries and international jurisdictions. Within these articles, you will find thousands of related links (including links to individual departments, agencies, etc., for countries) and extensive bibliographies of print resources.

Education

Kathy Schrock's Guide for Educators

school.discoveryeducation.com/schrockguide

This well-known directory for K–12 teachers and parents contains links to hundreds of sites, each with a brief annotation. You can browse by subject, grade level, etc. It is a good source for links to lesson plans, among other things.

EducationWorld

www.educationworld.com

EducationWorld contains an extensive browsable and searchable collection of education-related resources. The site is more a portal, not merely a directory, and contains much original content by the producers of the site (such as articles and lesson plans), as well as the links to other sites.

Education Atlas

www.educationatlas.com

Education Atlas is a clearly organized resource guide containing 45,000 education websites arranged in eight major sections (Online Degrees, Higher Ed, K–12, Early Childhood, Special Ed, Educators, Careers, and Study Skills). It also has categories for a variety of topics such as Home Schooling, Instructional Technology, and Regional (international).

News

Kidon Media-Link

www.kidon.com/media-link

Although a number of sites serve as directories of newspapers and other news sources on the internet, Kidon Media-Link is one of the most extensive and seems to have relatively few dead links (a common problem with some of the other news directories). The site is arranged by continent and then country, and provides more than 19,000 links to newspapers, news agencies, magazines, radio, and TV sites (Figure 2.7). (Additional news resource guides can be found in Chapter 8.)

Genealogy

Cyndi's List

www.cyndislist.com

This is perhaps the best known of the numerous genealogy directories and has links to more than 300,000 sites. You can browse through the 187 categories or take advantage of the search box. Both beginners and experienced genealogists should find it useful.

Travel

The Traveler's Web

www.extremesearcher.com/travel

The site for *The Traveler's Web* contains links to more than 500 internet travel resources covered in the book by the same name (and written by the author of the book you are currently reading).

GENERAL WEB PORTALS

Portals, or gateway sites, are sites that are designed to serve as starting places for getting to the most relevant material on the web. They typically have a variety of tools (such as a search engine, news, weather, and directories) on a single page, so that a user can use that page as the "start page" for his or her browser. Portals can often be personalized with regard to content and layout. Many serious searchers choose a portal, make it their start page, and personalize it. Thereafter, when they open their browsers, they have in front of

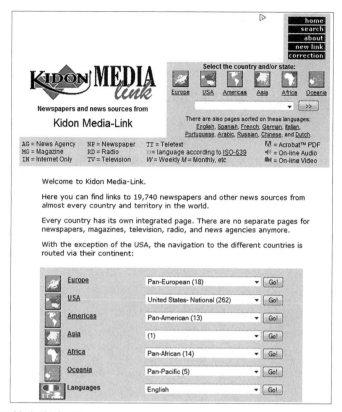

Figure 2.7   Kidon Media-Link main page

them such things as news headlines in their areas of interest, the weather for where they are or where they are headed, stock performance, and so on.

The portal concept goes considerably beyond the idea of web directories as we have been discussing them. However, this chapter seems the appropriate place to discuss them since general web portals, as with directories, embody the concept of getting the user quickly and easily to the most relevant web resources. In addition, the natures of directories and portals are melded so tightly that it is not feasible to try to totally separate them.

Well-known general portals include Yahoo!, AOL (www.aol.com), and Excite (www.excite.com). Most countries have their own popular general portals, for example, the French portal Voila! (www.voila.fr).

General portals usually exhibit three main characteristics: a variety of generally *useful tools*, positioning as a *start page*, and *personalizability*.

General Portals as Collections of Useful Tools

In line with the idea of a "gateway to internet resources," general portals provide a collection of tools and information that allows users to easily put their hands on information they frequently need.

Instead of having to go to different sites to get the news headlines and weather, or to find a phone directory, dictionary, search engine, and so forth, a portal can put this information—or links to this information—right on your start page. General portals usually include some variety of the following on their main pages:

- News
- Weather
- Stock information
- White pages

- Yellow pages
- Sports scores
- Free email
- Maps and directions

- Shopping
- Horoscope
- Calendar
- Address book

General Portals as Start Pages

Most general portals are designed to induce you to choose the site as your browser's start page. Because at least part of their support comes from ads, you may find some ads on the page, but portal producers know that the useful information must not be overpowered by ads or no one will come to the page. The overall thrust is to provide a collection of information so useful that it makes it worthwhile to go to that page first.

Personalizability of General Portals

Most successful general portals make their pages personalizable, allowing the user to choose which city's weather appears on the page, which stocks are shown, what categories of headlines are displayed, and so on. If you look around on the main pages of these sites, you will usually see either a Personalize link or a link to a My… option, such as My Yahoo!, which will allow you to sign up and personalize the page or will direct you to your personalized page if you have already done so. A Sign-In link will do likewise.

Yahoo!'s Portal Features

A look at Yahoo!'s main page offers a good idea of the types of things general portals can do. Yahoo! is undoubtedly one of the best of the general portals, particularly with regard to personalization features. In fact, a case could be made that for the serious searcher, Yahoo!'s personalized portal (My Yahoo!) is more important than the Yahoo! Directory (and with the disappearance of the directory from Yahoo!'s homepage, Yahoo!'s designers seem to agree).

TIP:

Follow these steps to make a chosen page your browser's start page:

- Internet Explorer: From the main menu bar, select Tools > Internet Options. Then under the General tab, enter the URL (including the http://) in the Home Page box. (You can enter multiple addresses to have additional "tabs" automatically loaded.)
- Firefox: From the main menu bar, select Tools > Options. Under the General tab, go to the Startup section and enter the address in the Home Page box.
- Safari: From the main menu bar, select Edit > Preferences. Under the General tab, enter the address for your start page in the Home Page box.
- Chrome: Click the wrench icon and then click Settings. Under the On Startup heading, enter the address using the Set Pages link.

Yahoo! has a number of portal features on its main, nonpersonalized page (www.yahoo.com). Some of them, such as news headlines, are displayed directly on the page, along with links to more than 20 other portal features, such as Autos, Real Estate, and Finance. Many of these links lead to more specialized portal pages provided by the site with, again, a collection of tools and links specific to the topic of that page. The best way to understand a portal such as Yahoo! is to lock yourself in your office and not leave until you have clicked on every link on the page. (Skip the ads, though.)

My Yahoo!

An example of a personalized general portal page (My Yahoo! at my.yahoo.com) is shown in Figure 2.8. Yahoo! provides one of the most personalizable general portals, with possibly the widest variety of choices, including many other Yahoo! "personal" products such as Yahoo! Mail, a calendar, and so on. It also provides personalized versions for many of its 70-plus country- or language-specific versions.

Some Other Popular General Portals

The following sites also all exhibit the three characteristics of general portals to varying degrees and with varying content. Determining which one is the best for any individual probably depends on what content is available on the portal and how it is presented. Try more than one before deciding. Most of the better-known general portals have dozens of options to choose from (many, many more if the portal allows you to add any RSS feed

Figure 2.8 My Yahoo! personalized portal page

you wish). Such items as Word of the Day and Pregnancy Watch may or may not be of interest to you. Your personal stock portfolio is handled very differently by various portals, and what data the portal displays and how it displays that data may make the difference in your choice. A portal may allow very detailed specification of what categories of headlines are displayed, or it may allow for only very general categories, and so on. The following portals, along with My Yahoo!, are among the best known in the U.S. For non-U.S. portals, take a look at the World section of Open Directory (www.dmoz.org/world), choose your country, and then search for the term portal in the relevant language.

Other selected examples of general portals include the following:

- Excite (www.excite.com): Once the best and still used by many people
- AOL (www.aol.com): The first popular general portal
- MSN (www.msn.com): The number of customizable content options has increased over the last few years.

One more resource related to general directories and portals is the following site.

Traffick: Frequently Asked Questions About Portals
www.traffick.com/article.asp?aID=9#what

This site provides a concise but quite informative overview and history of the web portal concept.

Summary

Remember that web directories provide sites that are evaluated and selected by human beings. With general web directories, the fact that sites are placed in categories to allow browsing makes these tools a good starting place when you want selected sites, when you want only a few sites, and when your question is general rather than specific. Specialized directories provide the searcher with at least *some* immediate "expertise" in knowing the most important internet resources for a specific subject area. Take advantage of one of the general, personalizable portals as a starting place, so you can easily go to your own selection of frequently needed information.

CHAPTER 3

SEARCH ENGINES: THE BASICS

General web search engines, such as Google, Bing, and Yahoo! Search, stand in contrast to web directories in three primary ways: 1) They are much larger, containing billions instead of a few million (or fewer) records, 2) there is virtually no human selectivity involved in determining what webpages are included in the search engine's database, and 3) they are designed for searching (responding to a user's specific query) rather than for browsing, so they provide more substantial searching capabilities than directories.

For someone using internet resources, a workable definition of a web search engine is a service on the web that allows searching of a large database of web resources by word, phrase, and other criteria. There is actually some ambiguity involved when we speak of *search engines*. From a slightly more technical perspective, when we use a site such as Google, we are utilizing a service that facilitates the searching of a database. In the narrower sense, the search engine is the program used by the service to query the database. Almost any site that provides a search box could be considered to have a search "engine." Here, when we speak of search engines, we will really be referring to a service, such as the three just mentioned, that provides searching of a very large database of webpages and may provide other services as well, such as translations and shopping.

HOW SEARCH ENGINES ARE PUT TOGETHER

To take full advantage of search engines, it is useful to understand the basics of how they are put together. Four major steps are involved in making webpages searchable by a search engine service. These steps also correspond to the "parts" of a search engine—the spiders, the indexing program and index, the search engine program, and the HTML user interface:

1. Spiders (aka crawlers): These are programs used by the search engine services to scan the internet to identify new sites or sites that have changed, to gather information from those sites, and to feed that information to the search engine's indexing mechanism. For some engines, popular sites (likely to have many links to them) are crawled more thoroughly and more frequently than less popular sites. Tied into this crawling function is a second way for webpages to get identified—by the process of submitted URLs. A link found on most search engines' sites will let someone submit a URL, and with the exception of those pages that are identifiable as spam (pages that are designed to mislead the search engine and search engine users and/or illegitimately lead to high rankings) or pages that are unacceptable for other reasons, the pages will be indexed and added to the database.

2. The indexing program and the index: Once a new page is identified by the search engine's crawler, the page will typically be indexed under virtually every word on the page. Other parts of the page may also be indexed, such as the URL, metatags (see Glossary), the URLs of links on the page, and image file names. Based on the content of a page, the indexing program may derive other characteristics to be indexed, such as language.

3. The search "engine" itself: This is the program that identifies (retrieves) those pages in the database that match the criteria indicated by a user's query. Another important and more challenging process is also involved: determining the order in which the retrieved records should be displayed. This "relevance-ranking" algorithm usually takes many factors into account, such as the popularity of the page (as measured by how many other pages link to it), the number of times the search terms occur in the page, the relative proximity of search terms in the page, the location of search terms (e.g., pages where the search terms occur in the title of the page may get a higher ranking), and other factors.

4. The HTML (HyperText Markup Language) interface: This HTML-based interface is what gathers query data from the user (the "search page"); the homepage and advanced search pages of the search service are the parts we usually envision when we think of a particular search engine. These pages contain the search box(es), links to the various databases that are searchable (images, news, etc.), and perhaps a number of other features.

HOW SEARCH OPTIONS
ARE PRESENTED

Exactly what search options are available varies from search engine to search engine. With any particular search engine, some available options are presented on the homepage, but on the advanced search page, usually several more options are clearly displayed. Options are typically made available 1) by means of a menu, or 2) by the searcher directly qualifying the term when it is entered in the main search box.

An example of the menu approach is shown in Figure 3.1, where (in Yahoo!) a pull-down menu allows the term entered in the box to be qualified. In this example, the search is requesting that only those pages be retrieved that have the term *antioxidants* in the *title* of the page.

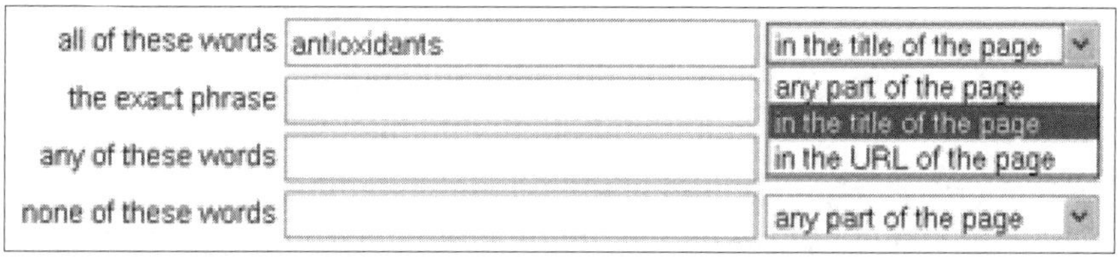

Figure 3.1 Example of the menu approach to qualifying a search term

Figure 3.2 shows an example of qualifying a term directly. Here (in Google) the *intitle:* prefix is inserted to do the same thing as shown in the menu example in Figure 3.1. (Whenever using prefixes such as this to qualify a search term, be sure not to put a space on either side of the colon.)

Figure 3.2 Example of using a prefix to qualify a search term

Usually you have a choice as to which approach to use. The menu approach is easier in that you do not need to know the somewhat cryptic prefixes. If you do know the prefixes, you may accomplish your search more quickly and easily.

TYPICAL SEARCH OPTIONS

A number of search options are fairly typical. These include phrase searching, language specification, and specifying that you retrieve only pages where your term appears in a particular part (field) of the record, such as the title, URL, or links. Now that major engines include more than just HTML pages, for some engines you can also specify file type (webpages, PDFs, Excel files, etc.). Every engine also offers some form of Boolean operations. Each of these options provides added capabilities for being able to control the recall and precision of the search. (See Chapter 1 for a discussion of recall and precision.)

The following gives a quick look at why you might want to use (or not use) those options. Table 4.1 near the end of Chapter 4 identifies which options are available in which engines, and the search engine profiles in Chapter 4 provide some details for using the search options in the major engines. Expect occasional changes in exactly which options are offered by which engines.

Phrase Searching

Phrase searching is an option that is available in every search engine, and perhaps surprisingly, it can be done the same way in all of them. To search for a phrase, put the phrase in quotation marks. For example, searching on *"Red River"* (with quotation marks) will ensure that you get only those pages that contain the word *red* immediately in front of the term *river*. You will avoid records such as one about the red wolves of Alligator River. This technique can greatly increase the precision of your search results and, at the same time, at least in this example, will not damage your recall. In other words, almost every record retrieved will in some way have something to do with Red River. As for recall, use of quotation marks will not cause you to miss any records dealing with Red River. Whenever your concept is best expressed as a phrase, be sure to use quotation marks. You are not limited to two words; you can use several. For example, to find out who said "When I'm good I'm very good, but when I'm bad I'm better," search for a few of the words together, such as *"when I'm bad I'm better."*

Some engines automatically identify common phrases, and most engines give a higher ranking to pages in which your terms appear next to each other. To be sure, though, that you are only getting records with your terms adjacent to each other and in the order you wish, use quotation marks.

Title Searching

This is often the most powerful technique for getting to some highly relevant pages quickly (high precision). It may also cause you to miss some good ones, but what you do get has an excellent chance of being relevant. All the major engines have this option, and most of them let you search titles by means of either menu options or prefixes (see Figures 3.1 and 3.2).

URL, Site, and Domain Searching

Doing a search in which you limit your results to a specific site allows you, in effect, to perform a search just of that site. Even for sites that have a "site search" box on their homepage, you may find that you get better results by doing a site search in a large search engine. If you want to find where on the FBI site the term *internship* is mentioned, use a search engine's advanced search page and specify the term *internship* in the search box and *fbi.gov* in the box that lets you specify the site (or domain or URL). Most engines will let you accomplish the same thing using a prefix. For example, in Google, Yahoo!, Bing, and Ask.com, you could search for:

> *internship site:fbi.gov*

Most engines allow you to be more specific and search a portion of a site, for example (in each of the four engines just mentioned):

> *internship site:baltimore.fbi.gov*

As well as specifying an exact site, you can, in some engines, specify that you want a term to be anywhere in the URL by using the inurl: prefix, for example:

> *members inurl:aiip*

In many search engines, domain searching is identical to URL searching. The use of the term, though, points out that you can use this approach to limit your retrieval to sites having a particular top-level domain, such as .gov, .edu, .uk, .ca, or .fr. This strategy could be used to identify only Canadian sites that mention tariffs or to get only educational sites that mention biodiversity.

Link Searching

There are two varieties of link searching. In one variety, you can search for all pages that have a hypertext link to a particular URL; and in the other, you can search for words contained in the linked text on the page. In the former, for example, you can check which webpages have linked to your organization's URL. In the latter, you can see which webpages have the name of your organization as linked text. Either variety can be very informative in terms of finding out who is interested in either your organization or your website. It can be very useful for marketing purposes, and it can also be used by nonprofits for development and fundraising leads. Also, if you are looking for information on an organization, it can sometimes be useful to know who is linking to that organization's site.

This searching option is available in some search engines on their advanced page and/or on the main page with the use of prefixes. Engines may let you look for links to an overall site or to a specific page within a site. If you want to search exhaustively for who is linking to a particular site, definitely use more than one search engine. In link searching, the difference in retrieval is even more pronounced than in keyword searching.

Language Searching

Although all of the major engines allow you to limit your retrieval to pages written in a given language, they differ in terms of which languages can be specified. The 40 or so most common languages are specifiable in most of those engines, but if you want to find a page written in Esperanto, not all engines will give you that option. If you find yourself searching by language, be sure to look at the various language options and preferences provided by the different engines, particularly if a non-Western character set is involved.

Searching by Date

Searching by date is one of the most obviously desirable options, and most major engines provide such an option. Unfortunately, it may not have much meaning. Through no fault of the search engines, it is often impossible to determine a definitive "date created" or the "date of publication" of the content of the page. To get around this, engines may use the date when the page was last modified or the date on which the page was last crawled by the engine. When searching webpages, keep this approximation in mind and do not expect much precision. (In other databases that an engine may provide, such as news or groups, the date searching may be very precise.)

Searching by File Type

Since the 1990s, most search engines have been indexing a variety of non-HTML pages, including Adobe Acrobat files (PDFs), Word documents, Excel files, and others. There are times when you may want to limit your retrieval to one of those file types. For example, if you wanted to print out a tutorial for Dreamweaver, you might prefer the more attractive PDF over the format of an HTML page. If you want a nice summary of a topic, try finding a document in PowerPoint. Collections of statistics on a specific topic can sometimes be easily identified by limiting your retrieval to Excel files. Specifying file type may not be required very often, but at times, it will be very useful.

Boolean Search Options

In the context of online searching, Boolean searching basically refers to a process of identifying those items, such as webpages, that contain a particular combination of search terms. It is used to indicate that a particular group of terms must all be present (the Boolean AND), that any one of a particular group of terms is acceptable (the Boolean OR), or that if a particular term is present, the item is rejected (the Boolean NOT). These relationships are represented by the dark areas in the Venn diagrams shown in Figure 3.3.

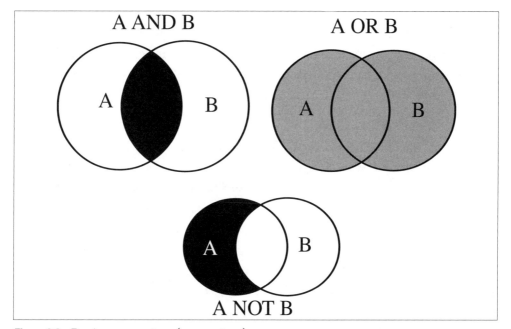

Figure 3.3 Boolean operators (connectors)

Very precise search requirements can be expressed using combinations of these operators along with parentheses to indicate the order of operations. For example:

(grain OR corn OR wheat) AND (production OR harvest) AND oklahoma AND 1997

The use of the actual words AND, OR, and NOT to represent Boolean operations has been downplayed in web search engines and has been replaced in many cases by the use of menus or other syntax. (In no major web search engine do you actually type *AND*.) Even if you have never typed an AND, OR, or NOT, you have probably still used Boolean. (One point here being that Boolean is "painless.") If you choose the "all the words" option from a pull-down menu, you are requesting the Boolean AND. If you choose the "any of the words" option from a menu, you are specifying an OR. Because all major search engines automatically AND your query terms (if you do not specify otherwise), any time you just enter two or more terms in a search box, you are implicitly requesting an AND (even if you do not realize it).

It is important to note that the use of Boolean provides tremendous control over recall and precision. When using other techniques that increase recall, you can often damage your precision because techniques that increase the number of records retrieved may cause a smaller portion of your results to be relevant and vice versa. With the use of Boolean, however, you can often greatly improve your recall without increasing the portion of nonrelevant records (and, again, vice versa). For example, if OR is used to find synonyms for a search term, recall can be greatly enhanced and records retrieved can be just as relevant.

Varieties of Boolean Formats
As with title, site, and other search qualifications, Boolean usually provides two options for indicating what you want: 1) a menu option, or 2) the option of applying the syntax directly to what you enter in the search box. Using the menu option can be thought of as "simplified Boolean" or "simple Boolean." An example of a Boolean menu option is shown in Figure 3.4.

With the syntax approach, the exact syntax used varies with the search engine. All major engines now automatically AND your terms, so when you enter:

prague economics tourism

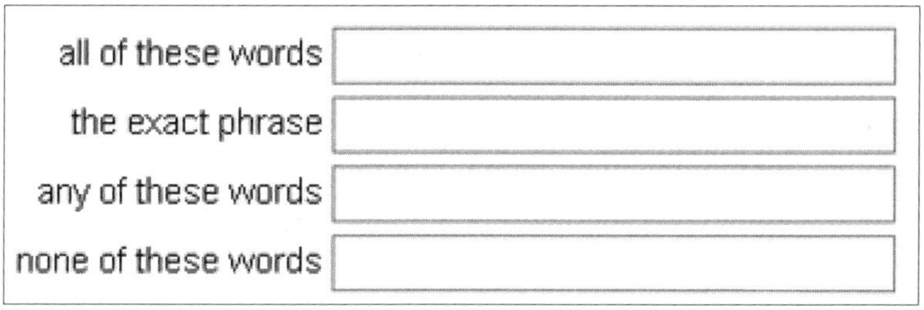

all of these words	
the exact phrase	
any of these words	
none of these words	

Figure 3.4 Menu form of Boolean options (and phrase option)

what you will get is more traditionally described as:

prague AND economics AND tourism

Figure 3.5 shows an example of Boolean syntax (from Yahoo!'s main search page).

roma population (hungary OR hungarian) | Search

Figure 3.5 Example of Boolean syntax

Full Boolean

Even though most engines provide syntax to allow near-maximum Boolean capabilities, engines have asserted their independence by varying the particular syntax used for entering a Boolean expression. For example, Google does not require parentheses when using an OR, but Bing and Yahoo! do require parentheses around ORed terms.

Table 3.1 shows how a typical Boolean-oriented search would be structured in the major search engines. For all practical purposes, a search engine can be considered to have full Boolean capabilities if it provides for all three Boolean operations (AND, OR, and NOT).

SEARCH ENGINE OVERLAP

It is important to recognize that no single search engine covers everything. Due to differences in crawling, indexing, and other factors, each engine's database includes and delivers webpages that the others do not. In some searches, if you search a second engine, it may significantly increase the number of unique records you find. Searching a third and fourth engine can also yield records not found by the first engines. Therefore, if you need to be exhaustive—if it is crucial that you find everything on the topic—do your search in

Table 3.1 Boolean Syntax at Major Search Engines

Search Engine	Boolean Pattern	Full Boolean?	Expression
Ask.com	A B OR C - D	No	"endangered species" maryland OR virginia -rockfish
Google	A B OR C - D	Yes	"endangered species" maryland OR virginia -rockfish
Bing	A (B OR C) -D or A (B OR C) NOT D	Yes	"endangered species" (maryland OR virginia) -rockfish
Yahoo!	A (B OR C) -D or A (B OR C) NOT D	Yes	"endangered species" (maryland OR Virginia) -rockfish

NOTE: Since Google and Ask.com ignore parentheses anyway, the following will work in Google, Bing, Yahoo, and Ask.com: "endangered species" (maryland OR virginia) -rockfish

at least two search engines. (At the end of this chapter, you will see why metasearch engines are *not* the solution to this problem.)

RESULTS PAGES

One of the most useful things a searcher can do is to take a few extra seconds to look not just at the titles of the retrieved webpages, but also at the other things included on results pages and at the details provided in each record. Most engines provide some potentially useful additional information besides just the webpage results. At the same time that they search their web database, they may search the other databases they have, such as news, images, and video. Among your regular web search results, you may find some news headlines that match your topic; a link to images, audio, or video on your topic; background information; and more.

One thing offered on search results pages by all of the major engines is a spell-checker. If you misspelled a word, or the search engine thinks you might have, it may graciously ask something like "Did you mean?" and give you a likely alternative, or it may rather presumptuously assume that you were wrong and give you the results for what it thinks you wanted. If it was indeed a mistake and it didn't automatically search for the correct spelling, just click on the alternate suggestion to correct the problem.

Be aware of Sponsor Results or Sponsored Links on results pages. These are ads for websites, and they are there because the site has paid to appear somewhere on the search engine's results pages. Most major engines keep ads more-or-less easily identifiable, for example, by putting them on a very light pink background or off to the side of the page. When placed at the top of the results pages, though, they may send less experienced users to an ad while thinking they have gone to a regular search result.

Also look closely at the individual web results records. In most search engines, results from individual websites are "clustered," that is, only the first one or two highly ranked records from any site will be shown, and there will be a link in the record leading you to "More from this site" or "Show more results from …", etc. If you are not aware of these links, you may miss relevant records from that site.

One other option you will notice on search results for some engines is a Translate This Page link. If a page is written in a language other than the language in which you are searching, in some cases, you may see such a link attached to the record. Click on it to receive a machine translation of the page. As with other machine translations, what you get may not be a good translation, but it will probably be an adequate translation, in that it will give you a good idea of what the page is talking about. Also keep in mind that only "words" are translated. The translation program cannot translate words displayed on a page that are actually images rather than text. (Many purists flagrantly reject the use of these translation tools. That attitude, it can be argued, is analogous to saying I should never attempt to read a German newspaper article because my own translation will have a lot of mistakes, that being totally ignorant of the content of the page is better than having just a general idea of what is being said.)

SEARCH ENGINE ACCOUNTS

For many features provided by the major search engines, you must have an account, particularly for using features that involve customized services such as personalized portals, email, search histories, etc. In most cases, signing up for these free accounts requires your divulging only a bare minimum of personal information (sometimes just an email address). (For any readers who may be intensely spamophobic, you may find it worthwhile to know that the author has accounts with all the major search engines, and some minor search sites as well, and has yet to identify any email spam that is the result of having signed up with them.) Considering the benefits these account provide, it is worth the minute or so it takes to sign up.

SPECIALTY SEARCH ENGINES

Numerous specialty search engines are available. Some are geographic (focusing on sites from one country), and some are topical (focusing on a particular subject area). To locate examples of these, check out the following category in Open Directory (www.dmoz.org): Computers > Internet > Searching > Search Engines > Specialized.

There are indeed some other search engines out there that are comparable in size to the engines discussed in this book, particularly the Chinese search engine Baidu (www.baidu.com) and the Russian search engine Yandex (www.yandex.ru). If you search in either Chinese or Russian, you may want to consider using those, although some English-language searching is possible in both. In the case of Baidu, be aware of the censorship restraints imposed by the Chinese government on Baidu's content.

METASEARCH ENGINES

Metasearch engines are services that let you search several search engines at the same time. With one search, you get results from several engines. (They should not be confused with metasites, another term for specialized directories, which were discussed in Chapter 2.) Considering the usefulness of using more than one engine, the metasearch idea seems compelling—and it is indeed a great idea. However, the reality is often something else. You may find that you like a particular metasearch engine and have legitimate reasons for using it, but it is important to note some particularly important shortcomings.

First, though, it should be noted that this section addresses the free sites on the web that allow the searching of multiple engines. There are also metasearch programs (software) that can be purchased to help you search multiple engines. These client-side programs may do a more complete job, but they involve downloading (and eventually purchasing) a program and sometimes involve several more steps to get to your results.

Free metasearch engines on the web are numerous. New ones frequently appear, and older ones disappear just as quickly. Among the better known are Dogpile, Ixquick, Yippy, MetaCrawler, and Search.com. They can cover portions of a large number of search engines and directories in a single search, and they can sometimes be useful in finding something very obscure.

However, each metasearch engine usually presents one or more (and sometimes all) of the following drawbacks:

1. They may not cover most of the larger search engines. If you have a favorite metasearch engine, see if it covers Google, Yahoo!, Bing, and Ask.com.

2. They may only return the first 10 to 20 records from each source. If record No. 11 in one of the search engines was a great one, you may not see it.

3. Most search syntax does not work. Some metasearch engines let you search by title, URL, and so on, but most do not. Some do not even recognize even the simplest syntax: the use of quotation marks to indicate a phrase.

4. Some present paid listings first (without necessarily identifying them as such).

Also, by now you know that on search engine results pages, the additional content presented (besides just the listing of websites) can often be very valuable. You usually lose this with metasearch engines.

Where metasearch engines can provide definite value is when they truly offer something above and beyond what you get in a single regular search engine. An example of this kind of feature is the subject clustering of results provided by Yippy (www.yippy.com).

If you find that a metasearch engine meets your needs, use it. However, they are not the solution for an exhaustive—or even a moderately extensive—search.

SEARCH ENGINE SHORTCUTS

Several search engines, particularly Yahoo!, Google, and Bing, provide shortcuts for quick answers, including phone numbers, stock prices, calculations, conversions, and so on. With these, you can just enter a brief statement in the main search box and click on search, and an answer will appear at the top of the results page. Shortcuts will be discussed in Chapter 4.

KEEPING UP-TO-DATE ON WEB SEARCH ENGINES

To keep up-to-date with what is happening in the realm of web search engines, take advantage of the sites listed in the section "Keeping Up-to-Date on Internet Resources and Tools" in Chapter 1.

CHAPTER 4

SEARCH ENGINES: THE SPECIFICS

Chapter 3 provided an overview of search engines, how they work, and their common features. This chapter, however, provides detailed profiles of each of the top search engines. The descriptions give an overview of the service, take a look at the features on the homepage and advanced search page, and call attention to any notable additional features.

For some features, such as news and image databases, only a brief mention is given in the profile because the subject is covered in detail in a relevant chapter elsewhere in this book. As you use these engines, expect to occasionally find new features, new arrangements of homepages, and other changes.

The engines presented here are the four most popular among serious searchers, or at least, English-language searchers. (If you look at many published lists of the most popular search engines, you will often see AOL Search listed among the top five. It is not discussed here because AOL is still the "internet on training wheels," and its search interface and results are "enhanced by Google," as its search page says. It provides no significant search features or content beyond what Google itself provides.)

See Table 4.1 at the end of the discussion on the major search engines for an outline of which options are available in which search engines.

GOOGLE

Within about four years, Google (www.google.com) went from being the new kid on the block to being the favorite search engine for the majority of users. For the most part, its high standing stems from using the popularity of a webpage as a major ranking factor, its simplicity for the casual user, and its vigorous efforts to increase both the size of its database and the provision of additional features and types of content. In ranking records, Google puts considerable emphasis on the popularity of a webpage, measured by how many other pages link to that page and the popularity of those linking pages. (Webpages are known by the friends they keep.) Google was the first major engine to provide a cache feature to let you go to a cached copy of the page as it looked when last indexed by the engine. Besides webpage searching, Google also provides excellent image, video, news, blog, and shopping databases, plus more specialized searches such as for journal articles and books, as well as an increasing number of non-search services including email, satellite images, and maps. The last time Google officially reported the size of its database, way back in 2005, it contained more than 8 billion records.

Google Homepage

One of the reasons Google is so popular is its insistence on a simple, uncluttered homepage (Figure 4.1). Even though the homepage is simple, exploring the few links on the page will uncover several features.

The homepage includes the following items:

- Search box: Enter one or more words (up to 32). Use a minus sign in front of a term to exclude that term (Boolean NOT). You can also use OR, as well as several prefixes such as intitle:. Google will ignore small, common words unless they are within quotation marks.

- I'm Feeling Lucky: Takes you directly to the page that Google would have listed first in your results (mostly a gimmick).

Figure 4.1 Google homepage

Across the top of the page, you'll find links to Google's various databases and other services. The exact links you see may change, as Google occasionally switches which databases and services have direct links on the main page and which are found under More. The databases and services include:

- +You: Links to your Google-provided personal, social networking page, Google+.
- Images: This leads to one of the largest image search databases on the web.
- Maps: Find maps, directions, a business directory, and a search for much of the world, plus driving directions (and where appropriate, walking directions and directions for public transit) and satellite images.
- Play: Get access to Google's "entertainment" hub, where you can download apps, songs, books, and movies, and sync them among your desktop, laptop, tablet, smartphone, and ereader.
- YouTube: Find videos on YouTube (owned by Google).
- News: Search 25,000 English-language news sources going back 30 days (plus a news archives search going back much further, and searches for news from other languages and countries).
- Gmail: Use Google's free webmail service.
- Drive: Use Google's online collaborative software applications (word processor, spreadsheet, presentations, etc.).
- Calendar: Get organized with a sharable online calendar.
- Videos: Search any video in Google's own YouTube plus video from other sites.
- Groups: Search groups (forums) including Usenet postings back to 1981, groups that are created on Google by Google users, and other forums found on the web.
- Shopping: Browse Google's shopping database.
- Books: Search full text of millions of books, plus the ability to view actual pages from many.
- Scholar: Search scholarly literature from peer-reviewed journals, preprints, theses, books, etc.
- Finance: Check out this portal for financial news and information.
- Blogs: Find blogs using Google's blog search.
- Photos: Create online photo albums using Google's Picasa.
- Reader: Get access to Google's RSS reader.
- Translate: Try out Google's translation services for more than 60 languages.

- Even More: Takes you to the page that lists virtually all of the major services provided by Google.

If you are signed in to Google, there will be some other links found on the upper-right side of the homepage. There, you will see your user name, under which you'll find the following options:

- View Profile: Allows you to view the personal profile that you have if you use Google+.
- Account Settings: Change your password; simultaneously log in to different accounts within the same browser; add alternate email addresses to your account; connect your YouTube account to your Google account; edit your Google+ profile; delete your entire Google account; and view and enable or disable your web history.
- Privacy Settings: Control your privacy settings with regard to your Google profile, your "circles" (of friends, etc.) in Google+, and photos and notifications in Google+. From here, you can also access your Dashboard, where, in one place, you can see and modify settings for all Google services such as Google Calendar, Google Books, your Android device, Blogger, Google Drive, etc.

If you use Google+, next to your user name you will also see a Notifications link, which lists recent notifications you have received on Google+, and a Share link, which enables you to share photos, video, and links with people you are connected to through Google+ and other social networking sites.

There are some additional links at the bottom of the page. These may include a link to Google+ as well as a link to change the background image for the page and links for information on advertising, the company, and sometimes a featured service. The About Google link leads to information about Google as a company.

Google Advanced Search

As with other engines, most Google searches can most easily be accomplished by putting one or more terms in the homepage search box. If you need enhanced capabilities, Google's advanced search page also provides all the common field search options (title, domain, link, language, and date), as well as some less common ones (Figure 4.2). The biggest challenge may be in remembering where Google hid the link to the advanced search page (under the gear wheel icon on results pages).

You will find the following on Google's advanced search page (in roughly this order):

- Boxes to perform simple Boolean combinations ("all these words," etc.)

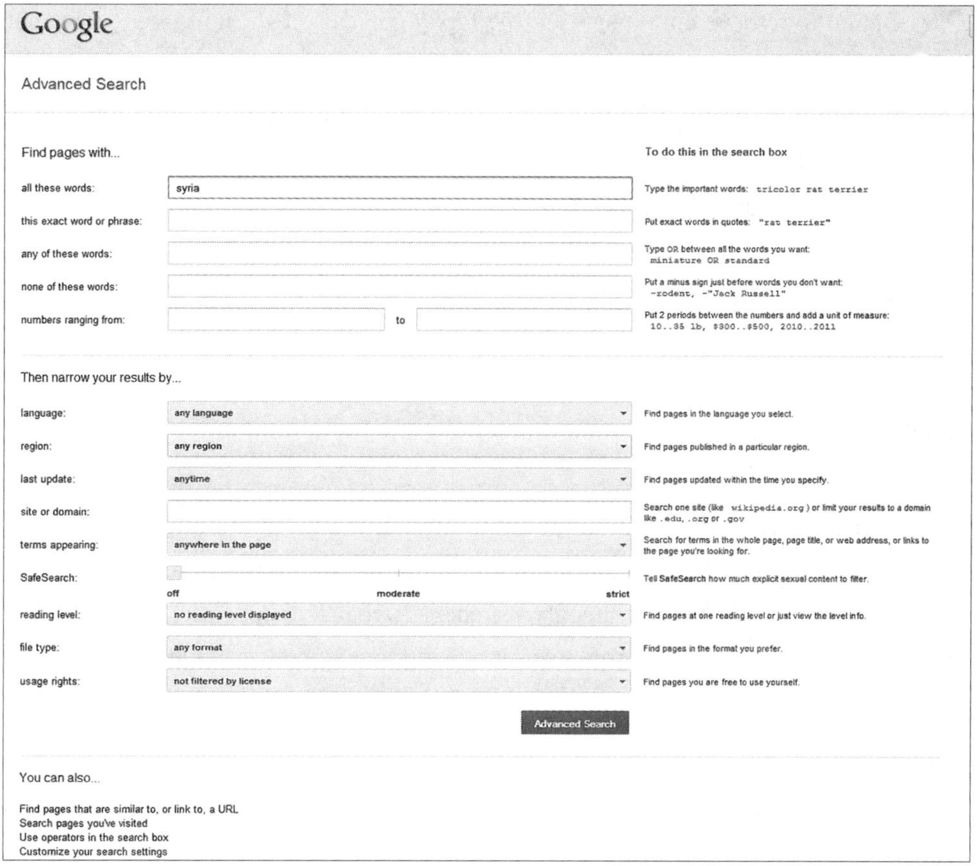

Figure 4.2   Google's advanced search page

- Numeric range option to limit retrieval to pages containing numbers with the range you specify (for years, dollars, etc.)
- Choice of searching for documents in all languages or any one of 46 languages
- Region menu to limit to pages from a particular country
- Last update (anytime, past 24 hours, past week, past month, past year)
- Box to limit to a particular site or domain
- Menu to limit retrieval to title, text, or URL fields, or within the links on the page
- A filter option (SafeSearch) to block adult content
- Choice of reading level (No reading level displayed, Annotate results with reading level, Show only basic results, Show only intermediate results, Show only advanced results).

- Option to retrieve only a specific file type (.pdf, .ps, .dwf, .kml, .kmz, .xls, .ppt, .doc, .rtf, .swf)
- Usage Rights menu to limit retrieval to material that can be used, shared, modified, and so on above and beyond "fair use," without infringing on copyright (this material has a Creative Commons [www.creativecommons.org] license)
- Page-specific tool to "Find pages [that are] similar to the page" whose URL you enter in the box or pages that link to a specific URL or to "Find pages that link to the page" (enter the URL of the page of interest)

At the bottom of the advanced search page you will find links leading to explanations of other features and settings.

Search Features Provided by Google

Using the menus on the advanced page and prefixes on the main page, Google provides field searching for all of the commonly searchable webpage fields (title, URL, link, language, date), plus searching by file format, date range, country, usage rights, and for "similar" pages.

Boolean

On the homepage, Google automatically ANDs all of your words. You can also use a minus sign to NOT a term, and you can use one or more ORs (the OR must be capitalized):

> *warfare chemical OR biological –anthrax*

This search expression would find all records that contain the word *warfare* and also contain either *chemical* or *biological*, but would eliminate all records containing the word *anthrax*.

(Since Google believes that it knows more about what we want than we do, if your query has several terms and Google finds nothing, it will sometimes ignore one or more of your terms. In other words, it may tell you there are matching records when, in fact, there are none.)

On Google's advanced search page, simple Boolean is done by use of the "all these words," "any of these words," and "none of these words" boxes.

Title Searching

Searches can be limited to words appearing in the page title in one of two ways. First, on the advanced search page, you can enter your terms in the search boxes, then choose "in the title of the page" from the "terms appearing" pull-down menu.

Second, on the homepage, you can use the prefixes *intitle:* or *allintitle:*. The *intitle:* prefix specifies that a certain word or phrase is included in the title:

> *intitle:online*
> *intitle:"online strategies"*

Use *allintitle:* to specify that all words after the colon be included in the title but not necessarily in that order. For example, the following would retrieve titles with both words somewhere in the title, not necessarily in the specific order:

> *allintitle:nato preparedness*

These prefixes can be combined with a search for a word anywhere on the page:

> *summit intitle:nato*

You cannot achieve this kind of combination using the menus on the advanced search page because your single menu choice (where your terms show up) will apply to all terms you enter in the search boxes.

URL, Site, and Domain Searching

If you want to limit retrieval to pages from a particular URL, it can be done in a way parallel to title searching. You can do it either using menus on the advanced search page or using prefixes on the homepage. On the advanced search page, enter a URL (or a top-level domain such as .edu or .ac) in the "Site or domain" box.

On the homepage, you can use the prefixes *site:*, *inurl:* or *allinurl:*

> *site:yale.edu*
> *inurl:bbc*
> *inurl:"bbc.co.uk"*
> *allinurl:news co uk*

To do a site search for a specific topic, on the advanced search page, enter terms for your topic in the search boxes and the URL in the "Search within a site or domain" box. A site search can be done on the Google homepage using the site: prefix, as follows:

hybrid site:ford.com

Link Searching

To find pages that link to a particular site, perform the search on the Google homepage by using the *link:* prefix. For example, to find pages that link to the Modern Language Association site, search for:

link:mla.org

Interestingly, although in its retrieval algorithm, Google puts much emphasis on linkages between sites, its *link:* search feature returns very few of the sites that actually do link to the page in which you are interested.

Language Searching

To limit retrieval to sites in a particular language, use the Language menu on the advanced search page. The default is "any language," but you can choose any one of 47 languages. If you want to set a particular language or languages as your default choice, use Google's Search Settings page. On that same page, you can also request that the Google search pages appear in any one of 149 languages (including Bork! Bork! Bork!, Elmer Fudd, and Klingon, as well as real languages).

Searching by Date

The Last Update window on the advanced search page allows you to limit results to pages that are new in the past 24 hours, past week, past month, or past year. Keep in mind that date searching is only an approximation because the origination date or last updated date is often not clearly identified on most webpages. Date searching has improved somewhat, but most webpages don't have a clearly defined date for search engines to work with, so when you search by date for recent items, your results may largely be from blogs and news sites.

Searching by File Type

Using the File Format menu on the advanced search page, results can be limited to any of the following formats: Adobe Acrobat (.pdf), Adobe Postscript (.ps), Autodesk DWF

(.dwf), Google Earth (.kml, .kmz), Microsoft Excel (.xls), Microsoft Word (.doc), Microsoft PowerPoint (.ppt), rich text format (.rtf), and Shockwave Flash (.swf).

On the Google homepage, you can accomplish the same thing (or exclude files of a particular type) by using the *filetype:* prefix. For example, if you want to print out a 1040EZ IRS tax form, search for:

1040EZ IRS form filetype:pdf

Searching for Related (Similar) Pages

You can search for pages that are similar to a particular page by using the *related:* prefix on Google's homepage:

related:searchengineland.com

Searching by Other Prefixes

The following prefixes can be used on the Google homepage to search for other specific information:

- **cache:** – Enter a URL after the colon to get Google's cached version of the page (*cache:www.cas.org*).
- **info:** – Enter a URL after the colon and you will be shown the record for that specific site and given links that take you to a) "similar" sites, b) sites that link to the site, c) all webpages indexed from the site, and d) pages that contain the URL as a term on the page (*info:cyndislist.com*). A link to the cached version of the page is also provided.
- **stocks:** – Enter a stock symbol after the colon to get stock quotes (*stocks:csco*).
- **inanchor:** – Use this to find pages that have a specific word in a link on the page, such as clickable text that contains that word (*inanchor:anadarko*).
- **allinanchor:** – Use this prefix (followed by one or more words) to find pages that have links containing your search terms (*allinanchor:extreme searcher*).
- **numrange:** – Use to find any pages that contain a number that is within the range you specify. You can also specify units (feet, meters, dollars, miles per gallon, etc.) using either the abbreviation or the full unit name. It doesn't always work perfectly but overall is very powerful (*american pottery numrange:1900..1920*). Actually just using the range, with the two periods but without the prefix, also works just as well

(*american pottery 1900..1920*). You can do a less-than or more-than search by leaving out the first or last number (*skyscraper height numrange:1000.. ft*).

"Wildcard" Words

Google allows the use of one or more asterisks for "wildcard" words (not to be confused with truncation, which is a technique for searching wildcard characters within or at the end of a word). You can use the asterisk for unknown words in a phrase search. The use of *each asterisk insists on the presence of one word*:

> *"erasmus * rotterdam"*

That search will retrieve "Erasmus Universiteit Rotterdam" and "Erasmus von Rotterdam." It will not necessarily retrieve any "Erasmus Rotterdam" records.

For a search that will retrieve "Erasmus University of Rotterdam" but not necessarily the "Erasmus Universiteit Rotterdam" records, try:

> *"erasmus * * rotterdam"*

If you want "Franklin Roosevelt" and "Franklin D. Roosevelt" as well as "Franklin Delano Roosevelt," search for:

> *"Franklin Roosevelt" OR "Franklin * Roosevelt"*

Synonym Searches

As with other search engines, Google really tries to be helpful. To do so, in some cases at least, it automatically recognizes and retrieves words that it considers "synonyms," a term that Google defines rather broadly to include word variants and closely related words. For example, a search on *diet* may also retrieve pages with the word *diets*, without you specifically asking it to do so. This makes it easier for searchers in that it means that it is not necessary to "OR" a lot of similar words. This in general is probably good, but Google's implementation of the idea is also a bit unpredictable.

You can force Google to search for synonyms by adding a tilde in front of a search term:

> *apples children ~nutrition*

In some cases at least, searching *~nutrition* causes items to be retrieved because terms such as *nutritional, eating, food,* or *health* are on the page.

However, there are times when you don't want Google to be so helpful, and you only want one specific word. You can insist that a term be searched exactly as you entered it by placing the term in quotation marks. For example, if you want the family name, "Price" but find you are getting things about "pricing" you may want to try: *"price."*

Search Suggestions

As you enter your query, Google will offer you search suggestions as you type (see Figure 4.3), typically based on searches that other people have done using your terms, searches you have done, searches using your terms based on your location, and so on. This is closely tied to Google Instant, which was mentioned earlier. With Google Instant turned on ("on" is the default; it can be turned off under Google Settings), you will see two things happen: 1) As you search, you will see Google autofill the search box with a statistically based likelihood of what Google thinks that you want, and 2) Google will instantly show results based on that likelihood. Whether or not Google Instant is on, as you type, a list of suggested searches will appear immediately beneath the search box. If you see one that appeals to you, click on it.

Definitions

Google will deliver two kinds of definition: definitions that come from regular dictionaries such as *Merriam-Webster*, and definitions that come from glossaries Google has found on various websites. The latter are particularly useful for words that will not be found in standard dictionaries, such as slang, acronyms, neologisms, and technical terms.

To get to a definition, type in *define* followed by a word for which you want a definition:

   define mashup

Figure 4.3 Google search suggestions

If the term is found in one of the standard dictionaries, you will see a definition and often a speaker icon that you can click on to hear the word. Beneath the dictionary entry, you may see links to other definitions and a More Info link that, when clicked, will take you to other definitions found on the web. If no standard entry is found, you will immediately be shown the definitions found on the web.

Calculator

For a quick arithmetic calculation, you can use the Google search box. Enter *46*(98-3+32)*, and Google provides the answer. For addition, subtraction, multiplication, division, and exponents use +, -, *, /, and ^, respectively. Google seems to want to hide the neat details about using this feature, but if you do a search on *Google calculator help,* it should lead you to more details or maybe even to wherever Google is currently hiding the instructions.

Metric-Imperial Conversions

From the main search box, you can easily convert measurements between metric and imperial systems for all common units of length, volume, mass, and temperature. (See Google's calculator help page for details on this.)

> *32 feet to meters*
> *30 km to miles*
> *8 liters to quarts*
> *68 f to c*

You can combine this with the calculator function (e.g., *32 mi/gal to km/litre* and also currency conversions such as *434 euros to usd*).

Some Miscellaneous Points About Search Statements on Google

Remember these points about search statements on Google:

- The order of words in your query may matter in terms of how Google ranks the results. Try placing your more important search terms at the beginning of your query.
- Until 2012, in Google searches, most punctuation was ignored, except for special cases, such as searches for C++. Now, you can effectively include most common punctuation symbols in your Google search (e.g., *b&b*).
- As with all major search engines, capitalization is ignored.

Google Results Pages

On Google results pages, it pays to look closely at the entire page and also at the content of the individual records (Figure 4.4). Among the reasons for this are that more and more options for refining your search now appear on the left side of search results pages and within the results list itself.

Google always searches its other databases whenever you do a web search. If your topic has been in the news recently, above, below, or among your results you will see a section "News for …" with a couple of headlines and a link to more. Click on the headlines to go to the news stories, or click on the title of the section to go to the full search in Google News.

Most importantly, on the left side of your results page, you will see a rather extensive list of ways in which you can narrow your results. Exactly what options appear will vary with your search and because of changes in the options that Google offers. Typically, there are three main ways to refine your results:

- Type of results: Use this to tell Google to only retrieve items from one of Google's more specific collections such as images, maps, videos, news, shopping, and blogs.

    A More link expands the list of options to include choices for categories such as

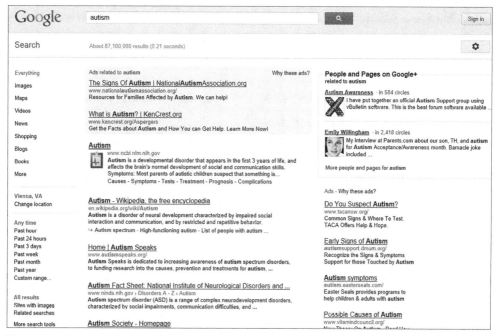

Figure 4.4   Google search results page

books, places, flights, destinations, discussions, recipes, applications, and patents. Choose any of these to not just narrow to that kind of content but to be given further narrowing possibilities specific to the kind of content. For example, if you click on Images, new options will be shown for narrowing results by size, color, type (face, photo, clip art, line drawing), and so on.

- Age of results: Choose results from the past hour, 24 hours, week, month, or year. You can also choose a specific date range. When you make one of these choices, you are given an additional sort option (by relevance or by date).

- Other characteristics: Use this set of options (titled "All Results") to narrow your results to pages that have images (giving you thumbnails next to each result), find related searches, see dictionary entries for your term, specify reading level, find results that are "local" to your location, or get translated foreign pages on your topic. The Verbatim option is a way of telling Google to search *just* the term you told it to. Use this when you don't want Google to be "helpful" (or presumptuous, annoying, and aggravating) by automatically including Google-designated synonyms, related terms, and so on in your results. Google rather frequently adds or deletes options found in this section.

Note that the first list will instantly appear, but to see the latter two, you may need to click on a Show Search Tools link found there.

You may also see a place on the left that identifies your location (either where Google is guessing that you are or a location that you have set). A link is provided for you to change your location.

In some cases, different and unexpected narrowing options based on your exact search may appear in the left margin. For example, search on *cornbread* and you may find options to narrow your results by specific ingredients, cooking time, and calorie count.

On the main part of Google results pages, there is the expected list of records, but a closer examination may reveal a number of things that are easily missed. If Google "thinks" you may have misspelled a search term, you may see a "Did you mean" message, with a suggested alternative spelling. If Google is pretty sure that you misspelled it, it will instead say "Showing results for," having automatically searched for what it assumes is the "right" spelling. Google, though, is humble enough to provide a link that will search for exactly what you typed.

It has already been mentioned that Google searches its other databases, such as news, images, videos, and maps. You may also find a wide variety of hopefully relevant odds and ends, dependent upon your search terms, upon what is happening in the world, and upon what the Google programmers have been up to. You may find the following among your results: recent notable quotations relating to your search topic, election results if you are in an elections season, suggested albums, and other features.

If you are signed in to Google+, you may see "Personal Results" appearing among your results. These are tips, photos, and posts made by the people you are connected to on Google+ or on YouTube. A line above the results list will tell you how many matching personal results you have for the current search. You can click on the link there to see *only* those results. Icons near the top of the page allow you to turn this feature on or off.

As you hold your cursor over individual results in the list, note the double right arrow that appears. Hold your cursor over the arrow to see a thumbnail of that page (Figure 4.5). Just above the thumbnail, you will usually see links for Cached and Similar. By clicking the Cached link, you will be directed to a cached copy that Google stored when it retrieved the page. This feature is especially useful if you click on a search result and the page is not found, or it is found but the terms you searched for do not seem to be present. Clicking on the Similar link will lead to pages with similar content. Take advantage of this capability to find related pages that may be difficult to find otherwise.

Within some individual records, there are what Google calls "sitelinks" and "rich snippets." For many records, Google will automatically list, particularly in results near the top of the results list, what it refers to as sitelinks, which are selected links to help you easily navigate that site. "Rich snippets" are actual bits of data and other information or links for places, people, organizations, product (and other) reviews and ratings, videos, stocks, lists, recipes, and so on—breadcrumbs that show a page's position in the hierarchy within a site. For example, in a search for *concerts Cleveland*, four of the first

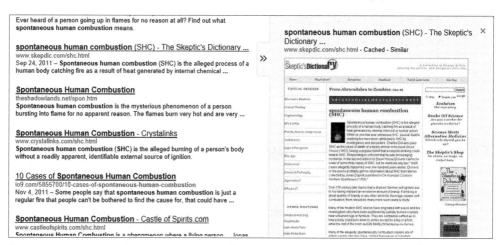

Figure 4.5 Example of individual records (with cursor held over one of them)

10 records contained snippets and two showed clickable links to other places in those sites; one record contained three items from a list that existed on the page, and one contained clickable links to specific concerts listed on the webpage.

If you encounter a record for a page that is in a language other than the one in which you are searching, you will see a link to Translate This Page into your search language. If your search results include any Adobe Acrobat, Adobe Postscript, Excel, PowerPoint, or Word files, a link (Quick View or View as HTML) will be available to display that result as HTML or as a Google Doc (discussed later in this chapter).

On search results pages, you can simply click on links at the top of the page to have your current search done in alternate Google databases (images, video, etc.).

Finally, on search results pages, you will notice a gear wheel icon that leads to a list of options, including the following:

- Search settings
  - SafeSearch filters: These specify various levels of adult content filtering.
  - Google Instant predictions: This provides users with immediate answers, even while you are still typing in your search, based upon what you have typed up to that point. Turn this feature on or off, or only have Google do it when your computer is fast enough. When turned on, your results pages are limited to a maximum of 10 results per page.
  - Results per page.
  - Where results open: You can have your selected results open in a separate window if you wish.
  - Blocking unwanted results.
  - Web history: This provides a list of searches you have done and the sites you have visited.
- Advanced search
- Search help
- Web history

Other Searchable Google Databases

In addition to its main database of webpages, Google provides searchable databases of images, groups, news, videos, blogs, products, maps and satellite images, books, and journal articles. Using Google's main search box, you can also search databases of businesses and stock prices. The images, video, maps, news, and shopping databases are accessible by clicking the appropriate link at the top of Google's main page (and on many other Google pages). Other databases can be accessed by the More link at the top of the page. Because the Google images, groups, news, and shopping databases are discussed in some detail in the chapters that follow, they are only mentioned briefly here.

Images

Google has one of the largest searchable image collections on the web, with billions of images. Details on image searching are covered in Chapter 7.

Google Groups (Discussions)

Google provides access to the Usenet collection of newsgroups, going back to 1981 and containing hundreds of millions of messages. In 2005, Google added its own user-created groups (forums). Access to this database is also available by clicking on Discussions on the left side of Google results pages. This will also lead to forums that are found elsewhere on the web, not just from Google Groups. More details on Google Groups are available in Chapter 5.

News

Google's news search is reachable through the link on the Google homepage or directly at news.google.com. It covers over 25,000 news sources and is updated continually. Most records are retained for 30 days, but the site also provides a search of a large archival collection of news. Read more about news searching in Chapter 8. Also in the news category, Google provides a search of blogs (weblogs) at www.google.com/blogsearch.

Google Shopping

Formerly known as Froogle, Google's shopping database contains pages of products for sale that Google has identified by crawling the web and also contains product information submitted by merchants. For more details on Google Product Search, see Chapter 9.

Google Maps

The map searches provided by various search engines all allow you to access road maps and driving directions plus they allow you to locate businesses in or near a particular city or other location. In the case of Google, its map search combines a search of a yellow pages database, information it has found from crawling the web, and its maps and satellite images databases to provide not just names, phone numbers, and addresses of businesses but also an accompanying (draggable) road map with the locations of the businesses shown, with options to get driving directions, a satellite view of the location, and for some areas, photos, traffic conditions, weather, and webcams (Figure 4.6). Google Maps now covers much of the "drivable" world, with satellite photos at least of virtually

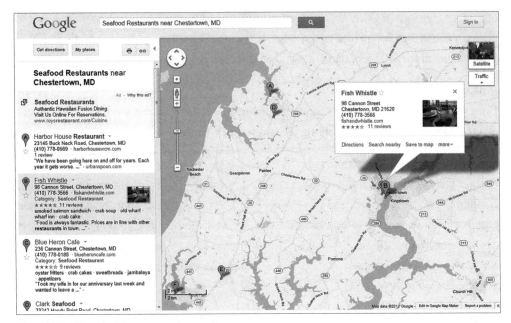

Figure 4.6 Google Maps search result

the entire planet. Google Maps is very closely integrated with Google Earth, which will be discussed shortly.

To find businesses, enter the topic (e.g., restaurants, hotels, pet massage) and the location. For location, you can enter a city or ZIP code (or post code or postal code) and/or city, state, and country (e.g., *pizza Doha Qatar*). You can also be more specific as to the location, for example, *london hotel near westminster*. Results show both a list and the map.

For a rapidly increasing number of cities, towns, and even some rural areas, and in an increasing number of countries, Google Maps (and Google Earth) now provide Street View, with draggable and tiltable horizontal (360 degrees) and vertical panoramic photos of real streets. Taken by special Google vehicles systematically roaming the streets, these photos provide a street-level view of what someone who is actually there would see (but, perhaps obviously, not in real time). Search for a location, click on the place-marker "balloon," and look for a link for Street View, or from the controls on the left of the map, drag the "little man" to the area of interest.

One way Google has integrated content that previously was available only on Google Earth is seen when you hold your cursor over the Map box on the upper right side of the map. A menu will pop up allowing you to view photos, weather, etc. on the map. This feature allows you to easily see and learn things about a location that you may never have expected and to get to a wide range of related information quickly and easily.

One additional very important feature of Google Maps is the My Places section (formerly My Maps), which enables anyone who has a Google account to easily create a mashup (what Wikipedia describes as "a website or web application that seamlessly combines content from more than one source into an integrated experience"). Though mashups can refer to the mixing of lots of different kinds of data on the web, the most common mashups involve integrating information into a Google Map. (Those maps you've probably seen in numerous places that have a "balloon" you can click on are mashups.) Other sites provide opportunities to incorporate their data with other data, but Google Maps is the most popular source, and Google makes the process unbelievably easy. If you want a map that shows points of interest to you, a map that you can point people to on Google Maps, email to people, or put on your website, you can easily do so using Google's My Places. Plus, you can add text, images, and video links to the balloons. If you want to get an idea of the possibilities that mashups can offer, a great collection of them can be found at Google Maps Mania (googlemapsmania.blogspot.com).

Google Book Search

Through arrangements with publishers and several major libraries, Google Book Search provides bibliographic information on and, in many cases, access to the full text of a large collection of both new and old books. Google Book Search is discussed in some detail in Chapter 6.

Google Scholar

Google Scholar covers peer-reviewed papers, theses, books, preprints, abstracts, articles, court opinions, and technical reports. The availability of this scholarly material on Google is a result of agreements with publishers, associations, universities, and others, allowing Google to index databases that search engine crawlers usually cannot penetrate (Deep Web material). For more on Google Scholar, see Chapter 6.

Google Blog Search

Google's Blog Search has the intention of covering any blog that provides a site feed (either RSS or Atom). Blogs can be searched using the same operators as a regular Google search and the following fields prefixes can be used: *link:, site:, intitle:, inblogtitle:, inposttitle:, inpostauthor:, blogurl:*. The first three of those are the same as in a regular web search, and the remaining ones are unique to blog searching (but hopefully self-explanatory).

Google Blog Search does not have an advanced search page of its own (just the regular web search advanced search page). However, on blog search results pages, you can narrow results to blog homepages or by time (past 10 minutes, past hour, etc.), as well as sort results by relevance or by date.

Patent Search

The 8 million patents in Google Patent Search come from the U.S. Patent and Trademark Office (USPTO) and are all full-text searchable. As of this printing, Google includes patents back to 1790 but does not include the most recently issued U.S. patents. Researchers should also be aware that the Google Patent Search does not provide the level of searchability of some other patents databases. In perspective, the USPTO's own site (www.uspto.gov) is completely up-to-date (updated every Tuesday when patents are issued), but full-text searchability on the USPTO site is available only from the beginning of 1976. Both the Google site and the USPTO site contain full images of all patents in the database.

While Google's interface is simpler and/or more intuitive than the interfaces for USPTO's own site and for commercial patent search services, Google offers fewer search options. Google provides searching by nine fields—in contrast to the 31 fields searchable on the USPTO site and more than 80 fields searchable on some commercial patent search services. Google's Advanced Patent Search page allows use of the usual combination of text search boxes (all the words, phrase, at least one of the words, without the words), plus search options for the following fields: Patent Number, Title, Inventor, Assignee, Current U.S. Classification, International Classification, Patent Type/Status, Issue Date, and Filing Date. Alternatively, most of these search options are available on the main page by means of Google's Boolean connectors and the following prefixes: *patent:, intitle:, allintitle:, ininventor:, inassignee:, uspclass:,* and *intlpclass:.*

Google Earth

In addition to being a tool for serious research, one of the most "fun" tools offered by Google is Google Earth (Figure 4.7), a searchable database that provides aerial/satellite views of places on the entire planet. Google Earth is also notable because it represents effective integration of a variety of trends and technologies, including nontextual content search and retrieval (in this case maps and images), streaming data, local search, and sharing.

Google Earth is a combination of a downloadable program and online data that provides satellite and aircraft imagery and allows users to integrate and superimpose their selection of related data.

Figure 4.7 Google Earth

Once the program has been downloaded, Google Earth's main page presents a control console and an image of the Earth. Click on an area of your choice, and then zoom in on exactly what you want to see—your own backyard, Maui, or Timbuktu. You can also zoom directly to your destination by typing in an address. At an "altitude" of your choice, you can have Google Earth superimpose roads, railways, schools, parks, hotels, restaurants, and other landmarks, as well see political boundaries, weather, photos, driving directions and more. You can tilt and rotate your image and "fly" over an area, and for some metropolitan areas, you can see 3D images of buildings and terrain. You can add your own placemarks and annotations and even share these with others.

Images are available for the entire world, with higher resolution versions for many locations, especially major cities. Google Maps search features and road maps are provided for most major metropolitan areas as well as non-urban areas. For the lower resolution sites, such as remoter parts of the world, the resolution will enable you to at least see major geographic features and towns. The higher resolution sites allow you to identify something the size of a car or smaller. A more powerful version, Google Earth Pro (with higher resolution and more sophisticated tools), is available for an annual subscription fee.

Google Earth includes rapidly increasing amounts of subject content associated with locations. Spend some time browsing the Layers and Places panels on Google Earth to get a feel for the possibilities. Content is provided by Google partner organizations and by the public at large. Searching for content on Google Earth can be done by using its search panel or by searching on regular Google. To find Google Earth subject content (text, videos, images, etc.) through a regular Google search you can use the "file type" search option and specify .kml and .kmz files (the two file types for Google Earth content). Along with your subject terms, either use the *filetype:* prefix in the main search box (e.g., *filetype:kml*) or use the corresponding menu on the advanced search page. Alternatively, in Google's main search box, simply try your topic and the phrase *"Google Earth."*

Stock Search

Enter a ticker symbol for a U.S. company in Google's main search box, and you'll get current stock quotes, prices, volume, and links to more information about the stock and the company from multiple finance and market-related sources (MSN Money, CNN Money, etc.). This information, which will appear above the regular Google search results, is an example of search engine "shortcuts" discussed in Chapter 3.

Google Toolbar

The Google Toolbar is a free downloadable feature that allows you to add the Google search box and additional features as a toolbar on Internet Explorer. If Firefox is your preferred browser, you can get much of the functionality of the Google toolbar by downloading various Firefox add-ons. To find the add-on, search for *firefox add-ons* and the tool of interest (e.g., *firefox add-ons autofill*). If you use Google Chrome, there are many add-ons that can be downloaded to serve the functions described in the next paragraph. In Chrome, click on the wrench icon, and choose Help and then Extensions.

For the Google Toolbar for Internet Explorer, you can add buttons to your toolbar to take you immediately to feeds, Google tools such as Gmail and Google Drive, and other features and "gadgets." Go to the More link on the Google homepage (then to the Even More link) to find out about what the Google Toolbar provides, including:

- Google search: With the toolbar showing, the search box always appears on your browser screen.
- Search options: The pull-down menu to the right of the toolbar search box provides for searches of images, maps, news, and so on, plus Search Site, which allows you to search only the pages of the site currently displayed. (This can also be done in any Google search box by using the *site:* prefix.)
- Highlight: This allows you to highlight your search terms (each word in a different color).

- Spell check
- Autofill: This allows you to automatically fill out forms on a webpage.
- Translate: When you open a page that is in a language other than your search language, the Translate Toolbar will appear just above the page. Click the Translate button there to translate the page into a language of your choice. Use the wrench icon on the Google Toolbar to change your default language settings.

Your choice of buttons for a variety of other Google services can also be included. The Google Toolbar can be customized to include most of the features (image search, etc.) on the regular Google homepage.

Other Google Interfaces, Features, and Content

The folks at Googleplex, Google's headquarters, let no grass grow beneath their myriad computers. While on one hand, some Google announcements receive inordinate attention, others receive relatively little press, and even less attention from the majority of Google users. Informal polling indicates that many Google users have not even clicked on more than one or two of the links on the Google homepage to see what is there, and even many very experienced searchers have not taken time to fully explore everything Google offers. The following Google offerings include some of the more significant features, content, and interfaces that may be easy to miss. Most of these can be found at the top of Google's homepage or through the More link above the search box on that page:

- Google+: "Google Plus" is Google's social networking site, its competitor to Facebook. With it, you can share photos, updates, videos, links, and so on, and converse with your friends by chat or by webcam. You can create "circles" of friends, family, acquaintances, and people you are following. Information (links, likes, etc.) from people you associate with through Google+ can, if you wish, be integrated into your regular Google search results in the form of "personal results." When you are signed into Google and are signed up for Google+, a link for it will appear at the top left of your page, as a plus sign followed by your Google name. Google+ is one more golden opportunity to provide Google with even more personal and intimate information about your life, your likes, your activities, your location, and your friends.
- Alerts (alerts.google.com): This feature enables you to be automatically notified of news stories, blog postings, video, and discussions on topics of your choice. These are discussed in Chapter 8.

- Gmail (mail.google.com): Google's free email service provides standard email functions and virtually unlimited storage, and comes with an integrated voice and video chat, and online phone call options.

- Bookmarks (www.google.com/bookmarks): Google provides an easy-to-use bookmarks option that can be utilized wherever in the world you are, accessible through Google Toolbar for Internet Explorer and Google Chrome, or at www.google.com/bookmarks. If you are a Firefox user, try an add-on such as GBookmarks, which provides access to your Google bookmarks.

- Google Hangouts: Google's own service for video chat is Google's competitive answer to Skype. Hangouts is accessible through Gmail and Google+, and allows videoconferencing for up to 10 people simultaneously.

- Finance (www.google.com/finance): This finance portal page provides stock information, news, and a personal stock portfolio. (Compare this to Yahoo!'s Finance section.)

- Calendar (www.google.com/calendar): This personal online calendar can be viewed by day, week, month, or the next four days. You can also share with others, have multiple calendars, get email reminders, import events from other calendars, send invitations for events, and more.

- Blogger (www.blogger.com): Blogger, owned by Google, lets you create a blog of your own.

- Picasa (picasa.google.com): This free downloadable program allows you to store, edit, and organize photos locally on your computer and online with Picasa Web Albums.

- Mobile (www.google.com/mobile): Google provides a number of its services, such as Search, Maps, Gmail, Blogger, Calendar, and YouTube, in a format compatible with your mobile device.

- Video: Google's video search is discussed in Chapter 7.

- YouTube: Google's famous video sharing site is discussed in Chapter 7.

- Custom Search Engine (www.google.com/cse): With this tool, users can construct a custom search form that searches only websites or webpages that the user specifies (one site or page or many), with further capabilities to tag sites with keywords enabling further narrowing by those categories. Sites can be shared with others or with the general public, and the search form can be housed on your own website or on a page that Google provides.

- Drive (drive.google.com): Drive (formerly Google Docs) is a suite of web-based, collaborative productivity tools, including a word processor, spreadsheet, slide presentation program, forms generator, and drawing tool. Documents are stored on Google's servers but can be uploaded from, or downloaded to, your own computer or mobile device and are compatible with a number of formats such as Microsoft Word, PowerPoint, and Excel. One of the biggest advantages is the collaborative nature of this feature, making it very easy for those you choose to share in creating, editing, and using documents.

- Sites (sites.google.com): This free website service allows users to easily create a website and allows others to share in editing and managing it and to embed other Google services such as Google Drive, Google Calendar, etc.

- Chrome (www.google.com/chrome): Google's own version of a web browser is intended to compete with Internet Explorer, Firefox, and other browsers. With Google Chrome, you will find some Google-specific features not available in other browsers, such as voice search. (When on a Google search page, by clicking the microphone icon in the search box, you can speak, rather than type, your search.)

- Wallet (www.google.com/wallet): Here you can store your credit card and shipping information so that you don't have to deal with logins, passwords, and other information for each online merchant.

- Reader (www.google.com/reader): This is a feed (automatic website and news updates) reader that allows you to easily subscribe to, organize, and read RSS and Atom feeds of your choice.

- SketchUp (sketchup.google.com): This is a free, downloadable, computer-aided-design (CAD) program with which you can create 3D models of buildings, places, inventions, spaceships—anything you want. If you haven't used such a program before, it may take an hour or more to begin to get comfortable with it, but you will be amazed at what it can do and will be even more amazed that it is free.

- Latitude (www.google.com/latitude): If you wish to share your location with friends, this provides a map that shows your location and the location of friends who are sharing their locations.

- Modcrator (moderator.appspot.com): This is a discussion platform where you can set up a "series" discussion, open it up to those whom you wish to participate, and have them vote.

BING

After a long period of promises, MSN delivered its "new" MSN Search in 2004, with a new interface and a crawler of its own (rather than, as previously, using someone else's). Analogous in more ways than one to Microsoft's Millennium Edition operating system, the delivery of MSN Search was fairly quickly followed, in late 2005, by the release (in beta mode) of Windows Live (live.com), Microsoft's "new" new web search engine. By late 2006, MSN Search was no longer available, having been replaced by Live or "Live Search," which in 2009 was enhanced and renamed as Bing (www.bing.com). Bing has a different look and feel than the old MSN Search, with a main page that has the now-usual minimalist search engine interface but with a large, attractive photographic background image. In line with Bing's "decision engine" marketing theme, Bing enhances its search results with useful "facts," gathered from selected websites, particularly in the areas of travel, health, shopping, and local information.

Bing Homepage

The attractive but simple Bing homepage (Figure 4.8) provides the following search-related features:

- Search box: In the search box, terms you enter are automatically ANDed, and you can use OR, NOT, and several prefixes.

Figure 4.8 Bing homepage

- Links to other databases: Databases such as Images, Videos, Shopping, News, Maps, and Travel can be searched by using the links above the search box.
- Search History: This link appears only if you are signed in and shows a list of your recent and frequent searches. If you are signed in, there will also be a link to Hotmail.
- A link to the MSN portal page.
- Sign-In: This link at the top of the page enables participation in the Bing Rewards program, connecting with Facebook (so that Facebook items will appear on your results pages) and connecting to your Microsoft account. The "Microsoft account" is actually your Bing account, and by signing in, you can more fully utilize Bing features. These include enabling search history, creating Bing alerts, adding Bing map collections, and gaining full access to the Bing Webmaster Center and the Bing Developer Center.
- Regional: This link allows you to choose from about 40 country versions of Bing.
- Preferences: The gear wheel icon leads to a Preferences page where you can turn the SafeSearch adult content filter on or off; turn search suggestions on or off; set the default location for local search and other geographically significant searches; and specify the language in which you would like the search interface to appear. Other links on that page lead to preferences for having search history on or off and links to clear and see search history; viewing and updating your Bing Rewards account; the Bing Finance page (MSN Money); and more than 50 country/language versions of Bing.

A changing variety of additional features and promotional "beta" is also included on the homepage. Move your cursor around on the background image to discover some hidden "hot spots" that provide information about the subject of the photo. (See the example of this in Figure 4.9.)

Bing Advanced Search

Bing had been providing a very simplified set of advanced search options as part of its results pages, but in 2012, it removed all of those options. The search refinements that were previously provided can still be accomplished but now only by the use of prefixes, as discussed in the following sections.

Figure 4.9 Bing main page "Hot Spot"

Search Features Provided by Bing

Boolean

All terms you enter are automatically ANDed. You can use the OR (or |) connector, but you should be sure to enclose your ORed terms in parentheses. To exclude words, you can use either *NOT* or a minus sign in front of the word. (To facilitate copying and pasting your query into another engine, you may prefer to use the minus for the NOT.) For example:

> *muskrats (recipe OR cooking) –baked*

Bing automatically searches for some variant word forms such as plurals (*recipes* when you search for *recipe*). You can insist on just one form by placing a plus sign before the term, for example, *+recipe*. A search statement can have up to 150 characters, including spaces.

Title Searching

To limit your search to pages that have your term in the title, you must use the *intitle:* prefix. You can use this with quotation marks for a phrase. To specify multiple words without insisting on a specific phrase, reuse the prefix:

> *intitle:handel*
> *intitle:"George Frideric Handel"*
> *intitle:handel intitle:biography*

Site, Domain, and URL Searching

To find all the pages that Bing has indexed for a particular site (up to two levels deep), or for a subdomain of a site, use the *site:* prefix:

> *site:fujifilm.com*
> *site:fujifilm.com/support*
> *shadows site:fujifilm.com*

This prefix can also be used to limit your retrieval to a specific top-level domain:

> *esters saponification site:edu*

Bing accepts a *url:* prefix, but it only retrieves the one record for that specific URL.

Language Searching

To search for items in a particular language, use the *language:* prefix with the two-letter code for the language:

> *biographie clemenceau language:fr*

Searching by File Type

You can search by file type by using the *filetype:* prefix:

> *photoshop tutorial filetype:pdf*

This prefix works for .html, .txt, .pdf, .doc, .xls, .dwf, and .ppt files.

Searching by Other Prefixes

In addition to the prefixes just covered, the following can be used in Bing:

- **loc:** – It doesn't always work, but enter *loc:* or *location:* followed by two-letter country code (*Fledermaus location:de*).
- **contains:** – Use to find pages containing a link to a particular media filetype, such as mp3 or wma (*Janice Joplin contains:mp3*).
- **inanchor:** – Use to find pages that have a particular word in the text of a link (*Texas restaurants inanchor:dallas*).
- **inbody:** – Use if for some obscure reason you want to identify pages that have a term in the body of the pages as opposed to the title, etc. (*inbody:frog*).

- **ip:** – Use to identify sites that are hosted on a particular ip address (*ip:207.57.95.6*).
- **prefer:** – Use for adding emphasis to a term for ranking purposes, although only occasionally does this seem to work (*"la rochelle" france prefer:marinas*).
- **feed:** – Use this to find pages that have a feed on your topic (*feed:boating*).
- **hasfeed:** – Use this to retrieve a page that contains terms you are searching for and that has a feed (*certification hasfeed:boating*).

Bing Results Pages

Associated with its one-time claim of being a "decision engine," Bing integrates some useful "facts" into search results lists, utilizing content from selected Deep Web websites, particularly in the areas of travel and local information. Do a search for a particular city, and you will find that your results listing may contain suggested deals and links to book a flight.

Elsewhere on results pages, you will find other enhancements for navigating through a search. Depending on the search, results pages may also show a list of related searches, related news headlines, and selected images from Bing's images database or links to videos. Bing also displays, if you are signed in, a useful, clickable list of searches you have recently done.

As with results pages for other engines, Bing search results are ranked by relevance. Individual webpage results listings include the page title, a brief description or snippet of text, and the URL (Figure 4.10). Some records will also show links to more specific topics/pages within that site, and non-English pages may show a Translate This Page link. Beside the URL for most sites you will find a "down arrow" that will take you to a cached version of that page.

Just as Google will display "personal results" (if you are logged in), Bing may likewise show some results based on your connections to other people. In the case of Bing, it has partnered with Facebook and may show news articles, local results, and other links related to your search that your friends on Facebook have indicated that they like.

Other Searchable Bing Databases
Images

An image search in Bing produces significantly smaller numbers of results than does a similar search in Google, but the results may on average have higher relevance (greater precision), since Bing is apparently a bit more conservative in terms of the words it tends to associate with an image on a webpage. On image search results pages, you can narrow

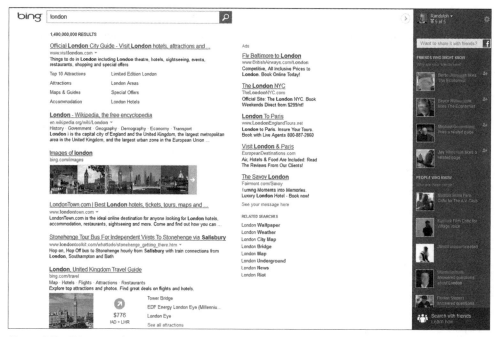

Figure 4.10 Bing results page

your results by size, layout (square, wide, tall), color (full color, black and white, or a specific dominant color), style (all, photograph, clipart, line drawing), and people (all, those images just showing faces, or those showing head and shoulders).

Video

The video search found on Bing covers a collection of commercial and noncommercial sources plus content from video sharing sites. Among other sources, you will find video here from YouTube, CNN, BBC, USAToday, AOL, MTV, ESPN, Hulu, CBS, Daily Motion, and Metacafe. On video search results pages, just hold your mouse over the thumbnails for an immediate preview. See Chapter 7 for more on video search.

Shopping

Bing has an extensive, easily browsable, and searchable shopping site, with access to products from major and minor online stores. On the left of results pages, you will find narrowing options by store, price, and brand, as well as options specific to the item for which you searched. (Search for "window shades" and you can narrow to cellular, roller, Roman, or horizontal.)

News

Bing's news search covers thousands of news sources worldwide, including news services, newspapers, and other sources. You can also use it to easily set up an RSS feed or free news alerts on specific topics for once-a-day, twice-a-day, or weekly delivery.

Maps

Bing's Maps Search provides searches for locations and businesses, with road maps for much of the world and aerial views for the entire world, driving directions (and routes for public transit or walking), and yellow pages–type information for many countries. It also incorporates imagery from what was formerly known as Virtual Earth (MSN's formidable competitor to Google Earth). For a number of cities, you will also find excellent "Birds' Eye" views, taken from planes and providing more detailed photos with more perspective.

Bing Maps now provides a My Places feature, which allows you to create your own map (a mashup) that can be shared with others, with your chosen annotated location, paths, areas, etc.

Travel

Bing's Travel section, which is what was previously known as FareChase, is a flight and hotel reservations site with booking capabilities and price comparisons, plus predictions of the best time to purchase a reservation, based on pricing histories.

Entertainment

Throughout Bing, you may notice a heavier emphasis on entertainment than found in other search engines. The Entertainment link found under More near the top of Bing's main page will lead to information on and sections about, music, movies, TV, and games. If you are signed in, for movies and music, you will see information for local events, show times, and more, and from the TV section, you can watch actual episodes of a number of series.

Other Bing Features and Content

Stock Search

Enter a ticker symbol in the search box and get current real-time quotes, charts, links to company news, etc.

Calculator

As with other engines, you can use Bing's main search box as a calculator. For addition, subtraction, multiplication, division, and exponents use, respectively, +, -, *, /, and ^. Parentheses can be used to nest operations, e.g., (12+2.1-1)^2. Unlike the calculator functions provided by other search engines, with the Bing calculator you can also solve some equations. For example, enter *8x + 5 = 244*, and it will tell you that the value of *x* here is 29.88.

Other Bing Instant Answers

As well as solving equations and getting stock quotes, there are a variety of other facts that Bing will provide directly from the search box. Enter *define* and a word to get a definition. Enter *flights from* and a city to get flight deals. Enter a flight number to get its status. Enter a shipper and a tracking number to track a package. Enter a holiday and a year to find the date for that holiday that year. Bing provides even more, so don't hesitate to try just about anything in the search box.

YAHOO!

Yahoo! (www.yahoo.com) made a series of dramatic changes over the last decade or so, moving away from primarily a directory function to search function. In 2004, Yahoo! created its own new webpage database to challenge Google's database and developed extensive databases for images, video, local, news, and shopping, as well as providing a search of the Yahoo! Directory. However, beginning in 2010, Yahoo! no longer provided a web search technology or a web database of its own. Yahoo!'s web, image, and other searches are now "powered by" Bing. For the two engines, you will see basically the same search results, although the order of results may sometimes differ. Overall results pages still will be a bit different because of some added features that Yahoo! provides that Bing doesn't, and vice versa. Yahoo!'s main strength lies in the numerous services (other than search) it provides through its main, general portal page and its personalized portal, My Yahoo!.

The My Yahoo! feature has provided perhaps the best general portal on the web, with a broad collection of additional content that the user can selectively choose to have appear on the user's personal My Yahoo! page. Yahoo! also provides a minimalist, streamlined Yahoo! Search page (search.yahoo.com; see Figure 4.11).

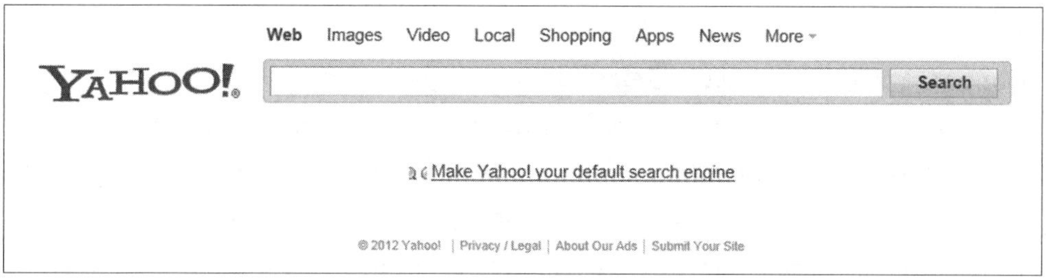

Figure 4.11 Yahoo! Search page

Yahoo! Homepage

The Yahoo! homepage is in the format of a general portal, with sections for search, news, and weather, Yahoo! Mail, and direct links to more than 20 Yahoo! services and sections, plus a link to More Y! Sites, which gives access to over 70 Yahoo! features and services. (For a really good feel for the range of things that Yahoo! provides, spend some time on that page.) The search section at the top of the Yahoo! main page is virtually the same as on the streamlined Yahoo! Search page and on personalized My Yahoo! pages. From any of these pages, you can search the web database, or you can choose an alternate database such as Images, Video, Local (yellow pages), or Shopping. Exactly which alternate database options appear may differ somewhat, but the More link above the search boxes provides links to all other searchable databases and to All Search Services, a page that lists all of Yahoo!'s search-related services. As you enter your search terms in the box, you will see a list of suggested searches appear beneath the search box. Hold your cursor over any of the suggestions; in the box to the right, you may see related news headlines, "top sites," or other related information for that suggested topic. From the main Yahoo! page, if you would like to go to Yahoo!'s streamlined search page (one that looks more like Google's homepage), click on the Search button without entering anything in the search box.

All three interfaces—Yahoo!, My Yahoo!, and the streamlined Yahoo! Search page—provide the following:

- Search box: In the search box, AND is implied between terms, and you can use OR, a minus sign for NOT, parentheses for nesting, and any of several prefix qualifiers.
- Advanced search: For some unfathomable reason, for a long time, Yahoo! has not put an Advanced Search link directly on the main pages, but, rather, tucked it away under the Options link. There you will also find a link to the Preferences page.
- Links above the search box provide access to searches of alternate databases (Images, Video, Local, Shopping, News, Apps, and More), described in greater detail later in this section.

Yahoo! Advanced Search

Users who manage to find their way to Yahoo!'s advanced search page will find extensive and easy search functionality (Figure 4.12), including the following:

- Boxes to perform simple Boolean combinations ("all of these words," "any of these words," or "none of these words"), plus a box for phrase searching
- Options to limit to a particular top-level domain or a specific domain or site

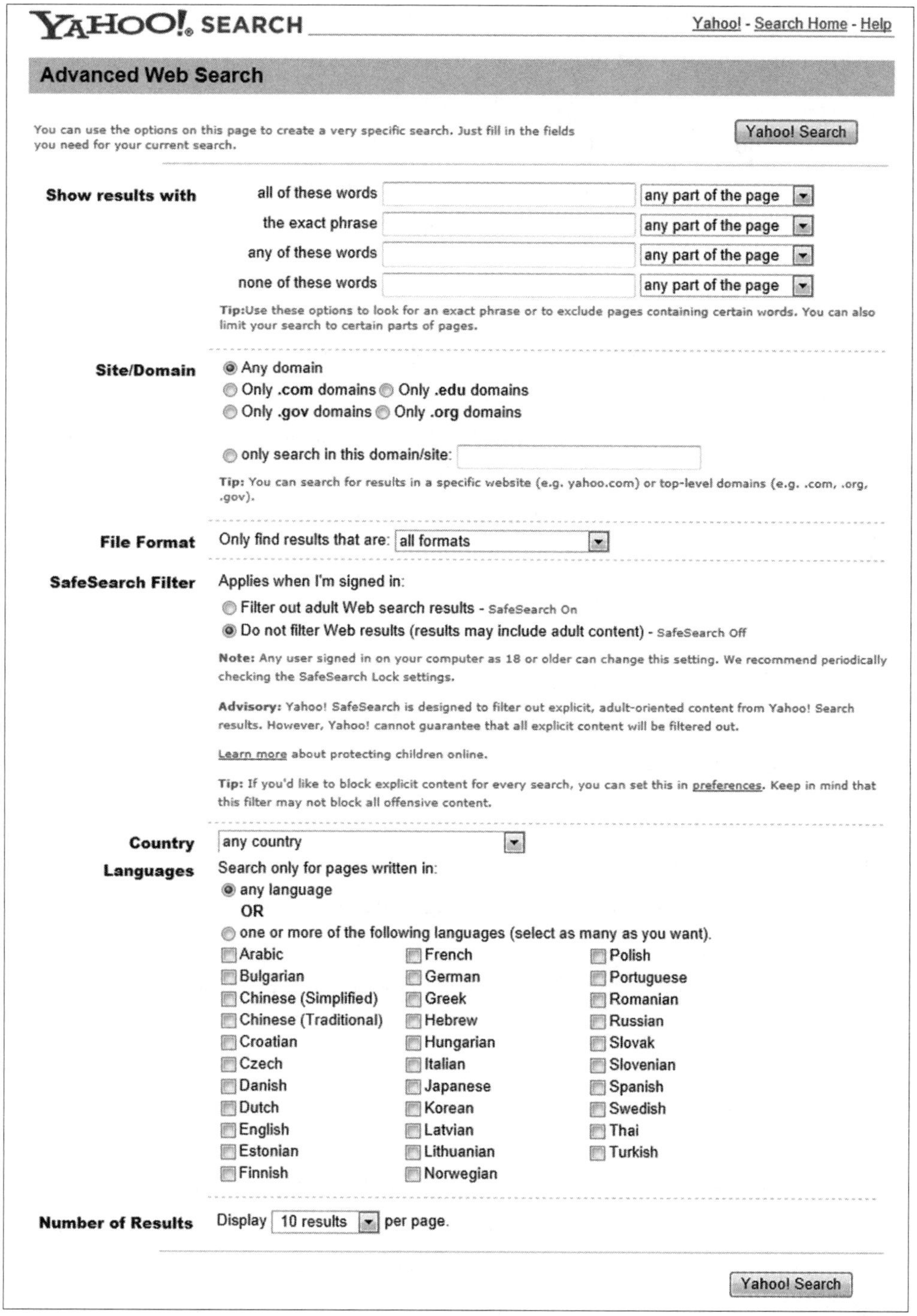

YAHOO!® SEARCH _____ Yahoo! - Search Home - Help

Advanced Web Search

You can use the options on this page to create a very specific search. Just fill in the fields you need for your current search.   [Yahoo! Search]

Show results with

all of these words [_____] [any part of the page ▾]

the exact phrase [_____] [any part of the page ▾]

any of these words [_____] [any part of the page ▾]

none of these words [_____] [any part of the page ▾]

Tip: Use these options to look for an exact phrase or to exclude pages containing certain words. You can also limit your search to certain parts of pages.

Site/Domain
- ◉ Any domain
- ◯ Only .com domains ◯ Only .edu domains
- ◯ Only .gov domains ◯ Only .org domains
- ◯ only search in this domain/site: [_____]

Tip: You can search for results in a specific website (e.g. yahoo.com) or top-level domains (e.g. .com, .org, .gov).

File Format Only find results that are: [all formats ▾]

SafeSearch Filter Applies when I'm signed in:
- ◯ Filter out adult Web search results - SafeSearch On
- ◉ Do not filter Web results (results may include adult content) - SafeSearch Off

Note: Any user signed in on your computer as 18 or older can change this setting. We recommend periodically checking the SafeSearch Lock settings.

Advisory: Yahoo! SafeSearch is designed to filter out explicit, adult-oriented content from Yahoo! Search results. However, Yahoo! cannot guarantee that all explicit content will be filtered out.

Learn more about protecting children online.

Tip: If you'd like to block explicit content for every search, you can set this in preferences. Keep in mind that this filter may not block all offensive content.

Country [any country ▾]

Languages Search only for pages written in:
- ◉ any language
  OR
- ◯ one or more of the following languages (select as many as you want).

☐ Arabic	☐ French	☐ Polish
☐ Bulgarian	☐ German	☐ Portuguese
☐ Chinese (Simplified)	☐ Greek	☐ Romanian
☐ Chinese (Traditional)	☐ Hebrew	☐ Russian
☐ Croatian	☐ Hungarian	☐ Slovak
☐ Czech	☐ Italian	☐ Slovenian
☐ Danish	☐ Japanese	☐ Spanish
☐ Dutch	☐ Korean	☐ Swedish
☐ English	☐ Latvian	☐ Thai
☐ Estonian	☐ Lithuanian	☐ Turkish
☐ Finnish	☐ Norwegian	

Number of Results Display [10 results ▾] per page.

[Yahoo! Search]

Figure 4.12 Yahoo!'s advanced search page

- File format option to retrieve only a specific file format (HTML, PDF, Excel, PowerPoint, Word, and text)
- SafeSearch filter for blocking adult content
- Country origin option to limit to any of over 90 countries
- Language option to limit to one or more of 32 languages
- Choice to specify the number of results per page (10, 15, 20, 30, 40, and 100)

Yahoo! Preferences Page

With the Yahoo! Preferences page (found under the Options link on Yahoo!'s search pages), you can edit a number of options that govern what happens during a search when you are logged in under your Yahoo! account. These include Search Direct (selecting whether search suggestions appear); SafeSearch (limiting "adult content"); SearchScan (identifying potentially harmful websites); languages (limiting results to specific languages); and Display and Layout (opening results in a new window, setting number of results per page, and having the Show More From This Site link appear with records).

Search Features Provided by Yahoo!

Yahoo! offers a variety of limiting and other search features, both on its advanced search page and from its main search box.

Boolean

When you enter multiple terms (e.g., *national debt*) in the Yahoo! main search box, an AND is implied and you will only get back pages that use all of the terms. To OR two or more terms, place OR between the terms and be sure that the ORed terms are enclosed in parentheses. You can also use a NOT or a minus sign in front of a term to exclude pages that contain that term:

> *(oil OR petroleum) reserves iraq –war*

As with other search engines, Yahoo! ordinarily does not always search "stopwords" (very small words such as articles and prepositions). You can "force" it to do so, though, by putting a plus sign in front of the term. Stopwords are automatically searched when they are searched as part of a phrase, using quotation marks, for example, *"in the limelight."*

On Yahoo!'s advanced search page, you can use simple Boolean by means of the search boxes at the top of the page in the "Show results with" section ("all of these words," "any of these words," or "none of these words").

Title Searching

For high precision searches and/or to locate a specific title, you can limit your retrieval to only those pages where your terms appear in the title of the page. Do this either by using the "in the title of the page" option in menus that appear on the right side in the "Show results with" section of the advanced page or use the *intitle:* prefix in Yahoo!'s main search box:

> *intitle:"gross national product"*
> *intitle:Syria*
> *inspection protocols intitle:fire*

URL, Site, and Domain Searching

With Yahoo!, you can limit your retrieval to pages from a particular site or kind of site by using the advanced search page or by using the *site:* prefix.

On the advanced search page, use the Site/Domain radio buttons to limit your search to *.com, .edu, .gov,* or *.org* top-level domains. For other domains, enter the top-level domain extension (*uk, fr, mil*, etc.) or combinations of these (e.g., *co.uk*) in the text box there. In that box, you can also specify a particular site (e.g., *cruisemates.com*).

In Yahoo! search boxes, you can use the *site:* prefix to accomplish the same thing. This can be combined with subject terms or other prefixes such as *intitle:*. The *site:* prefix can also be used to limit to a top-level domain (.edu, .com, .org, .uk, .fr, .ca, etc.):

> *site:chrysler.com*
> *human cloning intitle:ethics site:edu*

The *url:* prefix is used to find the Yahoo! record for a specific site:

> *url:onstrat.com*

Language Searching

Use the Language checkboxes on the advanced search page to search any of 32 languages. Toward the bottom of Yahoo!'s main page, you will find a link to Yahoo!'s

International sites. That link will lead to the Yahoo! sites for more than 60 countries, each site in the language or languages of that country.

Alternatively, you can also use the *language:* prefix, followed by the two-letter code for that language:

> *epinal language:fr*

Searching by File Type

The File Format pull-down menu on the advanced search page lets you narrow your search to any one of the following document types: Word (.doc), Excel (.xls), PowerPoint (.ppt), Adobe PDF (.pdf), and text (.txt).

In Yahoo! search boxes, you can search for type of file by using the *filetype:* prefix:

> *glacial melting filetype:ppt*

Searching by Country

Yahoo!'s advanced search page lets you limit your search results to pages that are identified as coming from any one of over 90 countries. The results are approximate and will both miss some pages and misidentify others.

Searching by Other Prefixes

Since Yahoo! uses Bing's database and search technology, prefixes that work in Bing also work in Yahoo! (see the exact list on pages 103–104).

Conversions

To find measurement conversions easily, use Yahoo!'s main search box and enter the conversion you want:

> *238.5 miles to kilometers*
> *19 celsius to fahrenheit*

The conversion feature works for most common units of length, weight, temperature, area, and volume. Abbreviations will usually work (m, in, ft, etc.); sometimes they won't.

Calculator

For a quick calculation, enter your problem in Yahoo!'s search box instead of pulling up a calculator:

46*56.98

13^2/(46*3)

For addition, subtraction, multiplication, division, and exponents, use +, -, /, and ^ respectively. You can also nest using parentheses, e.g., 15*(14+43).

Stock Search

Stock quotes, charts, and news are available by entering the ticker symbol in the Yahoo! search box. The stock information will be shown at the top of the results page. The main Yahoo! site provides quotes for U.S. markets.

Yahoo! Results Pages

Records on Yahoo! search results pages are listed (ranked) according to their relevance to the search terms (Figure 4.13).

In addition to the expected parts of a results listing—a title that links to the page, a snippet of text showing search terms that matched, and the URL of the page—you may also find the following, depending on the record (Figure 4.14):

- Cached: Clicking on this link will take you to an archived version of the page. Use this when you encounter a "Page Not Found" message or when the word for which you searched is no longer on the current page.

- More From This Site: When there are additional matching pages from a site, if you have so chosen this on the Yahoo! Preferences page, this link will appear and allow you to see those pages.

- Enhanced Results: Some results will be enhanced with more detail and links to specific parts of that site.

Additional Content Displayed on Search Results Pages

Above your results list, if you have searched for a topic that is in the news, you may see headlines on that topic. Elsewhere among your list of results, you may find links to relevant images and videos. If you have searched for a city, you will usually see a city guide above your regular results list and links on the left to major attractions there. On the left of the page, you will also see the following:

- Filter by time: With this option, you can narrow your results to the last day, week, or month.

- Related searches: Search topics others have used that relate to your search terms.

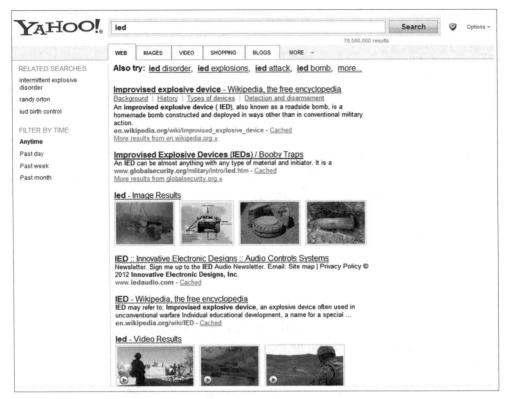

Figure 4.13   Yahoo! results page

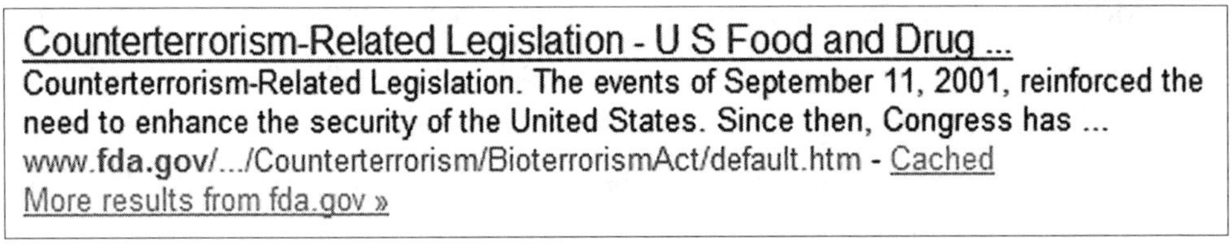

Counterterrorism-Related Legislation - U S Food and Drug ...
Counterterrorism-Related Legislation. The events of September 11, 2001, reinforced the need to enhance the security of the United States. Since then, Congress has ...
www.fda.gov/.../Counterterrorism/BioterrorismAct/default.htm - Cached
More results from fda.gov »

Figure 4.14   Example of an individual record in a Yahoo! search result

- Trending searches: This list, similar to related searches, will appear if your search topic is currently popular.

Just above your results listings, you may also find other related items, depending upon the topic you searched. If Yahoo! senses that you misspelled one or more of your search terms, the message "Including results for ___. Show only ___." pops up. It indicates that Yahoo! has actually searched for what it "thinks" you wanted, but at the same time offering a link to change the search to exactly what you typed in. For example:

Including results for *parliament*. Show only parliament.

Yahoo! will provide an "Also try" option, another list of suggested searches, in this case, other searches that include words you used in your search.

Other Searchable Yahoo! Databases

Yahoo! also provides access to several major additional databases via the links above the search box on its main page: Images, Video, Local, and Shopping. (The choice of databases changes fairly frequently.) A More link there leads to links to Answers, Directory, News, and other Yahoo! databases. There are at least a score of databases that can be found here or within the various Yahoo! sections on the Yahoo! main page: The Autos section has databases of new and used car prices; the Health section has databases of health-related articles and other health information; Jobs is an employment database (provided by Monster); the Movies section has databases of films; Yahoo! Travel contains Yahoo!'s implementation of the Travelocity database; and so on. The major offerings are described in the following section very briefly since they are covered in more detail in later chapters. The best way to get to know what searchable databases Yahoo! offers is to start with Yahoo!'s main page and spend time browsing the links you find there.

Images

Yahoo!'s image database (images.search.yahoo.com) is an extensive collection of images found on websites or provided by large images sources such as Panoramio. See the section on searching images in Chapter 7.

Video

Here you can search the millions of videos that Yahoo! has gathered directly from video sharing and distribution sites such as YouTube, Dailymotion, Metacafe, Hulu, etc. Use the Video link above Yahoo!'s main search box or go to video.search.yahoo.com to begin your search. For more details on Yahoo!'s video search, see Chapter 7.

Shopping

Yahoo! Shopping (shopping.yahoo.com) is easily searchable and is one of the web's largest online shopping sites, with millions of products and tens of thousands of merchants (see Chapter 9).

Local

Yahoo! Local (local.yahoo.com) features a directory of U.S. businesses. (If you access Yahoo! from one of its international sites, check the main page to see if Yahoo! has a similar service for your country.)

To search for a business, enter a name or type of business (*Saks, Macys, plumber, pizza, interpreter,* etc.) in the left search box on the Local Search page and, in the right-hand search box, either a ZIP code or the name of a city and the two letter postal code for a state. Yahoo! will retrieve a list of matching businesses with the name, phone number, and address of the business, a rating (by Yahoo! users), and the distance from your own default location. A map is shown with the matching hits, and links are also provided for driving directions, reviews, sending the information to a phone, and for further details on the business. You will also find, on the left of the results page, links to narrow your search by such things as category, location, distance, etc. The Category link lists related business categories for either narrowing or expanding the topic of your search. Click on one of the names in the results listings to get more detailed information, including the business web address (if there is one) and a map with a Find Nearby link to locate nearby similar businesses, ATMs, hotels, parking, and movie theaters.

If you go directly to the Yahoo! Local site at local.yahoo.com, you will find a "City Guide" for your default location, with browsable business directory categories, a map, a list of upcoming local events, and user-recommended restaurants and other businesses.

Yahoo! Directory

You can search Yahoo!'s traditional web directory by clicking on the Directory link (found under More above the search box) or going to dir.yahoo.com and entering your search terms in the search box. A search will yield a list of any matching categories and matching sites.

News

The Yahoo! news search (news.yahoo.com) covers thousands of news sources in 35 languages. This is discussed in detail in Chapter 8.

Apps

With Yahoo! Apps (apps.search.yahoo.com), you can browse or search Yahoo!'s database of Apps for either the iPhone or Android devices. For each result, you will see a brief description, a link to full details of the app, a rating (1–5 stars), and the price. The left side of the search results page provides filters by device (iPhone or Android), price (free or paid), and category (news, games, weather, etc.), and results can be sorted by relevance or rating. For downloading, a link can be sent by text message to your phone, you can be redirected to the iTunes site or to the Android Market, or you can scan the QR code that is provided for each result.

Yahoo! Groups

Yahoo! Groups (groups.yahoo.com), which are all created by Yahoo! users, provides a very powerful communication tool. The content of "public" groups (those that the group creator decides can be public) is searchable and is an excellent place to gather advice and opinions. Yahoo! Groups are discussed in more detail in Chapter 5.

People Search

Yahoo! People Search (people.yahoo.com) is a directory of U.S. and Canadian phone numbers, mailing addresses, and email addresses. The main People Search page indicates that it provides information for "U.S. Phone and Address," but if you put the two-letter code for a Canadian province in the State box, you can also find listings in Canada. (Apologies are probably due from the Yahoo! folks.) For other countries, check the country-specific Yahoo! site for a People section. Although you can search by first name, last name, city, and state, you may be able to get by with as little as the last name, which means you may not have to know the state (or province) in which a person lives.

Yahoo! Toolbar

The free downloadable Yahoo! Toolbar, available for Internet Explorer and Firefox, provides easy access to most Yahoo! services, such as Search, Mail, News, Address Book, Bookmarks, Calendar, Alerts, Translation, and so on, regardless of what webpage is showing in your browser window. The Yahoo! toolbar also serves a function similar to a browser's bookmarks toolbar. Yahoo! provides a list of over 1,000 sites (a large proportion being news sites) you can add, plus the capability of adding custom buttons for any website you choose.

Other Yahoo! Features and Content

Here are just a few of the additional services that can be accessed either directly from Yahoo!'s main page or through the More Yahoo! Services link on that page:

- Address Book: Store addresses and related information for use with Yahoo! Mail, Yahoo! Groups, or the calendar, or just use it as a convenient place for storing any phone numbers and addresses. For the latter, it can be your "traveling" address book.

- Answers (answers.yahoo.com): Ask questions of other Yahoo! users and answer their questions.
- Autos (autos.yahoo.com): Research new or used cars and prices.
- Calendar (calendar.yahoo.com): Enter events and tasks, have email reminders sent to you, print events, tasks, and calendar pages in a variety of ways, and share your calendar.
- Finance (finance.yahoo.com): Access a broad range of statistics, advice, news, background, tools, and services related to finance and investing, along with a personal portfolio option.
- Health (health.yahoo.net): Find a range of information on diseases, conditions, and health-related issues, including a drug guide, health news, and expert advice.
- Mail (mail.yahoo.com): Sign up for Yahoo!'s robust web-accessible email service, one of the most-used free email services in the world.
- Messenger (messenger.yahoo.com): Send and receive instant messages.
- Mobile (mobile.yahoo.com): Access a variety of Yahoo! services on your cell phone or other mobile device.
- Movies (movies.yahoo.com): Find reviews, show times, trailers and clips, news, and more about movies and about what's in the theaters and what's out on DVD.
- Music (music.yahoo.com): Information, interviews, and videos about musicians, groups, and recordings.
- OMG! (omg.yahoo.com): OMG! is a celebrity-oriented section of Yahoo!, with photos, news, blogs, videos, and so on specifically about celebrities.
- Travel (travel.yahoo.com): Make reservations for airlines, trains, autos, vacation packages, and cruises, and read country and city guides.

ASK.COM

Ask.com (www.ask.com), formerly known as Ask Jeeves, has an interesting history going back to 1996. In its early days, it was not a search engine but rather a "question and answer" site, utilizing stored collections of answers and algorithms that made an attempt at understanding your question and then finding the probable answer.

When it purchased the Teoma search engine technology in 2001, Ask Jeeves was very obviously moving into the more standard search engine arena. Its transition was complete when, in 2006, it changed its name to Ask.com, retired the butler, and completely redesigned its interface. Briefly, in 2008, it decided to become the "married women's" search engine. In 2009, Ask.com decided to become part of the NASCAR scene, with a lot of attention to NASCAR on its pages and even a special NASCAR search engine. (A historical note: For the once-promising search engine, Northern Light, the emergence of a NASCAR fetish within its organization immediately preceded the doom of the search engine.) By mid-2009, the NASCAR period of Ask.com seemed to have run its course. In 2011, Ask.com headed back to its roots as a "Questions and Answers" engine, but it continues its search to find itself.

Ask.com provides, in addition to its web search, an increasingly emphasized database of Questions and Answers and additional databases, such as images and video. For that reason, the discussion of Ask.com that follows will briefly look at its general "web search" capabilities, but most emphasis will be on the contribution that Ask.com itself most actively promotes, its Questions and Answers approach to search.

Ask.com Homepage

The Ask.com homepage provides a search box, as well as tabs for "Search the Web" and "Q&A Community" and for searching the Images, News, Video, Local, and Reference databases. (The tabs for all but the first two the databases disappear on succeeding Ask.com pages.) Most of the rest of the homepage is used to provide examples of Questions and Answers (Figure 4.15).

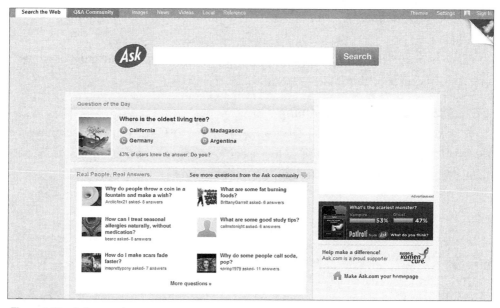

Figure 4.15 Ask.com homepage

Search Features Provided by Ask.com's Search the Web

For "Search the Web" queries, Ask.com offers basic Boolean and the ability to use prefixes to qualify a term. As you enter your search terms, you may see a list of "search suggestions" appear beneath the search box.

Boolean

As with other search engines, all terms you enter in the main search box are automatically ANDed unless you specify otherwise. You can also use an OR and a minus sign for a NOT:

> *deterioration concrete OR cement –bridges*

On the advanced search page (which interestingly only appears as an option if you are signed in to Ask.com), Boolean is available through "all the words," "at least one of the words," and "none of the words" options.

Title Searching

For higher precision, you can use the *intitle:* prefix to limit your retrieval to items where your term occurs in the title:

> *symbolism intitle:chrysanthemums*

On the advanced search page, you can narrow your search using "location of words"; one option is "in page title."

URL, Site, and Domain Searching

To limit to sites with a particular term somewhere in the URL, you can use either the *inurl:* or *site:* prefix. To limit retrieval to a specific site or to pages that come from a particular top-level domain (.com, .fr, .org, etc.), use the *site:* prefix:

> *inurl:nato*
> *NATO site:de*
> *nonproliferation site:un.org*

On the advanced search page, to narrow your search using "location of words," one option is "in URL."

Ask.com's Search the Web Results Pages

For each Questions and Answers result, you will see the title of the page, the URL, and a brief snippet. Depending upon your search, you may see within the results list an "answer" relating to your question (a descriptive paragraph, image, etc.), news headlines on the topic, a travel guide, thumbnails of images from Ask.com's images database, etc. To the right of the list, you may see a list of related searches and a list of related questions from the Questions and Answers database.

Q&A Community Searches

Using the Q&A Community tab on the Ask.com homepage, your question goes in a very different direction with quite different results. According to Ask.com, "We send your questions to those who are best qualified to answer them." If Ask.com finds the answer on the web, it delivers the answer immediately at the top of the page as an "answer," not just as a link. If the answer isn't found on the web, Ask.com uses its "matching technology to route the question to a qualified Ask.com user who can help."

For "Who, What, Where, When" searches (What is a transistor? or Who invented the transistor?), Ask.com can provide precise, quick, informative answers, with the information drawn from a wide variety of sources. On the other hand, before you rely on the quality of answers found there, especially the ones that come from the Ask.com "Q&A Community," spend a couple of minutes looking at the sample recent Q&As presented under that tab. Some answers are credible and even cite reliable sources. On the other hand, chances are very good that you, as a reader of this book, will be able to quickly come up with answers that more adequately meet the information quality criteria discussed in Chapter 1.

Other Searchable Ask.com Databases

Images

Ask.com's image search (www.ask.com/pictureslanding) is designed very similarly to that of Google and Yahoo!, but its database is apparently (based on retrieval numbers and the relevance of images retrieved) substantially smaller.

News

The news search on Ask.com (www.ask.com/news) provides a browsable news homepage and a search of a wide range of major news networks, newspapers, magazines, and blogs.

Video
Ask.com's video search (www.ask.com/video) uses blinkxTV for its content (see Chapter 7).

Local
Ask.com's local (business directory) search (www.ask.com/local), which just covers U.S. businesses, utilizes maps from Bing and business listings from Citysearch.

Reference
Ask.com's Reference section (ask.reference.com) is a collection of about 500 links arranged in 12 categories. The majority of the links lead to Wikipedia articles.

AskEraser
AskEraser is an optional setting that, when turned on, automatically erases your Ask.com search history from Ask.com's servers.

Settings
The Settings link at the top of the Ask.com homepage leads to a page where you can change the email address for notifications from Ask.com, volunteer to answer questions, change your password, display or hide your connections in your public profile, delete your account, open results in a new window, show or not show search suggestions, set adult-content filtering, and turn AskEraser on or off.

ADDITIONAL GENERAL WEB SEARCH ENGINES
The web search engines covered in this section are additional engines that the serious searcher should be aware of. For these, most searchers may not want to absorb the level of detail provided for the four engines just covered, but you should be aware of special features these provide, or at least be aware of the existence of the engines themselves. The "special features" point applies particularly to the first one, Blekko. The others are listed here, to some degree at least, for "historical" purposes.

Blekko
Another search engine with a weird name, Blekko (www.blekko.com) stands out for its innovative approach for filtering results to achieve high precision. You enter your term and follow it with a "slashtag," one provided by Blekko, by you, or by someone else.

Table 4.1   Features of Major Search Engines

	Ask.com	Bing	Google	Yahoo!
Boolean	*term term* (Defaults to an AND) *-term* (for NOT) *term* OR *term*	*term term* (Defaults to an AND) *-term* (for NOT) (*term* OR *term*)	*term term* (Defaults to an AND) *-term* (for NOT) OR *term* OR *term*	*term term* (Defaults to an AND) *-term* (for NOT) (*term* OR *term*)
Stemming	Some automatic stemming	Some automatic stemming	Some automatic stemming	Some automatic stemming
Title field	intitle:*term*	intitle:*term*	intitle:*term* allintitle:*term1 term2*	intitle:*term*
Site/URL field	inurl:*term* site:*term*	site:*term*	inurl:*term* allinurl:*term1 term2* site:*term*	site:*term*
"Links to" a site			link:*term*	
File type		filetype:*extension*	filetype:*extension*	filetype:*extension*
Language	Choice of 6 languages on advanced search page	*language*:xx Choice of 42 languages	Choice of 46 languages on advanced search page	*language*:xx Choice of 32 languages on advanced search page
Numeric ranges			nnnn..mmmm e.g., 1850..1899	
Media search	Images, video	Images, video	Images, video	Images, video
Similar pages			Yes	
Also shown on results pages	Related searches Related questions	Links to cached pages Shortcuts Related searches Search history Stock quotes News headlines	Links to cached pages Translation options Stock quotes Link to definitions, video, blogs, etc. News headlines	Related searches "Also try" Shortcuts Stock quotes News headlines
Other searchable databases	Maps News Shopping Reference Local	Places maps News Shopping Local Travel	Maps News Shopping Books Groups Scholar (journals) Blogs Earth Patents	Maps News Shopping Answers Directory, Jobs People Travel

Results are narrowed to websites that have a focus on the topic indicated by the slashtag. For example, *China/conservative* would get records on China from politically conservative websites. There are also some non-topical slashtags, such as date, plus some other features that make Blekko stand out for its approach to search.

Blekko Homepage

The Blekko homepage is very minimalist, with a search box, help and preferences links, and a number of "company" and "about" type links at the bottom of the page. Get started by entering some terms in the box and, if you know or wish to guess, a slashtag, for example, *lithuania/economics*. Refinement can take place on results pages.

Search Features

Blekko offers one major search feature, its unique slashtag approach. Slashtags are of three types: topical (created by Blekko); user (created by users); and built-in (algorithmically generated to identify characteristics of a page, such as date, blogs, etc.). Blekko has created over 400 slashtags for general use, including *allergies, anthropology, autism, Egypt, finance, genealogy, health, history, news, nutrition, reviews, Shakespeare,* and *wine*. On search results pages, you will find a link to Blekko's slashtag directory, which allows you to either search for slashtags or browse through lists. Of particular interest are slashtags that filter results for a particular "slant," such as *conservative* and *liberal*.

Blekko has also created a set of "built-in" slashtags that narrow by type of site, such as people, blogs, forums, etc. A *date* slashtag sorts search results by date and a *dr* slashtag allows you to enter specific year ranges (e.g., tornadoes/dr=2010–2011).

To create a slashtag of your own, click on the Create a Slashtag link (found on results pages), name your tag, and list the URLs you want covered. You can type the URLs yourself or use the Search for Websites feature provided there.

Blekko Results Pages

On search results pages, above the list of results, you will find the number of results and links enabling you to sort the results by date or by relevance (Figure 4.16). For each individual result, there will be a link to the page, a snippet of text, the URL, and some suggested slashtag links. A More link leads you to more suggestions.

Other Blekko Databases

On search results pages, you will see options for Images, Video, and Local. Clicking on one of these terms will, in effect, add that slashtag to your query and result in a display of items that have the corresponding slashtag (e.g., *nasturtiums/images*).

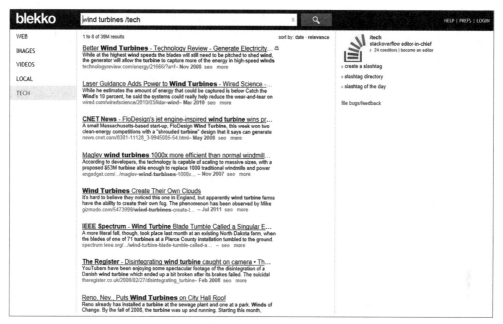

Figure 4.16   Blekko results page

Virtually Defunct Engines

There are four web search engines that have been around for a long time but whose current lack of functionality, features, interest, and size means that they do not offer anything of real significance to the power searcher. However, their names do come up occasionally.

HotBot (www.hotbot.com), which is one of the oldest web search engines, was once one of the most powerful, with some pioneering and unique features. After years of neglect and downgrading, there is virtually nothing left of its former glory, and the site is now merely a watered-down interface for Lycos.com.

Lycos (www.lycos.com) was once a major contender on the search engine scene. The searches it provides are now "powered" by Bing.

Once among the top three or four search engines, AltaVista (www.altavista.com) and AllTheWeb (www.alltheweb.com) are now Yahoo! properties. AltaVista's unique and powerful search technology (including truncation and the NEAR connector) was discontinued several years ago. A search at www.altavista.com will yield results from Bing and www.alltheweb.com takes you to Yahoo! search.

VISUALIZATION SEARCH ENGINES

Visualization engines provide a very different "look"—literally—at search results.

Instead of the traditional linear, textual list of retrieved items, results are shown on a map that displays conceptual connections spatially. Visualization continues to be an area of extensive research, and several sites demonstrate various visualization approaches. The conceptual and visual mapping done by these sites can be especially useful for a quick exploration of the concept possibilities, directions, and terminology for a particular search. Consider this approach for competitive intelligence and other searches where you need to start by understanding relationships rather than just browsing lists of results.

Leading visualization engines include TouchGraph and Quintura. Each uses the content of one or more of the larger search engines' databases. You will also see visualization approaches appearing in other sites, such as Silobreaker, which is covered in Chapter 8.

TouchGraph

TouchGraph (www.touchgraph.com) offers a dynamic and interactive display of the relationships between entities such as (in the case of the free demo sites it provides) webpages from the databases of Amazon and Google, and images from Facebook. To try TouchGraph, go to the Demo section of its site (www.touchgraph.com/seo). To do a TouchGraph SEO search, enter a term or a URL. To do an Amazon search, enter a keyword (title, author, etc.). For Facebook, log in to Facebook, and TouchGraph analyzes photos connected to your photos. The results are displayed by a network of lines connecting the various nodes or websites (Figure 4.17). From each, site lines radiate to the

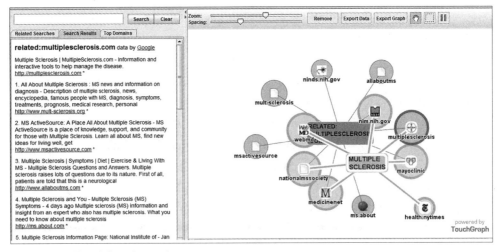

Figure 4.17 TouchGraph results page

sites to which they link. Double-click on one of the nodes and notice the new connections now shown.

Quintura

Of the two visualization engines discussed here, Quintura (www.quintura.com) is the newest. When you search on a term using Quintura, the most obvious feature you see on the results page is a "cloud" of terms—similar to a "tag cloud" but showing the "concepts" that Quintura has identified as dominant among the concepts found in the search results set, which it gets from the Russian search engine Yandex (Figure 4.18). Terms in the cloud have a size relative to their "importance," and the distance between terms is used to indicate the degree of connection. Details of hits are shown in a "regular" search results list beneath the cloud display. If you hold your cursor over one of the terms in the cloud, you will see the matching sites for that term. Double-click on the term and that concept is automatically added to your search and the new list and cloud are shown. In addition to webpage searches, Quintura also offers an image search (also from Yandex) and a video search (with results from blinkx). Quintura also provides a kids' version that utilizes content from Yahoo! for Kids.

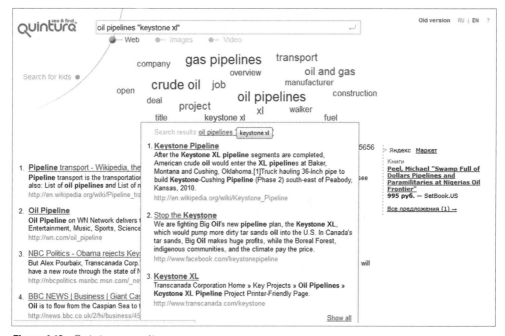

Figure 4.18 Quintura results page

SEARCH ENGINE COMPARISON SEARCHES

There are a number of sites that provide a comparison of results from various search engines. Unlike metasearch sites, which extract and amalgamate the top few results from multiple engines, these comparison sites give more of a side-by-side comparison, with a much truer look at what is actually available in each engine. Though each has a unique approach and may cover a different selection of search engines (and different types, such as web, images, blogs, video, etc.), you can get a feel for what this type of tool can do by taking a quick look at Zuula and TurboScout.

Zuula

Zuula (www.zuula.com) allows you to view the actual results from nine web search engines, displayed in separate tabs, with a single click (Figure 4.19). Zuula also provides a similar comparison for images (10 engines), video (11 engines), news (9 engines), blogs (6 engines), tags (7 engines), and job searches (3 engines).

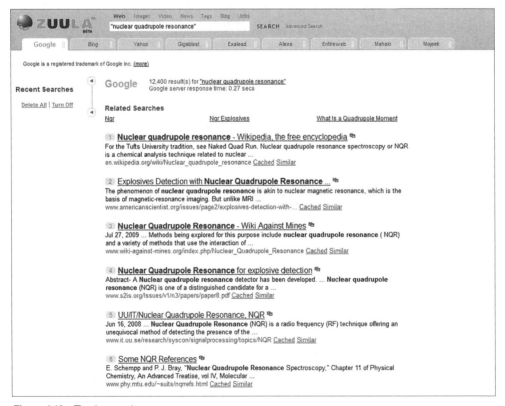

Figure 4.19 Zuula results page

TurboScout

TurboScout (www.turboscout.com) allows a quick look at the results from more than 90 engines, arranged under seven categories (Web, Images, Reference, News, Products, Blogs, Audio/Video). Enter your term or terms, click on a category, and then choose an engine.

CHAPTER 5

DISCUSSION GROUPS, FORUMS, NEWSGROUPS, AND THEIR RELATIVES

Groups, newsgroups, discussion groups, lists, message boards, and other online interactive forums are tools that are often under-used resources in the searcher's toolbox. Particularly for competitive intelligence (including researching and tracking products, companies, and industries), for other fields of intelligence (including security, military, and related areas), and for technical troubleshooting and advice, discussion groups and their relatives can be gold mines (and, analogously, the product is sometimes difficult to find and to mine). These resources can be essential when you need to see the subjective side of something—politics, travel, products, people, technology—anything where opinions can be useful. In general, groups, forums, and so on bring together, in one place, discussions on a specific topic or subject. The topic can be very broad or very narrow, but these sites are places where a range of people can contribute their knowledge or questions about the topic of common interest.

You may find yourself making use of groups without even realizing it. When you enter a "how-to" or troubleshooting query into a search engine, many of the best answers that come up are likely to come from groups. Indeed, if, for example, you run into a computer problem (you get an error message you don't understand and can't remedy, your software isn't behaving as it should, etc.), enter a few words describing the problem, or, in quotation marks, just enter a string of words from the error message. Chances are the most relevant answers returned may actually be on forums.

Groups, mailing lists, and a variety of their hybrids represent one aspect of the interactive side of the internet, allowing users to communicate with people who have like interests, concerns, problems, and issues. Unlike regular email, where you need the addresses of specific persons or organizations in order to communicate with them, these channels allow you to reach people you don't know and take advantage of their knowledge and expertise. This chapter outlines the resources available for finding and mining this information, and it suggests some techniques that can make it easier.

A major barrier to understanding these tools is the terminology. Though *discussion groups* is probably the most descriptive term applied to most of this genre, other terms are also used. *Newsgroups*, which was the first term used, usually have little to do with news, and *mailing lists* are definitely not to be confused with the junk mail you receive in either your email or traditional mailbox. Newsgroups, narrowly defined, usually refers to the Usenet collection of groups that actually originated prior to the internet as we now think of it. *Groups*, more broadly defined, includes newsgroups and a variety of other channels, variously referred to as discussion groups, bulletin boards, message boards, forums, and even (by dot.com marketers, primarily) communities. In this chapter, the terms *groups* and *forums* will be used interchangeably to refer to all of the incarnations just mentioned.

In terms of the type of communication channels they provide, it would not be unrealistic to include blogs in this chapter. However, the blog phenomenon is different enough to be addressed separately and is covered later in this book (see Chapter 10). Groups can be thought of as primarily a communal, participatory, democratic experience, whereas blogs are usually exclusively controlled, top-down, by an individual (with, however, some participatory possibilities). Though they existed prior to the creation of the term Web 2.0, the interactive, collaborative, sharing nature of groups makes the whole concept of groups very Web 2.0-ish.

Many groups provide both an online forum and a "mailing list" service. The biggest distinction between these two services lies in how the information gets to you. On the forum side, messages are posted on computer networks (e.g., the internet) for the world to read. Usually anyone can go to a group and read its content and, usually, anyone can post a message. With a mailing list, content goes, by email, only to individuals who subscribe to the list, and past messages usually are not accessible. Messages that appear in groups are usually more fully archived and, therefore, more retrospectively available than the content of something that is purely a mailing list.

Both groups and mailing lists can be moderated or unmoderated. With unmoderated groups (and lists), your posting appears immediately when you submit it. If the group or mailing list is moderated, your posting must pass the inspection of someone who decides whether to approve the posting, and, if it is approved, then posts it to the list. Among other things, this means that moderated groups and lists are more likely to have postings that really are directly related to the subject.

The messages within each individual group are usually arranged by "threads"—a series of messages on one specific topic, consisting of the original message, replies to that message, replies to those replies, and so on. Users can post messages to either the original message or to any of the replies, or they can start a new thread.

GROUPS OF GROUPS AND INDIVIDUAL GROUPS

Groups can be found on sites that offer a collection of many individual groups and on websites that host one or more groups relevant to the specific area of interest of that site. Collections of groups include the grandparent of all groups, Usenet, commercial portals such as Yahoo!, and sites such as Delphi Forums (www.delphiforums.com) and Yuku (formerly ezboard; www.yuku.com) that serve as hosts for discussion groups. Individual groups are found in such places as professional association sites and travel sites such as Lonely Planet. The next few pages will give an overview of the nature of these various collections and individual groups, and outline how you can most easily access them and participate.

Usenet

Before going into how and where to find groups of interest and how to search for specific messages of interest, a few words should be said, for background and historical purposes, about Usenet. Usenet is the original and probably still best-known collection of groups, created in 1979 at the University of North Carolina and Duke University by Jim Ellis, Tom Truscott, Steve Bellovin, and Steve Daniel. Usenet (a "users' network," originally spelled USENET) started as a collection of network-accessible electronic bulletin boards and grew quickly both in terms of use and in its geographic reach. Not only does Usenet predate the web, it predates the internet as most of us know it today. With the popularization of the internet and the web, however, Usenet access is now, for all practical purposes, through the internet (and in most cases through Google), and most users use a web-based interface rather than the older specialized software known as Usenet newsreaders.

Until probably the late 1990s, most Usenet access was through an Internet Service Provider (ISP), and messages were read and posted by means of special software called newsreaders or through such software built into browsers such as Netscape. ISPs received newsfeeds from the computers that hosted Usenet groups and then made that content available to the ISP's customers.

Web access to Usenet newsgroups first became widely available through a site called Deja News, which was created in 1996 and later became deja.com. It was great—until the people responsible for its design and marketing began to miss the point and decided to make it into a shopping site, with the newsgroup access relegated to a minor position.

Deja.com went out of business and can now best be remembered as an early pioneer of the dot-com bust.

To the rescue came none other than almost-every-serious-searcher's favorite site, Google. In 2001, Google bought Deja's remains, began loading the archive, and quickly added the capability to not just search Usenet postings but to post messages as well. By the end of the year, it had made a 20-year archive of Usenet postings available and easy to access. Details of how to make use of Usenet through Google is coming up a few pages from here.

Other Groups

Although Usenet is the best-known collection of groups, it is not the only one. Collections of groups can be found on commercial sites and portals such as Yahoo! and on group-hosting sites such as Delphi Forums and Yuku. Google's own user-created and hosted groups are not only now available but may be overshadowing the Usenet groups on Google. You will also find a lot of specialized groups on association and club sites, such as the Illinois Cycling Association, the Institute of Electrical and Electronics Engineers (IEEE), and the Australian Tarantula Association. These web-based groups vary considerably in terms of the appearance of the interface, but they all function in about the same way. For most sites, you can read what group members have posted without belonging to the group and without logging in. To post questions and other messages, you will probably have to join the group, although often your email address and a name (real or otherwise) is about all you need to do so. For most association sites, you must be a member of the association to participate in the discussions.

Resources for Locating and Using Groups

The following resources (and others) can be used to locate either *groups* of interest or *messages on specific topics*:

- Groups search engines: Certain search engines are devoted to searching large numbers of groups from sites across the web, among them Omgili (www.omgili.com) and BoardReader (www.boardreader.com).
- Google Groups (groups.google.com): Use this for searching Usenet groups, the newer Google Groups, and other groups that Google has identified on the web.
- Google's web search: This is useful for locating some non-Google and non-Usenet groups; search results will also include those things found by searching Google Groups.

- Yahoo! Groups (groups.yahoo.com): This search covers only groups on the Yahoo! site (there are hundreds of thousands of them).
- Delphi Forums (www.delphiforums.com): More than 8,000 active forums can be found on the Delphi Forums site.
- Yuku (www.yuku.com): Yuku is another provider of forum services.
- Big Boards (www.big-boards.com): Use this resource guide to locate very large message boards and forums.

Don't hesitate to simply use a search engine search to find a group. Searching on your topic and the term forum usually works well, as in the first example that follows. But if you want a more inclusive search, follow the second example:

physics forum

"multiple sclerosis" (forum OR "discussion group" OR "message board")

Sites of Associations Related to Your Topic

Look on the site of an association related to your search topic for an indication of a *forum*, *discussion*, or similar term suggesting the presence of a group. This tip also applies to locating mailing lists.

GROUPS SEARCH ENGINES

There are search engines designed specifically to search the contents of groups from across the web, not just content stored on their own site, as is the case with Google Groups and Yahoo! Groups. You can use these search engines either to locate individual messages that mention a topic or to locate forums that cover a broader area of interest you wish to follow.

Omgili

Omgili (www.omgili.com) searches more than 100,000 forums, newsgroups, and mailing lists. It differs from some of its competitors by providing significantly more "searchability," allowing the user to more precisely refine a search.

As with general web search engines, the search terms you enter in Omgili's main search box are automatically ANDed, and you can use quotation marks for phrases and a NOT to exclude terms.

Results pages will show the titles of topics and then snippets from each and links to the full threads. Above the list of topics are links to order results by date and to show questions. Also on search results pages, you can take advantage of three "slider bars" to narrow or broaden your search by time frame and by messages with a minimum number of replies or a minimum number of discussing users. More searchability is available by clicking on the Advanced Search link found on search results pages. There you will find options for narrowing your search by phrases, by language, and by occurrence in the title, topic, or replies, and for searching within a specific forum. For some of the options, there is a corresponding prefix *(intitle:, intopic:, inreply:)* that you can use directly in the search box on the main page. As for language, you can search in any language you wish by using search terms in that language as your search query.

On Omgili results pages, look at the "Buzz" graph that shows the frequency of occurrence of your search terms over the last month. (Click on Buzz Graph to get an HTML code for a free widget with which you can place a further customized chatter graph on your own website.)

BoardReader

With BoardReader (www.boardreader.com), you can search more than 100,000 unique message board domains. Links at the top of the main page allow you to search for posts (messages) that contain your terms or for forums about your topic. Other links there will limit your results specifically to messages on IMDb (the Internet Movie Database) message boards, to groups hosted on the Yuku group hosting website, to groups on the Lefora group hosting site, and to the video search option (provided by blinkx). Another search category, microblogs, searches Twitter.

On BoardReader's advanced search page, you can search using simplified Boolean, and by language, by date, or by domain, and sort results by time, by relevance, or by a combination of time and relevance. An advanced links search page allows you to search for messages that have linked to a specific URL or part of a URL ("path"). Like Omgili, BoardReader shows on results pages a graph indicating the recent frequency of occurrence of terms.

Using Google to Find Groups and Messages

When Google first got into the realm of groups, the main and only focus was on the Usenet collection, with its archives going back to 1981. In 2004, Google launched its own user-created groups, mimicking to a significant degree the types of groups offered by Yahoo!. The focus has now moved away from Usenet to Google's own groups. More recently, Google added threads and messages from many other sites on the web that have groups. Overall, Google lists more than 3 million groups. The following is a quick overview and some highlights.

Browsing Google Groups

From the main Google Groups page (click on the More link on Google's main page to get to the Groups link or go directly to groups.google.com), you can click the Browse All link to browse through the 12 main top-level hierarchies or browse by Region. After you choose a category, the pages will show options to filter those results by specific words and language.

As you browse throughout the levels, you will see links to additional lower levels in the hierarchy or related categories and, beneath that, specific groups at that level. Clicking on the group name will take you to the message threads for that group.

Searching for Groups and Messages

As you enter search terms in the search box on the main Google Groups page, specific suggested matches will appear beneath the box. If you don't click on one of those choices but click the search icon instead, both groups and messages will be retrieved, with "Groups matching ____" listed first, followed by messages that contain the terms (see Figure 5.1). Google will show all groups that have your term(s) in the group name or description, plus any threads containing that term. Those groups with your term in the group name will be shown at the top of the results. Click on the name of the group to go to the group. In the list of individual messages, click on the title of the message to see the messages plus other messages in the thread or click on the name of the group to see other messages in that group. Above the results list, there are links to sort either by relevance or by date.

You will in some places see references to specific Usenet groups (which are arranged in a hierarchy that at first glance appears a bit arcane). The hierarchy consists of 10 main top-level categories—alt (alternative), biz (businesses), comp (computers), humanities, misc, news, rec (recreation), sci (science), soc (social sciences), and talk (politics, etc.)— and thousands of other next-level hierarchies, based mainly on subject, geography, and language:

sci.bio.phytopathology
rec.crafts.textiles.needlework

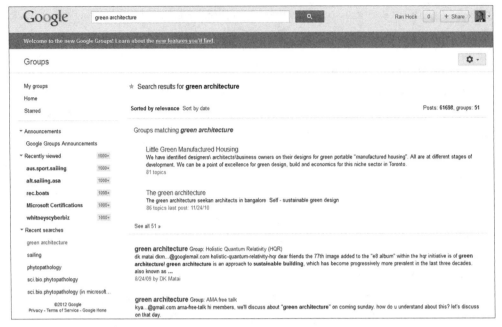

Figure 5.1 Google Groups results page

When you are on a results page and are viewing either a group or individual message, as you enter a new search, the search suggestions will now include options to search *within* that group either for topics or messages containing your new search terms.

When you have clicked to view a group that is open for public viewing, buttons will appear above the messages list for a "New topic" (to start a new thread within that group, if non-members can post to the group), "Mark all as read," and "Refresh," as well as to report abuse and see either a compact list view (all information on one line) or a standard view (two lines). As you proceed, you will see, depending upon the group, links to post messages, join groups, etc.

Joining a Group

If you click one of the Apply for Group Membership buttons, a window will appear asking you 1) how you want to read the group's messages (no email, once-a-day summary of activities email, digest email with up to 25 full messages in a single email, email for each message, or subscribe to emails for those topics to which you have posted), 2) which email address you wish to use, 3) the nickname you want to appear on your posts, and 4) other information you wish to share.

Posting Messages

Depending upon the "openness" of a group, how you post a reply will differ. For those groups that don't require membership to post, you can add your own new thread to a discussion by clicking the New Topic button that will appear when you are on the results page for a group. If you are looking at specific messages in such a group, use the red Post Reply button to add your messages to that thread. To reply to a specific message within a thread, you will see a green Post button after each message. There may also be a gray Post Reply button to the left of messages that has a pull-down window enabling you to reply directly to the author, view recent activity relating to that post, etc. As if those weren't enough places, beneath some messages, there will be a reply box. On one hand, if all of that seems a bit complicated, it is. On the other hand, it reflects streamlining that Google has done to deal with groups from a wide variety of sources (Google and non-Google, and various levels of public accessibility and membership possibilities).

Starting a Google Group

To start a new Google Group, from the main Google Groups page (or elsewhere), click on the New Group button.

Follow the next several steps, which include naming your group, providing a description, and selecting the level of public access. You can fill in just the basics (group name, description, group email address) or accept the defaults for a number of other options and get started very quickly. You can also take just a few more minutes and precisely tailor the access and management of the group to meet your specific needs. Those additional options include level of access in terms of who can view messages (selected users, managers of the group, owners of the group, anyone), who can post messages (managers, owners, members, anyone), who can join (anyone, only invited users, or by requested permission), etc. Using the several Advanced Settings options, you can specify the following:

- The degree to which members need to identify themselves
- Whether members' display names must be unique within the group
- Whether email addresses will be kept private
- Whether the group should be listed in the Google Groups directory
- Whether you wish to receive messages from Google regarding Google Groups
- Whether the group is suitable to anyone or only adults
- Whether topics can include discussions or questions or both
- Whether posting can be done by web or email or both
- Who can post on behalf of the group and who can invite new members

- Whether posts will be moderated and who will moderate and how, as well as appearance and lengths of subject lines, whether messages will be archived, and more

Using Web Search to Identify Non-Usenet, Non-Google Groups

You can also find group messages by doing a Google web search, then using the "discussions" narrowing option found on the left side of search results pages. This will retrieve messages that would be found in Google Groups, but without the convenience of the features provided by Google Groups. It will also retrieve messages from groups whose content is not included in Google Groups.

Using Yahoo! to Find Groups and Messages

Along with the groups search engines already mentioned and a Google Groups or Google web search, another place to find groups is Yahoo! (groups.yahoo.com, or look for a Groups link on Yahoo!'s homepage). If you want to create a group of your own, for free and with powerful options, perhaps the first place to go is Yahoo! Groups. Yahoo! Groups is actually a hybrid of groups and mailing lists, because for each group you can receive messages either at the Yahoo! website or by email. Yahoo! allows you to search or browse through the groups, post messages, and create groups of your own. There are hundreds of thousands of Yahoo! groups, some with thousands of members and many with only a single member. (Join one of the latter and brighten someone's day.) There are a dozen or so "duct tape" groups alone, including one for people who enjoy being taped up with duct tape.

Searching or Browsing for Yahoo! Groups

You can find Yahoo! groups of interest to you either by browsing through the 17 categories on the main Groups page or by using the search box there. Be aware that a search there only searches group names and their descriptions, not individual messages. However, once you have gone to the page for a particular group, the search box on that page will enable you to search for messages from within that group. Terms you enter in the search boxes are automatically ANDed. You can also use "-" (minus sign) to exclude a word. Yahoo! does automatically truncate, so a search for *environment* will also retrieve items that contain the word *environmental*.

Whether you use the search box or browse the categories to find groups on Yahoo!, the listing of groups that results will contain the name of each group, the description, the number of members, whether the archive is public or not, latest activity, whether it is moderated, and when it was created. If it is public, you can browse through the messages without joining the group. Clicking on the name of the group will show you more detail about the group, including the number of recent messages and so forth, plus a calendar showing numbers of messages posted each month (Figure 5.2). The number of members and volume of postings are usually important indicators of the potential usefulness of the group.

Joining a Yahoo! Group

After identifying a group of interest, if it accepts new members, click on Join This Group. If you are not signed in to Yahoo! you will be asked for your Yahoo! password. If you do not have a Yahoo! password, you can get one at this point. After joining a group, you can go to the homepage for the group and read and post messages. Delivery methods for messages include:

- Individual emails: To receive individual email messages
- Daily digest: To receive up to 25 of the posts for the day in one message
- Special notices: To receive update emails from the group's moderator
- Web only: The true groups approach, where you go get the messages, rather than receiving them by email

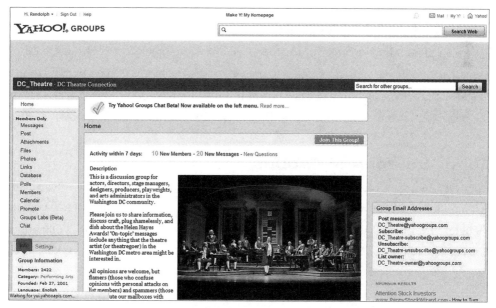

Figure 5.2   Yahoo! Groups description

Once you have joined one or more groups, when you are signed on and go to the Yahoo! Groups main page, you will be presented with a page providing links to all of the groups to which you belong. The Manage link there takes you to a page where you can edit your memberships, with options to change delivery methods, your profile, and your email address for the group, and also to leave a group.

On both the pages that list messages and on the message pages themselves, you have a variety of options, such as viewing the message in brief (simple) form or expanded form, viewing the sender's profile, and viewing the messages by date (using the "calendar" on the page). Though most Yahoo! groups don't take advantage of all of the possibilities, each group is provided with options for adding the following features and content: Files, Photos, Polls, Links, Database, Polls, Members List, and Calendar. The availability of these features takes Yahoo! Groups far beyond most of its competitors.

Starting a Yahoo! Group

Yahoo! is definitely one of the easiest—perhaps actually *the* easiest—place on the web to set up a group. A group of your own can be a great tool for a course you are teaching, networking and support groups, family, community organizations, and so forth, and you can set one up in 10 minutes or less.

You choose the category (although Yahoo!'s staff may change the category if they see it and feel the category is inappropriate), name the group, decide if it is to be public, moderated, and so on. Basically, all you have to do is fill in the blanks.

With Yahoo!'s large number of users and members, large number of groups, ease of use, range of options, and accessibility to both those who want to use and those who want to sponsor groups, Yahoo! Groups is a potent resource for those who wish to make use of the internet as a communications channel.

Other Sources of Groups

There are numerous other places where you will find groups, some large and some small, but most have considerably less reach and content than those available through Yahoo! or Google. Nevertheless, the group that may precisely meet your needs may be in one of the smaller collections. Two additional sources, not as large as Yahoo! but having both a large number of groups and members, are Delphi Forums and Yuku.

Delphi Forums

www.delphiforums.com

According to Delphi Forums, this site has more than 4 million registered users, 8,000 active forums, 100,000 messages a day, and more than 200 million total messages. As with Yahoo! Groups, you can read most messages with Delphi without registering, but to post messages, you must register. Registration is easy and free.

Delphi's lists are browsable using 23 categories (click on the Forums link on the main page to get to the categories). An advanced search link on the Forums page enables you to search for forums. Terms entered in that box will search both titles of groups and the content of the forum's homepage. When browsing through categories, you are also given a search option to search just within that category. On the pages for individual forums, look for the advanced search link, which will give you the opportunity to search the messages and by author, date, etc. "Basic" members can search three months back. Premium members can search as far back as a year.

You can create a free forum on Delphi, but for fuller capabilities (capability of conducting polls, etc.), premium services (DelphiExtra and DelphiPlus) are available. If it is really important that you find as many groups out there on your topic as possible, don't ignore a search on Delphi Forums.

Yuku

www.yuku.com

Yuku, the forums site formerly known as ezboard, provides a place for people to create forums, but it also provides "profiles" (social networking), photo sharing, and blogs. A search box on the homepage yields results from the Yuku forums.

Big Boards

www.big-boards.com

Big Boards is a resource guide covering more than 2,300 of the largest message boards and forums (measured by the numbers of members and the numbers of posts). You can locate discussions of interest either by using the Big Boards search box or by browsing through the 12 main directory categories (and more than 130 subcategories).

MAILING LISTS

Most of what can be said about the usefulness and nature of groups also applies to mailing lists. As mentioned earlier, the biggest differences with mailing lists are that 1) the message arrives in your email rather than you having to request to see messages, with every message sent to the list coming to you, 2) you have to subscribe, often providing identifying information (and may need to be a member of the sponsoring organization), 3) the content of mailing lists is less likely to be archived and searchable than for groups, and 4) although the email delivery mode makes it easier to access and ensures that you don't miss anything important, mailing lists postings have been known to fill up mailboxes and be a nuisance to deal with. The comparison is analogous to a company bulletin board compared to the inbox on your desk: Some information is more appropriately accessed by your going to the bulletin board periodically, whereas for some information, you would prefer to get a copy on your own desk. If, on a particular topic, you want to make sure you don't miss anything, a mailing list may better serve you.

One change that has occurred in the last few years is that the concept of mailing lists has, for many users, been obscured somewhat by the groups that were just discussed. Many people read, join, and participate in groups and, as part of that process, somewhere along the line indicate that they would like to receive messages by email (instead of, or in addition to, seeing messages by going to the group's website).

In other cases, users can join many mailing lists from many other types of websites just by clicking a link there that says you would like to be added to the website's mailing list. This has made joining a mailing list a much easier process than it used to be. Whether a specific mailing list is just one function of a group, is provided by a website, or exists by itself in "pure mailing list" form (i.e., just email delivery) probably doesn't and shouldn't make much difference, as long as you get what you need. What is said in the following paragraphs about mailing lists in some cases will be more descriptive of mailing lists that exist mostly on their own, not as a part of a "group" function.

The receipt and distribution of messages on the older "purer" form of mailing lists (those that are not just one function of an online group or those that are joined by just clicking a link on a website) are controlled automatically by "listserver" software. Lists are often referred to, inappropriately, as "listservs." LISTSERV is a registered trademark for listserver software produced by the L-Soft company, and the term (legally) should not be applied generically. Other frequently encountered mailing list managers are Majordomo, GNU Mailman, and Listproc.

For any kind of mailing list, you need to subscribe to participate. (How to find lists will be discussed shortly.) Some sites (e.g., lots of association sites and commercial sites) provide a nice web interface where you just have to fill in the blanks. Other sites provide instructions for sending an email message to the mailing list administrative address and tell you what command you need to put in the header or message in order to join. For example, you might be instructed to send a message to majordomo@alektorophobia.org with the message *subscribe fearofchickens* in the body of the message. The instructions will vary primarily depending upon the listserver software being used. You will usually receive a reply confirming your membership to the list and referencing an information file explaining how to use the list, ground rules, and so on.

The following are other important points about using mailing lists that are managed by listserver software:

- The email address to which you send administrative messages is different from the one you use for posting messages. It is a great annoyance to list members to see administrative messages in their mailboxes.
- Many lists offer delivery of a "digest" form in which a number of messages are bundled on a regular basis (e.g., daily or weekly). This is especially useful for lists that have a lot of traffic, and digests can avoid clogging up your email inbox. They may also have an option where you can suspend delivery while you are on vacation.
- Many (probably most) lists will provide an FAQ (Frequently Asked Questions) file or webpage, which is usually worth scanning.
- Some lists provide archives, many of which are searchable.
- Before you sign up, note (from descriptions you find of the list) the level of traffic. If you subscribe to several high-volume mailing lists, you will end up not being able to read them because of the hundreds of messages you receive. For high-volume lists, consider taking advantage of digest versions and "on vacation" options.

Tools and Techniques for Locating Mailing Lists

For many people, their first experience in using mailing lists is through organizations to which they belong. Numerous other lists of interest may be out there and, fortunately, there are some online sites that make them easy to find. Among these are Topica and L-Soft CataList. Yahoo! Groups and Google Groups could also be included among these "finding tools" since, as pointed out earlier, their groups also have an email option.

Topica Email List Directory

lists.topica.com

Topica's thrust is providing mailing list services to companies, associations, and individuals. Many readers who use mailing lists may have noticed that instead of associations managing their own lists, many have taken advantage of the Topica service. Topica (formerly liszt.com) hosts more than 100,000 email newsletters. In addition to association lists and lists created by individuals, many of Topica's lists are commercial, but keep in mind that these are opt-in lists—you only join if you want to join. They can be valuable for competitive intelligence purposes, as well as for keeping up-to-date on products and special deals from your favorite suppliers.

You can use the Topica List Directory and its search capability without signing up, but signing up will enable you to have a page that shows all the Topica lists to which you belong and will allow you to manage your subscriptions.

Lists of interest can be identified either by using the search box or browsing through the Topica categories. To browse, click on one of the categories on Topica's List Directory. To search, use the search box on that page. Click on your choice of items in the results list to get a detailed description. The list descriptions given usually make it easy to determine if this is a list for you (Figure 5.3). The description pages also make it easy to read and subscribe to (join) the list. On those and other pages, you will find how to (very easily) start a list of your own. (First ask yourself, "Does the world really need my list?")

L-Soft CataList, the Official Catalog of LISTSERV Lists
www.lsoft.com/lists/listref.html

As the name says, L-Soft CataList is the official catalog for the 60,000 public lists that use LISTSERV software. In addition to searching list names and descriptions, you can

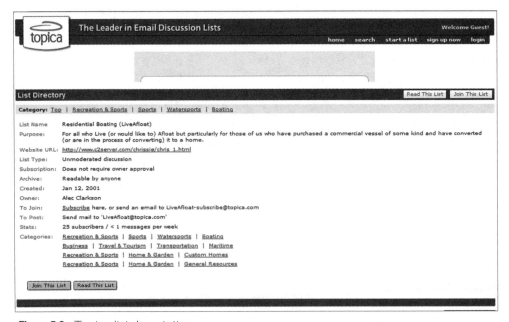

Figure 5.3 Topica list description

view lists by host country or view only those with 10,000 subscribers or more, or those with 1,000 subscribers or more.

INSTANT MESSAGING

Instant messaging, pioneered by AOL Instant Messenger with variations by Yahoo! and others, is another incarnation of online interaction for people and is a hybrid of groups and email. Although it was first populated mainly by teenagers—an extension of the historic evolution of hanging out on the street corner or occupying the family phone—instant messaging spread beyond that. Though instant messaging is still very much alive, its social role has largely been replaced by other technologies, particularly social networking sites such as Facebook and microblogging sites such as Twitter (see Chapter 10). Instant messaging has also achieved some degree of acceptance and utility in corporate environments.

If you haven't used or seen it, the way instant messaging works is that participants create a buddy list of people they want to interact with online on an immediate basis. You send a message to someone on your list, and it will pop up on his or her screen. People who use the same instant messaging service who are not yet a buddy but who want to talk to you can send you a message asking to talk. You also have the option of creating a chat room in which multiple people are invited to join the conversation.

NETIQUETTE POINTS RELATING TO GROUPS AND MAILING LISTS

Readers of this book most likely already have a good sense of Netiquette (internet etiquette), but some may profit by these selected points relating to groups and mailing lists:

1. "Lurk before you leap." Lurking or hanging around just observing a discussion without participating is definitely a good idea. It may involve just reading a few messages or a few threads, and you may find yourself ready to leap in and join the conversation in a matter of minutes. Read enough messages (and preferably the FAQ or similar documentation) to be sure that the conversation is at the level appropriate to your needs and knowledge. If a group is very technical, members can get annoyed at beginners asking extremely simple questions. If there is a searchable archive, check it out. Don't get caught trying to start a discussion about a topic that has already been beaten to death.

2. Don't use newsgroups or email lists for advertising. Depending on the group or list, there might be times when it would be acceptable to respond to a posting that may

have requested a service you provide, but be careful. You can easily irritate many people. In such a case, you can play it safe by responding directly to the poster by email, rather than responding to the group or list as a whole.

3. Don't get sucked into a flame war (an angry or unnecessarily strongly worded series of messages, aka flaming). Remember the sad truth that there are people out there who have nothing better to do than waste their time being nitpicky, rude, and generally obnoxious. The advent of groups and lists has become a wonderful channel for their frustrations and repressed feelings.

4. Only forward messages if allowed. Some associations, particularly, have rules regarding the privacy of messages, often relating to such things as client privilege and competitive intelligence. Follow those rules very carefully. This mistake can cause you to be banned from a group—and worse.

5. Use crossposting (posting the same message to multiple groups or lists) advisedly. It clutters up people's mail and time.

CHAPTER **6**

AN INTERNET REFERENCE SHELF

All serious searchers have a collection of tools they use for quick answers—the web equivalent of a personal reference shelf. The challenge is to make sure that you have the right sites on your shelf. This chapter provides a selective collection of sites that should be on most researchers' shelves. Different researchers have different quick-reference needs requiring different tools. For many of us, we may have found out about most sites through a friend or by simply stumbling across them but may not have systematically assembled a complete collection. Here we highlight reference tools that provide quick answers to some of the most frequently asked questions, from the mundane to the esoteric.

This chapter goes hand-in-hand with Chapter 2. For subject areas of interest to you, many of the resource guides of the types covered in Chapter 2 should be in your reference collection, much in the same way that the reference section of a library usually contains a good collection of resource guides. In addition to quick-answer sites, a number of resource guides for reference tools in particular areas, such as government information, and companies, are also included here.

Going from general to specific, we first look at some prime general tools, such as encyclopedias, and then move in the direction of tools that can provide specific bits of information. For many of the categories, as well as lists of specific sites, suggestions will be provided about using the resources effectively.

Remember that all of the links presented here, as well as links for all sites covered throughout this book, are available at www.extremesearcher.com. Also keep in mind, especially for this "quick answers" chapter, that many of these sites have a mobile version.

THINKING OF THE INTERNET AS A REFERENCE COLLECTION

Especially with the advent of widely available broadband connections, going to the internet rather than to print resources for frequently sought information has become the mode. With a little practice, web searching is clearly quicker and easier (and in some cases, such as telephone directory assistance, much cheaper). The biggest tricks are 1) being aware—simply understanding the range of quick-reference tools that are out there, and 2) getting in the habit of using them—remembering to use them and bookmarking them. Another trick is not to fall into the trap of always going to the internet first. (I have a dictionary right behind me that I often grab rather than reaching for the keyboard.)

The tools listed in this chapter provide a start in making sure the reader has a sense of the breadth and variety of quick-answer sites. The next step in understanding the range of these tools is to spend some time browsing through one of the several reference resource guides listed at the end of this chapter. Plan to spend at least 20 minutes poking around those sites. Almost anyone can find something new and interesting in them.

CRITERIA USED FOR SELECTING THE TOOLS COVERED

Selection of the tools covered here was based on several factors. The first factor is my own experience as a long-time internet user and former reference librarian, as well as my experience observing and talking with thousands (literally) of internet users from a wide variety of organizations and countries. The second factor is the measure of a site's utility for a wide range of users. Some sites were chosen because they provide good examples of the range of these tools, and others were chosen because they provide examples of particular features to look for when examining and using reference sites. In several instances, multiple sites serve basically the same function (such as the travel reservation sites). In these cases, more than one site is included in order to point out the differences and the utility of using more than one, rather than choosing a favorite and always going there.

TRADITIONAL TOOLS ONLINE

A number of online tools are electronic parallels to common print tools, including encyclopedias, dictionaries, almanacs, and the like. These are excellent sources for quick answers and for background relating to more specific research. In these (and many other) tools, a number of factors contribute to their usefulness. These factors are important to know in some circumstances, irrelevant in other circumstances, and often are the same ones to be considered when using print reference tools:

- Does the tool contain everything that the print version contains? Encyclopedia.com contains everything the print equivalent does (and more), whereas the free online version of *Encyclopaedia Britannica* contains only a portion of the paid version.

- Does it contain things the print version does not? Many online tools provide collections of links and often news headlines that the hard-copy version does not provide.
- How current is it? The version of Bartlett's *Familiar Quotations* available as part of Bartleby.com is the 1919 edition.
- Is the entire site free? Or is there a fee required to access part of the content? For many of the tools that require a subscription, the fee is not too high, and you may find the expenditure worthwhile.

The annotations for the sites discussed here, which are purposely brief and not intended to be reviews of the sites, include the major points that researchers should consider when determining whether to use the tool ("… too great brevity of discourse tends to obscurity; too much truth is paralyzing," according to Blaise Pascal in a quote located by using Bartleby.com).

ENCYCLOPEDIAS

Encyclopedia.com

www.encyclopedia.com

Encyclopedia.com not only includes 51,000 articles from the sixth edition of the *Columbia Encyclopedia* but also content from over 100 other encyclopedias (general, medical, science, etc.), dictionaries, and thesauri, as well as other sources. Articles from the *Columbia Encyclopedia* and some of the other reference tools are free, but for many of the sources, particularly journal and magazine and news articles, you will only get a description and an excerpt. To see the full article, you will need a paid subscription. Articles can be located by browsing through categories or alphabetically (look for the Research Categories link), or by searching (see Figure 6.1). For students and researchers, Encyclopedia.com automatically shows a citation at the end of each article formatted in MLA, Chicago, and APA styles.

Encyclopaedia Britannica Online

www.britannica.com

As the online version of the renowned *Encyclopaedia Britannica* (which ceased its printed version in 2012), this site provides *very* brief articles for free, but the vast majority of the content requires a subscription. Considering the quality of this encyclopedia, you may find that buying a subscription is well worth the price. With either the free or subscription version, you can browse or search, and results include the encyclopedia

Figure 6.1   Encyclopedia.com article

articles and carefully selected websites. Take advantage of the free images and other resources.

Wikipedia

www.wikipedia.org

Wikipedia, an internet-only encyclopedia, is by far the largest encyclopedia in existence. It is also an example of a *wiki* site, a collaborative project by internet users that allows easy input and online editing by any user (theoretically, at least). Because of this, intense debates have ensued about Wikipedia's quality, reliability, accuracy, and policies. But remember that no other encyclopedia has ever had as many editorial eyes examining the content, and in contrast to print encyclopedias, Wikipedia provides an extremely high level of currentness.

Wikipedia contains over 4 million articles in its English version, and it has versions in more than 100 other languages with more than 10,000 articles each (plus smaller versions for many other languages). It is both browsable and searchable.

HowStuffWorks

www.howstuffworks.com

HowStuffWorks is an example of a specialized but broad-reaching encyclopedia with articles on, indeed, how stuff works. Content is organized into categories for adventure, autos, culture, entertainment, home & garden, money, science, and technology, each with numerous subcategories. Find what you are looking for by browsing the categories or by using the search box, and explore subjects ranging from how solar cells work to how brainwashing works to how pop-up turkey timers work.

DICTIONARIES

YourDictionary

www.yourdictionary.com

YourDictionary is a resource guide that provides links to more than 2,500 dictionaries and grammars for more than 300 languages, as well as a variety of other language-related resources. The site features *Webster's New World College Dictionary*, *American Heritage Dictionary 4*, and others, but perhaps more important are the links to multilingual dictionaries and specialized subject dictionaries, including technical and scientific dictionaries. (Look for the category links, particularly the Other Dictionaries link, on the homepage.) The quality and extensiveness of the dictionaries varies, but for most languages, you will have a choice among a number of dictionaries. When you consider that relatively few libraries in the world have as many language dictionaries on their shelves as this site brings to your fingertips, you can better understand the potential of the web as a reference resource.

Dictionaries—Selected Examples

In addition to taking advantage of YourDictionary, you may find it worthwhile to bookmark one dictionary for each of the languages you are most likely to use. Following are some recommendations.

Figure 6.2   Merriam-Webster Online definition page

Merriam-Webster Online

www.merriam-webster.com

This is a full-featured English dictionary with pronunciation (with audio), parts of speech, etymology, inflected forms, and synonyms (Figure 6.2). It also provides a Spanish/English dictionary, medical dictionary, thesaurus, and a link to *Encyclopaedia Britannica*. One useful feature that isn't found in many online dictionaries is links to the next and previous words in the dictionary. Give the word games a try as well. An unabridged version is available for a subscription fee.

Collins

www.collinsdictionary.com/dictionary/english

For those who prefer British English, make use of the Collins English Dictionary, which provides audio pronunciations, origins, synonyms, usage examples, etc. On the site for this free online version of Collins, you will also find a thesaurus and translating dictionaries for French, German, and Spanish and a translator for translating text between a large variety of additional languages.

Diccionarios.com

www.diccionarios.com

This general Spanish dictionary, from the internationally known dictionary publisher, Larousse, also includes translating dictionaries between Spanish and nine languages—Catalan, Basque, English, French, Galician, German, Italian, Polish, and Portuguese—plus a Spanish medical dictionary. The extensive Spanish-language dictionary provides audio for pronunciations. Without a subscription, you may be limited in the number of lookups allowed.

LEO Deutsch-Englisches Wörterbuch

dict.leo.org

LEO contains more than 700,000 entries and provides a quick English/German and German/English lookup. You will also find audio pronunciations and a display of usage and extensive idiomatic expression examples. Take advantage of the advanced search for narrowing your results by category, word class, etc. Look under the information ("i") button for complete definitions from multiple dictionaries.

COMBINED REFERENCE TOOLS AND ALMANACS

Answers.com

www.answers.com

Go to Answers.com to get multiple resources very quickly and simply on one page: dictionary definitions, encyclopedia articles, maps, local time, a currency converter, statistics, etc. These come from hundreds of reference tools, including multiple general encyclopedias, specialized encyclopedias, dictionaries, a thesaurus, glossaries, travel guides, a company directory, a recipe collection, and more. Answers.com provides answers from those reference sources and from the Answers "community" (individuals who contribute answers). The downloadable 1-Click Answers application lets you do an ALT-Click on any word on your screen and go directly to the Answers.com page for that word.

InfoPlease

www.infoplease.com

No brief description can be a substitute for spending time exploring this site, which is much more than just an almanac. Explore each of the main sections: World & News, United States, History & Government, Biography, Sports, Arts & Entertainment,

Business, Calendar & Holidays, Health & Science, and Homework Center. The site contains the Information Please almanacs, an encyclopedia (Columbia Electronic Encyclopedia), InfoPlease Dictionary, InfoPlease Atlas, biographies, and more. Lots of little gems can be found, such as timelines, statistics, slideshows, country profiles, and so on. For non-U.S. users, the World & News section will move you away from the U.S. orientation of the homepage. One of the many interesting features is the Cite link, which shows you how to cite the item being viewed. When using the main search box, you can perform a search automatically on all of the almanacs, the encyclopedia, biographies, and the dictionary. Terms you enter are ORed, but items with all of your terms (AND) will be listed first. Quotation marks can be used to search phrases. By using the pull-down window near the search box, you can limit your search to specific almanacs, biographies, the dictionary, or the encyclopedia.

ADDRESSES AND PHONE NUMBERS

There are many places to go on the web for phone numbers and addresses worldwide. For a specific country, start by identifying the available directories by using a resource guide such as Infobel or Wayp International White and Yellow Pages, but don't expect 100 percent success (or even 70 percent) in any of the directories. Some of the directories may be incomplete or a bit dated; depending on the country and the website, some of the yellow pages are internet-only (without an equivalent print version) and may be fairly limited. However, some are quite extensive. Searchability and extensiveness of the white pages listed here also vary considerably. But if you ordinarily use telephone directory assistance, these sites will allow you to find many people a lot more easily and a lot less expensively. When searching, remember that names may be listed in a variety of ways (for example, with first initial instead of the full first name).

Infobel
www.infobel.com

Infobel provides access to phone directories for more than 200 countries and contains links to white pages, yellow pages, business directories, and email directories. Which of these are available depends upon the country.

Wayp International White and Yellow Pages
www.wayp.com

Wayp is a resource guide for white and yellow pages directories, arranged by continent and country. Click on the name of a continent to see which directories are available for each country.

Yahoo! People Search

people.yahoo.com

For finding addresses, phone numbers, email addresses, and more, Yahoo! People Search covers U.S. numbers and addresses, as well as provides a reverse phone number search (put in the number and see whose number it is) and an email address search that works reasonably well.

AnyWho

www.anywho.com

AnyWho has U.S. yellow pages and white pages, provided by AT&T. Searches are also available for reverse phone number lookups, addresses (from Intellius), maps (from Bing), and area codes.

WhitePages

www.whitepages.com and www.whitepages.ca

In addition to the usual name (person or business) and reverse phone number lookup, WhitePages can also provide you with information on neighbors. Enter an address to get names, addresses, and phone numbers of others in your neighborhood.

QUOTATIONS

The Quotations Page

www.quotationspage.com

This is a resource guide with a searchable database of more than 27,000 quotations from more than 3,100 authors. You can either search or use the subject directory (Life, Love, Success, Change, Friendship, Dreams, Happiness, Attitude, Character, Education, etc.). The Quotations Page is a great source if you are preparing a talk, an article, or a paper. Quote something from Lucius Accius, and people may think you have actually read his works.

Bartleby.com

www.bartleby.com

Bartleby.com belongs in the category of "outstanding" sites (Figure 6.3). Chief among its quotation sources is Bartlett's *Familiar Quotations* (1919 edition), but it also contains a wonderful collection of other quote sources, handbooks, anthologies, collected works of famous authors (including Shakespeare), and other reference tools. The content is primarily humanities, but Bartleby even throws in some science. The contents of all of these resources can be searched together, or you can use the pull-down windows from the main page or on the Reference, Verse, Fiction, or Nonfiction tabs to individually search more than 200 full-text works. The following list is just a selection of what is available at Bartleby.com:

Oxford Book of English Verse, 1919

Yale Book of American Verse, 1912

The World Factbook, 2008

Roget's International Thesaurus of English Words and Phrases, 1922

Bartlett, John, Familiar Quotations, 10th edition, 1919

Fowler, H. W., *The King's English*, second edition, 1908

Quiller-Couch, Sir Arthur, *On the Art of Writing*, 1916 and 1920

Quiller-Couch, Sir Arthur, *On the Art of Reading*, 1920

Sapir, Edward, *Language: An Introduction to the Study of Speech*, 1921

Strunk, William, Jr., *The Elements of Style*, 1918

The Bible, King James Version, 1999

Brewer, E. Cobham, *Dictionary of Phrase and Fable*, 1898

Bulfinch, Thomas, *The Age of Fable*, 1913

Frazer, Sir James George, *The Golden Bough: A Study in Magic and Religion*, abridged edition, 1922

Cambridge History of English & American Literature (18 vols.), 1907–1921

Eliot, Charles W., ed., *The Harvard Classics and Harvard Classics Shelf of Fiction* (70 volumes), 1909–1917

Eliot, T. S., *The Sacred Wood*, 1920

Shakespeare, William, *The Oxford Shakespeare*, 1914

Van Doren, Carl, *The American Novel*, 1921

Gray, Henry, *Anatomy of the Human Body*, 20th edition, 1918

Farmer, Fannie Merritt, *The Boston Cooking-School Cook Book*, 1918

Post, Emily, *Etiquette*, 1922

Inaugural Addresses of the Presidents of the United States, 1989

Robert, Henry M., *Robert's Rules of Order Revised*, 1915

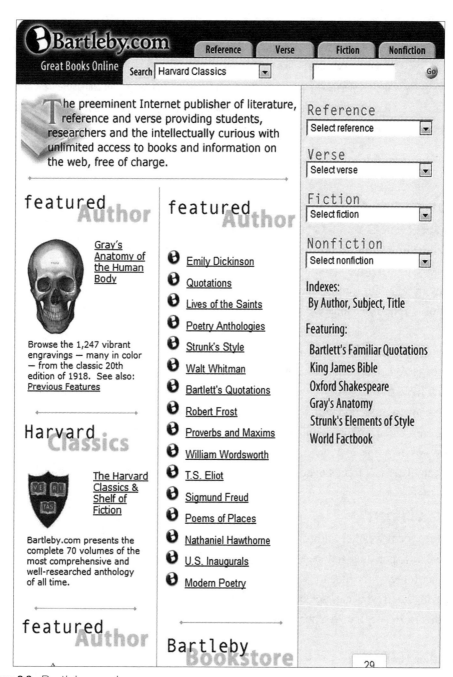

Figure 6.3 Bartleby.com homepage

TIP:

If a quotation sounds like an old famous quotation, try identifying it at Bartleby.com first. If you don't find it here, try a search engine and search for the quote as a phrase. Bartleby.com has the advantage of greater authority, while the search engines have wider reach and cover more current material.

FOREIGN EXCHANGE RATES/ CURRENCY CONVERTERS

If you travel internationally, have family or friends living in other countries, or purchase items outside your own country, you may frequently need to know the equivalent of your money in a certain foreign currency. There are many sites on the web that do these calculations. Yahoo! has one of the best.

Yahoo! Finance—Currency Converter

finance.yahoo.com/currency-converter

You have to look fairly closely on Yahoo!'s Finance page to find the link to the currency converter, so you will want to bookmark this specific page. You will discover that it provides a conversion calculator that handles more than 150 currencies. Under the converter box is a link to View 5 Day Trend, which leads to a graph showing fluctuations. You can also view trends over other time periods, ranging from one day to five years.

WEATHER

Both for local weather and for travel planning, a good weather site is essential. A good option is a personalized portal, such as My Yahoo!, that automatically supplies the weather forecast for the cities you specify. If you use a news site as your start page, look there to see if you can select weather information for specific cities. If you want a weather-only site, try Weather Underground.

Weather Underground

www.wunderground.com

Just enter the location to get weather for a particular place, including what seems like an endless collection of weather-related data and maps for locations worldwide. Sign in and change settings to have temperatures appear in either Fahrenheit or Celsius (or both).

MAPS

Perry-Castañeda Library Map Collection

www.lib.utexas.edu/maps

The Perry-Castañeda Library Map Collection is a tremendous collection of maps, plus links to gazetteers and so forth (Figure 6.4). Most of the more than 44,000 maps on this site are public domain, and no permission is required to copy or distribute them. (The CIA actually produces a large portion of the maps.) The site also has a fascinating collection of historical maps. Beyond the maps immediately on the site, there are links that lead to thousands and thousands of maps found on other sites. Take time to read the FAQ, especially for the useful tips on printing the maps. The General Libraries at the University of Texas should be thanked profusely for providing this resource.

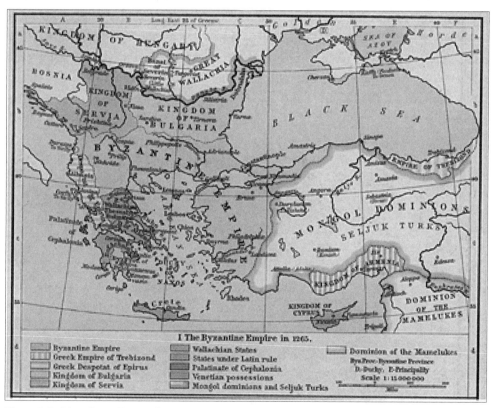

Figure 6.4 Map from Perry-Castañeda Library Map Collection

David Rumsey Historical Map Collection

www.davidrumsey.com

This collection contains more than 34,000 high-resolution maps and images online. It focuses on rare 18th- and 19th-century maps of North and South America, but it also includes historical maps of other continents. The various viewers provided on the site make it easy to navigate and examine the maps in detail.

GAZETTEERS

Global Gazetteer

www.fallingrain.com/world

This gazetteer provides a directory of more than 2.8 million cities and towns in more than 180 countries. Locate the place of interest by first browsing by country, then by region (state, provinces, etc.), and then alphabetically. Each place listed has a satellite or topographic image, latitude and longitude, elevation, population, weather data, nearby cities and towns, nearby airports, and more. Data is taken from the U.S. government's National Geospatial-Intelligence Agency and other public information sources.

World Gazetteer

www.world-gazetteer.com

Latitude, longitude, current population, other statistics, and maps are available at the World Gazetteer site for countries, administrative divisions, cities, and larger towns.

ZIP CODES

U.S. Postal Service ZIP Code Lookup

www.usps.com/zip4

If you have the street address, the U.S. Postal Service site can provide the nine-digit ZIP code. Enter a city and get a list of all ZIP codes associated with that city or enter a company name and address to get the company's ZIP code.

STOCK QUOTES

As with many other frequently asked reference questions, stock quotes can be found at numerous places on the web. For the searcher who needs stock quotes frequently, it will be worthwhile to investigate several sites and determine which one is the best for you by looking at ease of use, clarity of presentation, detail provided, personalized portfolio features, types of charts and graphs available, and presence of associated news stories. As with weather information, consider using a personalized portal, such as My Yahoo!, that can integrate selected stock information and a personalized portfolio into your start page. Remember that these free quotes are typically delayed by 20 minutes. If you use a major brokerage house or an online trading service, be sure to look at its site. You may qualify to sign in as a client and receive real-time data and order capabilities. Yahoo!'s Finance section is one example of the many sites that offer free stock information online.

Yahoo! Finance
finance.yahoo.com

The Yahoo! Finance site provides access to stock information, financial news, and so on for the U.S., Europe, and Asia. Its personal portfolio option is particularly strong, and you can create multiple portfolios to track you investments or interests. Yahoo! Finance also offers a wide range of RSS feeds on finance topics, advice articles, calculators, a glossary, and more.

STATISTICS

Although not every statistic you might want is available on the internet, finding statistics via the web makes locating a needed statistic amazingly easier than just a few years ago. The expanse of statistical information is immense, as is the amount that could be said about finding statistics on the internet. A few very basic hints and resources are provided here. Because the topic of statistics is so broad, you are often best off starting with one of the numerous resource guides. Other than resource guides, only a handful of specific sources for the most commonly sought statistics are given here.

Keep the following hints in mind:

- There are three main ways of finding statistics on the internet:
  1. Go to a site that you think may contain the statistic and search or browse. For example, try the relevant governmental department (e.g., *the Department of Agriculture for U.S. agricultural statistics*). Think about what agency or other organization would have an interest in collecting the data you are trying to find.
  2. Go to a collection of links to statistics sites (such as those listed later).
  3. Use a general web search engine such as Bing, Yahoo!, or Google. Far more statistical material is indexed by search engines now than was the case a few years ago, especially because of the indexing of PDFs, Excel spreadsheets, and other document types. A search strategy can often be very straightforward. For collections of statistics in a particular area, try a search such as *health statistics*. For

more specific statistics, try a combination of one or more subject terms plus the place and perhaps the year (for example, *avalanche fatalities norway 2012*).

- Good news: There is plenty of redundancy of identification and access; in other words, there are many routes online to the same statistic.
- When you find a statistics site you might use again, bookmark it. To make it easier to use bookmarks, create folders or tags to organize similar types of sites.
- On statistics sites, take advantage of site search boxes and site maps.
- Watch for terminology. Unless you are familiar with the topic, the terminology may not be obvious. The term *housing starts* may not be what you think to look for immediately when searching for statistics on the number of new homes being built.

BEOnline—Statistics

www.loc.gov/rr/business/beonline/subjects.php?%20SubjectID=56

This collection of links from the Library of Congress is not extensive (just under 100 sites), but it covers a wide range of carefully selected statistics sites, particularly for business, economics, and the social sciences.

OFFSTATS

www.offstats.auckland.ac.nz

Provided by the University of Auckland Library, this is an extensive collection of links from official statistics-rich sites around the world. You can browse by region, country, and subject or by combinations of those.

U.S. Statistics

USA Statistics in Brief

www.census.gov/compendia/statab/brief.html

This site contains selected tables from the venerable *Statistical Abstract of the United States*, including summary tables for a broad range of subjects, plus basic state population data (Figure 6.5). The full *Statistical Abstract of the United States* is available at www.census.gov/compendia/statab. The collection of data by the U.S. Census Bureau for this publication ceased in 2011. Beginning with the 2013 edition, publication will be taken over by ProQuest (www.proquest.com). (When the 2013 edition becomes available, the exact link to the site will appear on the webpage accompanying this book, www.extremesearcher.com).

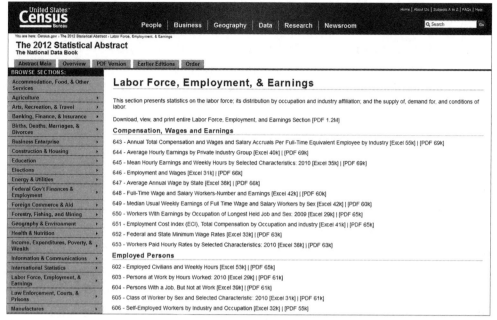

Figure 6.5   USA Statistics in Brief section listing

FedStats

www.fedstats.gov

FedStats contains links to statistics produced by more than 100 U.S. federal agencies. You can browse or use the search feature to search across agencies.

BOOKS

Most book searches on the internet fall into one of two categories: 1) finding information *about* books—in other words, what books are available on a particular topic or by a particular author—and verifying bibliographic information, or 2) trying to *locate the entire book online*. Unless the book was published close to a century ago, don't necessarily expect to get the complete book in full text online. Nevertheless, millions of books are currently available in full text, and the number has grown rapidly. If the book is in English or French and is by a famous pre-20th-century author, you have a pretty good chance of finding the full text online.

Finding Information *About* Books
—Bookstores

Keep in mind that the large online book vendors' sites are not just good for buying books, but they are also good for identifying books currently in print on any topic or out of print but still available for sale by used- or rare-book dealers.

Amazon

www.amazon.com

   Amazon lists millions of book titles (and lots of other products) for sale with good discounts. The site is searchable by keyword, author, title, subject, publisher, ISBN, publication date, condition (new, used, collectible), format (paperback, hardback, audio, etc.), age level, and languages, and it is browsable by subject. Click on Books, then on Advanced Search, for these search options. There you will also find additional options for narrowing and sorting your search results. As well as new books, Amazon also includes millions of used, rare, and out-of-print books from hundreds of booksellers. Take advantage of the book categories on the left of the book search page. As you are browsing, look for books labeled with Amazon's Search Inside the Book feature, which provides a search of the contents and images of selected parts of the book, including the covers, the table of contents, sample pages, the index, and more.

Barnes & Noble

www.barnesandnoble.com

   Competing head-to-head with Amazon, Barnes & Noble also provides access to millions of books (and other merchandise). The search box on its homepage lets you search books by author, title, or subject. Options on the left side of the pages enable you to browse by subject and narrow by price range and format. The site also has a collection of millions of out-of-print, used, and rare books from dealers around the world (use the submenus under the Books tab).

Finding Information *About* Books—
Bibliographic Databases

To find what books have been published at any time on any topic, go to the online catalog of one or more of the major national libraries. For English-language materials (although, of course, they are not limited to English materials), you might start with either The British Library or the U.S. Library of Congress.

Library of Congress Online Catalog

catalog.loc.gov

The Library of Congress Online Catalog includes 14 million records for books, serials, computer files, manuscripts, maps and other cartographic material, music, and audio/visual materials (Figure 6.6). The Basic Search option searches by title, author, subject, call number, keywords, and series and by LCCN (Library of Congress Control Number), ISSN (International Standard Serial Number), or ISBN (International Standard Book Number). Guided Search provides searchers with a greater number of options, and the OR, AND, and NOT options can be used by means of the pull-down windows and radio buttons.

The British Library

blpc.bl.uk

This site provides a search of 14 million books and more than 43 million other items, including journals, newspapers, sound recordings, and other materials. It covers items located in The British Library Public Catalogue, plus lots more. The main search covers the 10,000 pages of the library's website, 30,000 images, 14 million catalog records, and 9 million journal articles. These can be searched individually or in combination. Click on

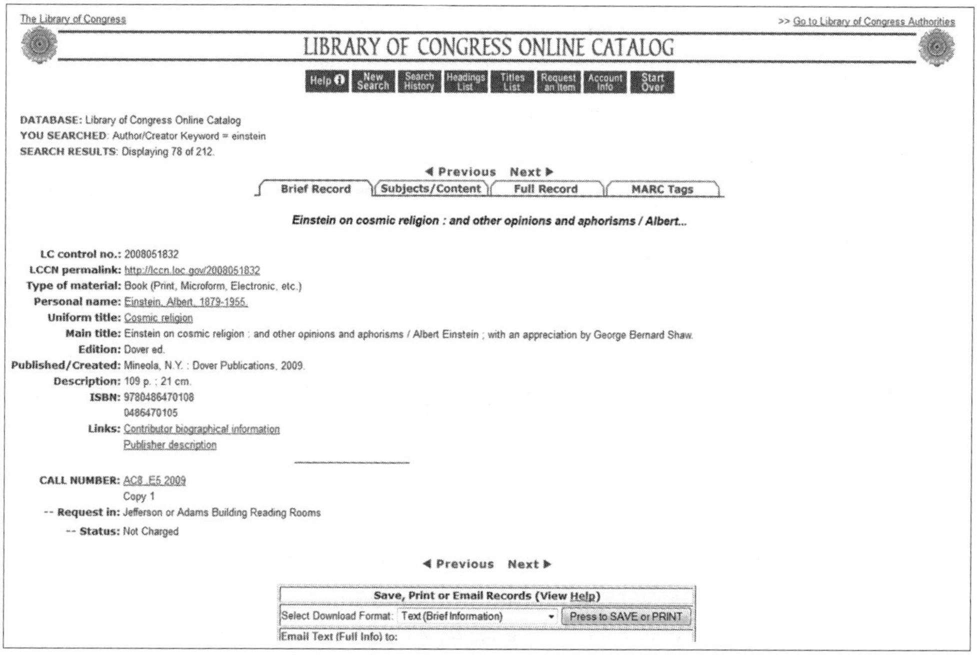

Figure 6.6 Bibliographic record page from the Library of Congress Online Catalog

the Advanced Searching link to get to more detailed search options for each of these collections. (To get to the advanced search page, under the Catalogues tab on the main page, click Explore the British Library. On the succeeding page, the Advanced Search link should be next to the search box.) The British Library site is far more than just a bibliographic search; the site also contains an impressive amount of multimedia content. Be sure to try the Turning the Pages section (Virtual Books) where you can view some books in a way you may never have before.

Google Book Search

books.google.com

Google Book Search offers a way to search a collection of both new and old books (plus some magazines), made possible due to Google's arrangements with publishers and several major libraries. More than 20 million books have been scanned and digitized. For books that are out of copyright, you can see the Full Book View with all pages of the book. For books under copyright, access will vary. You can see actual pages of the book (either the full book but more likely a "limited preview") if the publisher has given permission, although you will need to log in to your Google account in some cases. You can search using the same Boolean expressions as with regular Google (AND is implied, and you can use OR and a minus sign for NOT). You can also use the following prefixes: *inauthor:, intitle:, inpublisher:, date:* (e.g., *date:1960–2006*), and *isbn:*. On the advanced search page (look for that link at the bottom of search results pages), you can elect to search All Books, or Limited Preview and Full View Books, Full View only, or Google eBooks. Menus and boxes allow for searching by title, author, language, publisher, publication date, subject, and ISBN (or ISSN for magazines). Many books (Google eBooks) can be downloaded, 3 million of them for free.

Gallica

gallica.bnf.fr

Gallica, from the Bibliothèque nationale de France, provides access to 1.9 million documents, including over 370,000 books, plus maps, manuscripts, images, periodicals, music scores, and sound recordings. The advanced search option provides an extensive variety of search options, including field (title, author, text, subject, etc.), publication year, language, document type (all, map, manuscript, book, sound recording, image, periodical, score), in text mode, theme (Religion, Economy & Society, Literature, Languages, Sciences, etc.), and others. Most books are available in full text and are full-text searchable, and Gallica offers an audio mode option so you can listen to the book being read to you. Use the "Feuilleter en Flash" option to "leaf through" the book. The website is available in French, English, Spanish, and Portuguese.

Your Local Library's Online Catalog

For something more local, check the online catalog of your local library. If it has a web-accessible catalog, you'll find the site for the catalog easily through a search engine, or you may find it by going to the Library of Congress Gateway to Library Catalogs (lcweb.loc.gov/z3950/gateway.html).

Full-Text Books Online

If you are trying to find a specific work online, a search engine usually works quite well. However, it may be easier to use a site that compiles a large number of such works and that will enable you to browse by title or author. Bartleby.com provides more than 200 full-text books including a number of useful reference works. But for a collection of more than 30,000 books, consult Project Gutenberg; and for locating more than 35,000 titles, look at The Online Books Page. The vast majority of the works in these collections are no longer under copyright; with a few exceptions, they are all from before the 1920s. (Unfortunately, the increased availability of 20th-century texts threatens to be slowed by attempts by both the EU and the U.S. Congress to extend copyright virtually into perpetuity.) The functions of the sites discussed here are to some degree redundant with Google Book Search and Gallica, but these sites' simplicity, arrangement, and selectivity make them still quite worthwhile.

The Online Books Page
digital.library.upenn.edu/books

This resource guide contains links to more than 1 million books. The creator and editor of the site, John Mark Ockerbloom, founded it in 1993, and he has been adding to it ever since. To be included, a book must be legitimately available for free, contain the full text of a significant book in a European language, and must be a "stable, well-formatted text in a standard format." The site, which is easily searchable by author and title, is also browsable by author, title, subject, and serial title.

Project Gutenberg
www.gutenberg.org

Project Gutenberg, established in 1971, was designed to place online, in easily accessible format, as many public domain electronic texts (etexts) as possible. So far, it has provided more than 40,000 texts, from Cicero to the Bobbsey twins. Although the majority of books are in English, Project Gutenberg contains (a few) books in about 60 other languages. The breadth of texts available makes this an excellent research site but also consider it a source of etexts to read on your laptop or other mobile device. Because most of the books are stored in ASCII text, they require minimal storage space. (You will also now find a number of books in audio format and a small collection of sheet music.) All the books are in the U.S. public domain, no longer under copyright (therefore, almost all are from before 1923). For many of the books, the entire text is available in a single file, allowing a researcher to quickly find all references to a particular word in a text (by using the Edit > Find in This Page function of a browser). Using this approach (not just here but elsewhere), you can go to the text of *The Odyssey*, for example, and quickly find each and every mention of Telemachus, if you are inclined to do such things.

Bartleby.com

www.bartleby.com

For a partial list of the books covered by Bartleby.com, see the previous section on quotations.

HISTORICAL DOCUMENTS

EuroDocs: Online Sources for European History

eudocs.lib.byu.edu

A resource guide, the EuroDocs site provides links to Western European documents that are online in transcribed, facsimile, or translated form. They are arranged first by country and then chronologically. The site is now in a wiki format.

A Chronology of U.S. Historical Documents

www.law.ou.edu/hist

The Chronology of U.S. Historical Documents site contains links to more than 140 full-text documents from the pre-Colonial period to the present.

GOVERNMENT AND COUNTRY GUIDES

In lots of situations, information about specific countries is needed—basics such as population, names of leaders, flags, or maps, or more detailed information on economics, geography, and politics. Numerous resources provide this information, and those resources differ primarily in terms of amount of detail and categories of data covered.

Governments on the WWW

www.gksoft.com/govt

Governments on the WWW is an excellent resource guide. Arranged by continent and country, the links on this site connect you to official government sites (including individual sites for parliaments, offices, courts, and embassies), banks, multinational organizations, and political parties. Though the site has gone for years without updating, it is a unique, useful collection, and most links are still valid.

CIA World Factbook

https://www.cia.gov/library/publications/the-world-factbook/index.html

This regularly updated work provides easily usable yet quite detailed country guides. Data for each country is arranged in the following sections: Introduction, Geography, People, Government, Economy, Communications, Transportation, Military, and Transnational Issues. This is an extremely rich site, and even if you do not think you will use it frequently, you will find the time spent exploring it worthwhile. As an indication of how widespread the respect for this site is, the Basic Facts on Iraq section of the official site of the former Permanent Mission of Iraq to the U.N. (under Saddam Hussein) was mostly taken word-for-word from the CIA World Factbook.

U.K. Foreign & Commonwealth Office—Country Profiles

www.fco.gov.uk/en/travel-and-living-abroad/travel-advice-by-country/country-profile

The profiles here, prepared by FCO desk officers, provide general facts and background about the country, its history, politics, economy, and international relations. The latter section typically focuses on the relations between the country being profiled and the U.K.

U.S. Government

USA.gov

www.usa.gov

USA.gov, which is the official internet gateway (portal) to U.S. government resources, is a good starting place for locating information from or about government services and agencies. The site has four main divisions: Get Services, Blog, Explore Topics, Find Government Agencies, and Contact Government. Take advantage of the A–Z List of Agencies link found on the main page, which provides an alphabetic listing of federal government agencies and links to state, local, and tribal government information.

U.S. Government Printing Office—FDsys

www.gpo.gov/fdsys

Use this site to search the Federal Register, Code of Federal Regulations, Commerce Business Daily, Congressional Record, Government Manual, and other U.S. government databases, either singly or together.

THOMAS: Legislative Information on the Internet

thomas.loc.gov

THOMAS has a variety of detailed and easily searchable databases with information related to federal legislation, including bills and resolutions, activities in Congress, the Congressional Record, schedules, calendars, committees, presidential nominations, treaties, and more. It also contains links to the Senate and House websites and to other government information. This is an excellent place to start a search on legislation currently in process or on a specific topic, or for tracking a particular current bill.

Open CRS

www.opencrs.com

On an ongoing basis, the Congressional Research Service (CRS) of the Library of Congress produces a collection of highly respected, nonpartisan reports on a wide variety of subjects relating to current political events and situations. Unfortunately, Congress (which, perhaps obviously from the name, controls the Library of Congress) pointedly prevents CRS from distributing the reports directly (though some members have fought hard to change this situation). To "democratize" the availability of non-confidential CRS reports, the Center for Democracy & Technology created this website, which collects reports that have been released. The reports included here represent only a portion of the reports produced by CRS, but this site is a good starting place to find out, as far as currently possible, what reports have been made publicly available and to access those reports online.

U.S. State Information

Library of Congress—State and Local Governments

www.loc.gov/rr/news/stategov/stategov.html

The Library of Congress State and Local Government directory is a resource guide with a convenient collection of links to state, county, and local government information.

U.K. Government Information
Directgov—Website of the U.K. Government

www.direct.gov.uk

Directgov is a searchable and browsable collection of information, news, and links to U.K. public sector information, including both central and local government information. The content is arranged primarily by topic (Motoring, Education and Learning, Environment and Greener Living, etc.) and by audience (Parents, Young People, Disabled People, etc.). For a more detailed list of content, use the A–Z of Central Government link found on the main page.

COMPANY INFORMATION

Entire books have been written on finding company information on the internet. Anyone who searches for company information frequently will want to spend time with one of those books and may already be familiar with the quick-reference company sites included here. For those who have only occasional need for company information or who are just getting into the area, the following sites will provide a start.

First, we should cover a few basic pointers about tools for finding company information. It helps to start by thinking about what kinds of company information you might reasonably expect to find on the internet. You might think in terms of three categories:

1. Information that a company *wants* you to know, such as its stature, its products or services, and any good news about the company
2. Information that a company *must* let you know, such as information required by government laws and regulations (e.g., Securities and Exchange Commission [SEC] filings in the U.S. and Companies House filings in the U.K.)
3. *What others are saying* about the company

To state something that is rather obvious, to find out what a company *wants* you to know, start with the company's homepage. Depending on the company, you will probably find detailed background, products and services, company structure, press releases, and so on. To find a company's homepage, you can just enter the name in any of the major search engines. The company homepage will usually be among the first few items retrieved.

To find out what a company *must* let you know, first keep in mind that these regulations apply only to publicly held companies. Other companies typically do not have to divulge very much information publicly. For U.S. publicly held companies, SEC filings are available through several sites, including the SEC's own site. For public companies in other countries, the amount of mandated information is usually much less than that required of U.S. companies, but you can start by looking at the CorporateInformation website.

For the third category of company information—*what others are saying* about a company—some items to keep on your internet reference shelf are discussion groups (especially Google Groups and other groups sources discussed in Chapter 5) and news stories (through MSNBC, CNN, BBC, etc.). For some key news sites, see Chapter 8.

The resources just mentioned, however, are basically most useful for finding information about a specific company you already have in mind. Many company questions focus on "What companies are out there that match a particular set of criteria?" For example, who are some of the largest seafood packers in Maryland? What is the name of a plumber who serves my neighborhood? These questions are often answered by using directories or online yellow pages of the types listed earlier in this chapter.

Company Directories

Company directories on the web differ in terms of:

- Number and type (public, private, U.S., non-U.S.) of companies included
- Free, paid subscription, or pay-per-view
- Searchability (by name, industry location, ticker symbol, size, etc.)
- Amount of information provided about each company (usually the more companies included, the less information about each)

CorporateInformation

www.corporateinformation.com

This site, from Wright Investors' Service, provides tens of thousands of company research reports, profiles, and analyses for companies in 65 countries. Full company reports from Wright Investors' Service require a fee, but free snapshot reports are provided for thousands of companies worldwide. The advanced search permits searching by combinations of global region, industry category, company name or ticker symbol, and keyword. For many users, the most useful and unique part may be the links to company directories and other resources arranged by country. Click on Research Links, found under Tools on the main page, and choose the country.

Hoover's

www.hoovers.com

Hoover's provides information on public and non-public companies worldwide (Figure 6.7), on company executives, and on more than 600 industries. For much of the

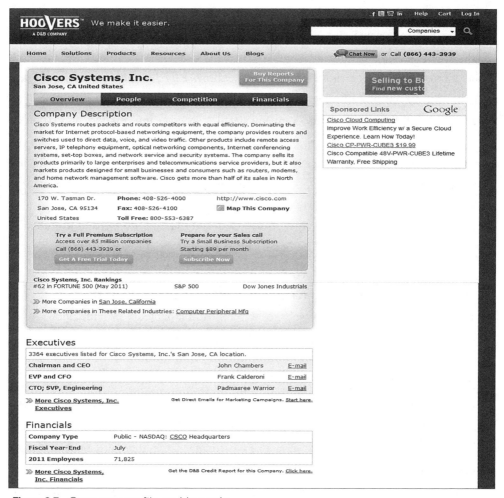

Figure 6.7 Company profile on Hoover's

information, a subscription is required, but especially for public companies, you will find very informative profiles with an overview of the company, perhaps basic financials, executives, etc. You will also find free overviews of hundreds of industries. The free portion is searchable by company name, ticker symbol, executive name, and industry. Spend some time exploring this site to get a feel for how much information is there.

ThomasNet

www.thomasnet.com

If you need to buy a manufactured product and want to find out who makes it or who can get it for you, this website is the place to go. This online version of the well-known resource formerly published as *Thomas Register* allows you to browse categories or to search by company name, product/service, or brand name. It covers more than 610,000 North American suppliers, manufacturers, distributors, and service companies, arranged under more than 67,000 categories. You can either browse by the categories or search, and searches can be narrowed by location, company type, ownership, and certification. The information you find will contain company profiles, contact information, and so on as well as links to websites. Also take a look at the White Papers section and click on the Guides link at the bottom of the page for fascinating information on manufacturing processes, product types, and related information. A companion site, Solusource (www.solusource.com), is a directory of suppliers around the world.

Also see the two product directories, Kompass (www.kompass.com) and Kellysearch (www.kellysearch.com) that are discussed in Chapter 9.

Company Phone Numbers and Addresses

Don't forget that the company's website will almost undoubtedly provide phone numbers. You can also check the phone directories listed earlier in this chapter.

ASSOCIATIONS

If you know the name of an association and need further information, usually the best place to start is with the association's homepage. From the other direction, if you need to find the names of associations that relate to a particular topic, there are a couple places to consider as starting points:

1. Use a search engine and search for the subject and terms such as association, society, organization:

   "solar energy" (association OR society OR organization)
   or
   solar (energy OR power) (association OR society OR organization)
   or just
   solar (association OR society OR organization)

2. Use the directory provided by the American Society of Association Executives.

American Society of Association Executives Gateway to Associations

www.asaecenter.org/Community/Directories/AssociationSearch.cfm

This ASAE Gateway provides links to thousands of association sites, which you can search by name, location, geographic scope, and organization type.

PROFESSIONAL DIRECTORIES

To find directories for a specific profession, try a search on the name of the profession and the word *directory*. It works sometimes; sometimes it doesn't. Two of the most widely useful directories, for physicians and lawyers, are listed here.

AMA DoctorFinder

extapps.ama-assn.org/doctorfinder

This AMA (American Medical Association) site offers "information on virtually every licensed physician in the United States" and includes more than 814,000 doctors. You can search by name, location, and specialty. Look on the main AMA site (www.ama-assn.org) under the Patients tab for additional resources such as the Atlas of the Human Body.

Lawyers.com

www.lawyers.com

Lawyers.com allows a search of 1 million attorneys and law firms in 170 countries by practice area, name, and location. Searches on Lawyers.com use the Martindale-Hubbell database, which will be familiar to any legal researcher.

OTHER INFORMATION ABOUT PEOPLE

Finding someone's phone number and address was discussed earlier. There is a lot more though that can easily (and legitimately and ethically) be found out. Sources include sites such as Facebook and LinkedIn (discussed in Chapter 10). A quick way to gather information on people from a variety of sources is the Pipl (pronounced like "people") site.

With regard to people searching in general, don't forget to use your imagination. Try the following if you are not finding the person you want or the amount of information you want on a person:

- Search for known or probable nicknames (*"Charles Stuart" OR "Chuck Stuart"*).
- Allow for the possibility of an unknown middle name or initial (in Google, *"Charles Stuart" OR "Chuck Stuart" OR "Charles * Stuart"*).
- Allow for inverted forms (*"Stuart Charles"*)

- Since you will often get hundreds of the "wrong" person with the same name, use professions, locations, and other qualifiers to help narrow your search: (*"Charles Stuart" OR "Chuck Stuart" opthamologist boise idaho*).

Pipl

www.pipl.com

Pipl is a specialized search engine that provides a simple search interface that can lead you to basic contact and other information about individuals from a wide range of resources. Pipl is programmed to go into a large number of Deep Web databases and extract information such as birthdays, former addresses, relatives, publications, etc. In doing so, it covers sites such as Amazon (for customer profiles), Facebook, phone directories, company databases, and fee-based services such as PeopleFinders and Intellius. It may be best to think of Pipl as providing "clues" rather than "facts." Pipl is making its best guess. Follow up on the sources it points to, or other sources, to confirm data that you intend to use.

Social Networking Sites as Research Tools

Obviously for researching living people and sometimes for researching other topics, consider social networking sites as possible resources. Though there are many social networking sites, the two dominant sites for these purposes are Facebook and LinkedIn, with Google+ edging its way in fairly rapidly. Twitter can also sometimes provide useful information about a person's interests and biases. To understand what search *topics* (beyond people searching) these tools are good for, think about the other kinds of content often found on these sites, particularly information about companies and other organizations for which a person has worked.

If you want to dig deeply, also check video-sharing, photo-sharing, and bookmark-sharing sites such as YouTube, Flickr, Picasa, and Delicious to see if your subject has an account there. If so, you may find out more about his or her interests and travels. For each of these sites, the challenge may be identifying whether the person has an account and what his or her account name (aka, "screen name") is. If and how you can do so may differ considerably from site to site. In Flickr, for example, in the main search box you can enter a name to be searched, and as you type, search options will appear beneath the search box, one of the options being Flickr members.

Be aware that as people have become more and sensitive to privacy issues, the chances of getting detailed information on people without your being friended by or connected to the person has decreased. Many people are significantly limiting the amount of information that is made public on the networking sites, and those same people are the ones who are less likely to friend or connect to someone they do not know.

The following descriptions focus on the search aspects of the site. Information on other aspects of these sites can be found in Chapter 10.

Facebook

www.facebook.com

By 2012, Facebook had about 1 billion users, with most of the individuals' pages providing at least a little information about the person, some providing extensive information. Many companies, organizations, groups, and other entities also have Facebook pages. A search in the Facebook search box will cover the names of pages (people, organizations, etc.), their basic information lines ("worked at," etc.), and other parts of Facebook pages. On search results pages, look on the left and you will see that you can filter your results by people, places, groups, apps, events, music, web results, posts by friend, public posts, and posts in groups.

LinkedIn

www.linkedin.com

LinkedIn provides networking with an emphasis on business connections. Content is primarily business-oriented (with members' profiles often resembling resumes), and communications and network connections usually have a business purpose. LinkedIn, because of the nature of its detailed resume-like content, can be one of the most effective sites for searching for information about people. LinkedIn particularly has become a site of interest to researchers who are doing company intelligence, since people often post information that provides clues as to what their companies are up to. Changes in positions held and other work-related events can provide very useful information about changes in a company's status and direction. It is understood that, because of this, some companies have cautioned their employees about giving out too much of such information.

LinkedIn has the most extensive advanced search page of any of the popular social networking sites, with over 20 searchable fields.

Google+

plus.google.com

Google+ (Google Plus) is Google's competitor to Facebook. As of this writing, it is significantly smaller than Facebook in terms of the number of individuals' pages and content in general, but with Google's ubiquity, it may one day become serious competition for Facebook. Results from users ("social search" results) are included in a regular Google search, but for the most effective search for social content, you may want to be signed in to Google+ and do your search from there. On Google+ search results pages, a drop-down menu will give you the following narrowing options: Everything, People and Pages, Google+ Posts, Sparks (news items), Hangouts (video chats), From Your Circles, From You, and From This Location.

Twitter
www.twitter.com

Searching on Twitter is quite simple. In the search box, enter names or words and resulting search results will include matching Twitter users and posts that contain your search terms.

LITERATURE DATABASES

As great as internet resources are, they definitely still do not cover all of what we think of as the world's literature. The majority of journal articles (especially those more than a few years old) are not available on the web in full text. But just as even a very large library owns only a small portion of extant literature, both a library and the internet at least provide pointers to the broader corpus.

You will find a number of bibliographic databases on the web that let you identify at least portions of what has been published on a particular topic, by a particular author, and so on. Many of these databases are available only through subscription, but many are available free. For books, you can go to major national libraries' catalogs, Google Books, and similar sites, and for journal literature, go to databases such as Medline, ERIC, and others. Depending upon the subject area and other factors, for much "scholarly research," sites such as IngentaConnect and Google Scholar may not be an adequate substitute for searching the proprietary, subscription literature databases found in libraries. Those "library" databases may provide more comprehensive coverage, provide greater clarity about the extent of coverage, and are more definitively scholarly and more searchable because of better commands, structure, and indexing.

For researchers, it is extremely important to take care in choosing your tools when doing a literature search. If all you need to do is get one or two articles to read for background on a topic, either the free bibliographic tools available on the internet or the more high-powered library databases (such as PsycInfo, INSPEC, BIOSIS, SciFinder Scholar, etc.) will probably suffice. However, if you are doing in-depth research, consider carefully the tool's coverage in terms of time frame, language, number and type of publications covered, and quality of indexing.

To identify bibliographic databases on the web for a particular subject, use the resource guides (discussed in Chapter 2) for that area. A good resource guide for any subject will clearly identify important literature databases in that area. For single-site (but not necessarily exhaustive) access to a broad range of scholarly journal literature, try ingentaconnect and Google Scholar. Other databases, such as Scirus (www.scirus.com), CiteSeer (citeseer.ist.psu.edu), and PubMed (www.ncbi.nlm.nih.gov/pubmed), provide similar access but to a smaller range of topics, such as science or business.

ingentaconnect

www.ingentaconnect.com

When you search the ingentaconnect site, you have access to more than 11,000 publications, mainly journals (from many fields) and more than 5 million articles. These publications include trade, scientific, and technical journals with coverage going back, in some cases, many decades. Take advantage of ingentaconnect's advanced search page. Ingentaconnect is searchable by keyword, author, publication, volume, and issue, and you can sort results by relevance, newest first or oldest first. Ingentaconnect is in the business of selling articles, and though a few articles are free, in most cases you will need to purchase the item in order to get the full document.

HighBeam Research

www.highbeam.com

Like ingentaconnect, HighBeam Research is in the business of selling content and provides a database that will locate articles for you. In the case of HighBeam, it covers more than 80 million articles from 6,500 publications, from the areas of business, technology, science, news, hobbies, and personal interest. In addition, its Reference search includes articles from encyclopedias, dictionaries, thesauri, almanacs, and other reference tools. Filters on search results pages enable you to narrow results by date, publication name, or publication type (magazines/journals, news releases, newspapers, reference works).

Google Scholar

scholar.google.com

Google Scholar is a collection of "peer-reviewed papers, theses, books, preprints, abstracts and technical reports," made available by agreements with publishers, associations, universities, and others. For searching, you can take advantage of Google's OR capability, plus the *intitle:, allintitle:, site:,* and *author:* prefixes. An advanced search page lets you use simple Boolean; search by author, publication (i.e., journal), or date (or date range). To get to advanced search, click the arrow on the right side of the search box. Clicking on a title on the results pages will take you to an abstract of the article, and in some cases, the full article. In addition to basic bibliographic information, you may find a link to the library (or other database) from which Google indexed the item and a link (for some books) that lets you find the book in a local library. Other links may lead you to articles that cite the article you retrieved and to sites where you may purchase the articles. Though what Google Scholar provides is impressive, keep in mind that its coverage and completeness are still less than that which may be available in more traditional bibliographic databases.

COLLEGES AND UNIVERSITIES

Peterson's

www.petersons.com

The Peterson's site offers a broad range of information for those looking for a school. From the search results pages, click on the Advanced Search link, from which you can select subject areas, majors, locations, and degree level. Elsewhere on the site, you can further filter your results by type of college (traditional colleges and universities, community colleges, online degrees), location, setting, student population, tuition, selectivity, and public or private. If you have a specific school in mind, you can also search by the name of the school. From results lists, use the Save School link to create a list of schools in which you are interested. Browse through the tabs on the tops of pages for an extensive range of other college-related background information, testing, admissions, and other topics.

College Board

www.collegeboard.com

The College Board site provides a variety of resources relating to the Scholastic Aptitude Tests (SATs) and other tests, plus information on finding a college and financing an education. A tremendous amount of practical advice is included, on such things as writing essays for college applications, transitioning to college, etc. Use the College Search tab to search College Board's database of 3,900-plus colleges by type of school, location, majors and learning environment, sports and activities offered, and other criteria. The My Colleges feature provides a useful side-by-side comparison of colleges you have selected from search results.

FACT-CHECKING SITES

Whether it comes from politicians on TV, fringe family by email, or overheard conversations from total strangers, we are constantly confronted with dubious information—sometimes half-truths or exaggeration, sometimes outright purposeful deception, sometimes the complete truth. Most of us don't have time to do the kind of research necessary to check all the facts needed to discover the "truth" or reliably assess the *degree* of truth.

Fortunately, there are several very reputable sites that do that for us and provide a more objective and balanced perspective. Three of the better known of those sites are described here. For all of these, the most effective way to search is usually to throw in four or five fairly specific terms from the story or, better yet, especially in the case of emails, use quotation marks and search for a several-word phrase copied directly from your source. (What appears to be a more and more common type of question that these sites can help us with is of the type, "Did Senator Rightwing *really* say that Senator Lefty is a Neanderthal nitwit?") If you think that any of these sites themselves are biased, check multiple fact-finding sites.

Snopes.com

www.snopes.com

Probably the best known (perhaps the first) site of this type, Snopes.com's greatest emphasis is on urban legends, including, according to Snopes.com, not just oft-told folklore-type materials but also "common fallacies, misinformation, old wives' tales, strange news stories, rumors, celebrity gossip, and similar items." In addition to the search function, Snopes.com provides 43 categories that you can browse on its homepage. Stories are rated as true, false, multiple truth values, undetermined, or unclassifiable veracity.

FactCheck.org

www.factcheck.org

In contrast to Snopes.com, the focus of FactCheck.org, from the Annenberg Public Policy Center, is politics. The main page features a depressingly large number of stories on currently circulating questionable statements, claims, quotations, and so on. A search box is provided, and the Archives link will take you to a page where you can browse by month, by section (Articles, Special Reports, Fact-of-the-Day, etc.), and by tag (for various political figures, topics, and issues). For the "Lighter side of spin," take a look at FlackCheck.org, a sister site to FactCheck.org.

PolitiFact

www.politifact.com

   This Pulitzer-Prize-winning site from the *Tampa Bay Times*, rather obviously, focuses on politics. PolitiFact's Truth-O-Meter rating scale has nine levels, ranging from "True" to "Pants-on-Fire." As well as the search box, take advantage of menu tabs, which will lead you to assessment of stories by state, by rating, by promises kept or broken, and by pundit. When on the Pundits page, click on the pundit's name to see a compilation of ratings for the pundit's statements.

TRAVEL

Travel is one area where you definitely need to know and use more than one website. Especially for travel reservation sites, don't count on any one always providing either the lowest cost flight or the itinerary that best suits your needs. On the other hand, loyalty to one site, and consequent heavier usage of that site, may get you special deals and discounts.

   When using the web for travel planning, don't think only of reservation sites. Take advantage of travel guides, discussion groups, and thousands of other sites that provide information on your destination, how to get there, and what to do and how to get around while you are there. (For a broader sampling of what is available, look at the companion site for the author's book on using the internet for travel, *The Traveler's Web*, at www.extremesearcher.com/travel.)

Destination Guides

Fodor's

www.fodors.com

   Fodor's, the print publisher, has a reputation for publishing what many travelers consider to be the best travel guides out there. Its website is an extremely rich resource with a useful collection of travel information, from what to see in a particular city to tipping practices worldwide.

Lonely Planet

www.lonelyplanet.com

   The Lonely Planet site is a down-to-earth online guide to world travel from another well-known publisher of travel guides. For an excellent travelers' discussion group, try the Thorn Tree Forum on this site.

Reservation Sites

Travelocity

www.travelocity.com

As with most other travel reservation sites, Travelocity provides airfare as well as rail fares and car rentals. Under Tools on flight pages, read the tips for identifying the lowest fares.

Expedia

www.expedia.com

Expedia sometimes has lower prices than Travelocity (and vice versa). Some users will prefer the way in which Expedia lets them search for fares and itineraries, and the way in which the results are presented.

Orbitz

www.orbitz.com

The third of the "big three" reservation sites, Orbitz provides differences in navigation and display of results. Compare the three to see which best suits your needs, but if you want the lowest price and best itinerary, check all three. On this and other travel reservation sites, check out the deals and the savings available by booking combinations of travel, hotels, and car rentals.

 TIP:

To find rail timetables, use a search engine and search for something such as *timetable Prague vienna rail.*

FILM

Internet Movie Database (IMDb)

www.imdb.com

Whether you are looking for current show times or a list of all of the movies in which Kevin McCarthy appeared, IMDb is the place to go. It is not just a database of movies, but a movie portal with many resources, including commentary, movie and TV news, new releases, etc.

REFERENCE RESOURCE GUIDES

The sites discussed in this chapter only scratch the surface in terms of what is available. For other reference shelf sites, consult the general reference directories (resource guides) discussed in Chapter 2.

CHAPTER 7

SIGHTS AND SOUNDS: FINDING IMAGES, AUDIO, AND VIDEO

Even for someone with a lot of web experience, it is sometimes hard to believe how much is available in the way of multimedia (images, audio, and video) resources on the web. Images are not only available, but they are searchable—not as searchable as we would like, but they are still searchable. Whether you need a photo of the person you are about to meet, or of the streets of a specific town in a remote country, or of an obscure microorganism, you have a pretty good chance of finding it on the web.

Audio and video files can be tremendously useful, whether you are using them for military intelligence purposes, for a discussion of Winston Churchill's "Finest Hour" speech in a history classroom, or for learning how to knit. This chapter summarizes what is available, provides some basic background and terminology for understanding and using these resources, points to the tools for finding what you need, and offers some techniques to do so most effectively.

THE COPYRIGHT ISSUE

Prior to using—or discussing—any of the resources here, the overarching issue of copyright must be considered. Although most people using the internet for research, teaching, and other professional applications already know about the issue and its implications, the importance of the copyright issue should be emphasized. The good news is that hundreds of millions of images, audio, and video files can be found easily on the web. The bad news is that you may not be able to use those images as you would like. Whenever you are using images (and any other original works) in any way, remember first of all that the vast majority of images and other artifacts on the web belong to someone: They are copyrighted. Some people (even some who should know better) still have the attitude that "I found it on the internet, so I can use it any way I want." As most readers of this book know, that's simply not so. This does not mean that you cannot use these types of files in a variety of ways, but it does mean that you must use them within fair use guidelines and other provisions of copyright law.

If you have found an image of interest and want to use it in a report, on your own webpage, or for other purposes, in most cases you cannot legitimately do so without getting the permission of the copyright owner. First, look on the site where you found the image. You may be lucky and find a copyright statement that specifies when, where, and how you may use images from that site. (For a good example of such a statement, look at the NASA statement at www.nasa.gov/audience/formedia/features/MP_Photo_Guidelines. html, but don't expect most sites to have such a clear statement with such minimal conditions.) For people in companies, universities, school systems, and other organizations, your organization may have published copyright guidelines for your use. For the layperson who is trying to understand and interpret the actual laws, it may be somewhat of a challenge. For a very basic understanding of copyright issues, look at the articles on copyright in the Patents, Copyright & Trademark section of Nolo (www.nolo.com).

IMAGES
Some Technical Background

To view images on your screen, no technical knowledge is required. If, however, you plan to save images and use them (remember copyright!) on a webpage, or print and distribute the image you save in any way, a few tips are in order.

Digital Image File Types

Web browsers can typically display only three image file formats: Joint Photographic Experts Group format (JPEG or JPG file extensions), Graphics Interchange Format (GIF file extension), or Portable Network Graphics format (PNG). The latter format is at present less common than the other two, but its popularity is increasing. Some search engines will allow you to narrow your image search by these file types, but it is unlikely that you will to need to do so.

Image Size

You will usually see image size referred to in pixels ("picture elements"), which are the space-related elements that make up a digital image. You can think of them as the "atomic" level of an image—the smallest unit of a digital image. An internet user can think of a typical monitor (with typical settings) as displaying about 72 or 96 pixels per inch (ppi). So depending on a number of factors, you can expect an image that has dimensions of 140 pixels by 140 pixels to take up about a 2" square on a typical screen.

Capturing Images

An image file can be saved by doing the following:

1. Hold your cursor over the image you wish to capture.
2. Click the right mouse button.
3. From the menu that pops up, choose Save Image As (in Firefox, Chrome, and Safari) or Save Picture As (in Internet Explorer).
4. Select the folder where you want to save the image and rename the file if you want. Do not assign or change a file extension. It is important that the original file extension (.gif, .jpg, .jpeg, or .png) be retained.

Editing Images

A discussion of image editing is beyond the scope of this book. However, since the object of an image search is often to get a print copy of the image, searchers may need to do some minor editing of what they find. Operations such as cropping (trimming) and resizing are fairly common and easy to do. Programs that can perform simple (or more complex) image editing are rampant. You can use free downloadable programs such as Google's Picasa or commercially available software that is very powerful, relatively easy to use, and not particularly expensive, such as Photoshop Elements. These are some programs, such as Pixlr (www.pixlr.com), where you can edit online. The latter programs are particularly useful when you are not working from your own computer. When you have decided on a program to use, do a quick search engine search for the program AND the term *tutorial*. There are ample good photo-editing tutorials out there.

Types of Image Collections on the Web

The web offers many image collections. Some are collections of the images found on billions of webpages, such as the image collections found on Google and Bing. Some are specialized by topic and represent the collections of specific organizations, such as the Australian National Botanic Gardens' National Plant Photographic Index (www.anbg.gov.au/photo/image-collection.html). Others are specialized by topic and represent the holdings of multiple institutions or sites, such as The Digital Scriptorium, which includes medieval and renaissance manuscripts (www.scriptorium.columbia.edu). Some collections are arranged by format or by application, such as the numerous clip art collections. Increasingly popular are collections of photos shared by individuals, such as those on Flickr and Picasa Web Albums. Another category, especially important for those who need good images that they can safely (legally) reuse in publications or elsewhere, is a commercial collection, such as Corbis.

Searchability of Images

Though millions of images can now be searched on the web, the search capabilities are still fairly limited, and search results can be rather "approximate." This is primarily because the amount and quality of indexing that can currently be done by search programs is quite limited. Technologies exist that can recognize objects within photos and can or will be able to see a picture of a tree, and without any text attached to the image, be able to tell that the tree is a tree, maybe even to identify it as a spruce and even as a blue spruce. Implementation of this image recognition on a large scale for web applications may take a while. Already, the ability to recognize images that contain faces has been implemented in some search engines and Google's Search by Image feature allows you to enter an image, instead of words, and find similar images.

In general, though, web search engines often do not have much to work with when identifying and indexing what a picture is showing. In many cases, the most that can be used for indexing is the name of the image file (e.g., sprucetree.jpg), an "alt" (alternative text) attribute that may be included in the HTML code, a caption if the image is in a table, and text that is near the photo. Indexing based on text near a photo becomes somewhat of a gamble and can account for many of the false hits that may occur in image search results. In some cases, image collections such as Flickr provide an opportunity for users to add tags to images that become part of the indexing, although this approach also carries with it some problems. That said, with a little imagination and a little patience and tolerance, the searcher can usually find a useful image quickly and easily using the collections and search techniques now available.

TIP:

When searching for images, start by limiting your query to one or two words. Most images only have very few words of indexing associated with them. If you search for *Boeing 747*, you will get substantially fewer good pictures of the plane than if you search for just *747*.

Directories of Image Resources on the Internet

As with almost any other type of internet content, there are specialized directories (resource guides) that offer easy identification of image collections. The two that follow are useful examples that can direct you to sites that contain collections of images. Like many specialized directories, the first directory is displayed on one long page. So, if you want to find a specific topic quickly, you may want to take advantage of your browser's Find In This Page option (under the Edit menu).

Digital Librarian: A Librarian's Choice of the Best of the Web—Images
www.digital-librarian.com/images.html

Here you will find more than 500 well-annotated links to image collections. For maps, check the companion Maps and Geography collection (www.digital-librarian.com/maps.html).

Image Collections Guides
www.lib.umn.edu/media/imageguide

Presented by the Libraries at the University of Minnesota, you will find very well-organized and annotated links to over 700 collections of images. A large portion of the entries were contributed by librarians worldwide who are members of the LibGuides Community.

Search Engine Image Collections

With images from the billions of webpages covered in their web databases, the major general web search engines provide not only access to possibly billions of images but also easy searchability (given the limitations on image searching previously discussed). As with a regular web search, use more than one engine. For any particular search, which images they retrieve will vary considerably as well as how many. Keep in mind that the number of images retrieved does not necessarily reflect the relevance of the images to your specific search. (Google, for example, usually finds by far the largest number of images, but it may be identifying images where your search terms were simply some-where on the same page as the image, not directly connected to the image.) Searchability and display of image results also differ among these engines.

Google's Image Search

Google says that it has the web's "most comprehensive image search," and there is a very good chance that the claim is true. To get to it, either click on the Images link on Google's main page or go directly to images.google.com. Once you're in Google Image Search (images.google.com), just enter your terms in the search box. Further search capabilities are found in the narrowing options shown on results pages and on the advanced image search page. The link for the latter is found under the Options ("gear") icon. Two features to be sure to explore are the face narrowing option and the Search by Image feature. The face option is found on search results pages. For the Search by Image feature, click the camera icon found on the Google Image search box.

Image Searchability—Main Image Search Page

On Google's main image search page, all terms are automatically ANDed. If you enter *temple esna*, you will get only those images indexed under both terms. Quotation marks can be used for phrases, and a minus sign in front of a term can be used to eliminate items indexed under that term. You can also use the OR as with a regular Google web search. To retrieve all images indexed under the term *temple* and under either *esna* or *khnum*, search for:

> *temple esna OR khnum*

You can also use the prefixes used in Google's web search. For images, the *site:* prefix will limit image retrieval to a particular website. This can be used in combination with other operations such as the OR. For example, images of either a corn or maize kernel from the U.S. Department of Agriculture site are available by searching for:

> *corn OR maize kernel site:usda.gov*

Advanced Image Search Page

Using Google's advanced image search page (Figure 7.1), you can:

- Use the Find Results boxes for simple Boolean (all these words, any of these words, or none of these words).
- Specify a phrase search by using "this exact word or phrase" (using quotation marks around the phrase in any of the boxes works just as well).
- Limit by image characteristics, including size, aspect ratio, and predominant colors.
- Narrow by content type for any content, faces, photo content, clip art, or line drawing. For faces, Google is using a technology that enables it to quite effectively identify images that are probably faces. Definitely try this when searching for people.
- Limit by images published in a particular country.
- Retrieve images only from a specific domain (such as .gov or fda.gov).

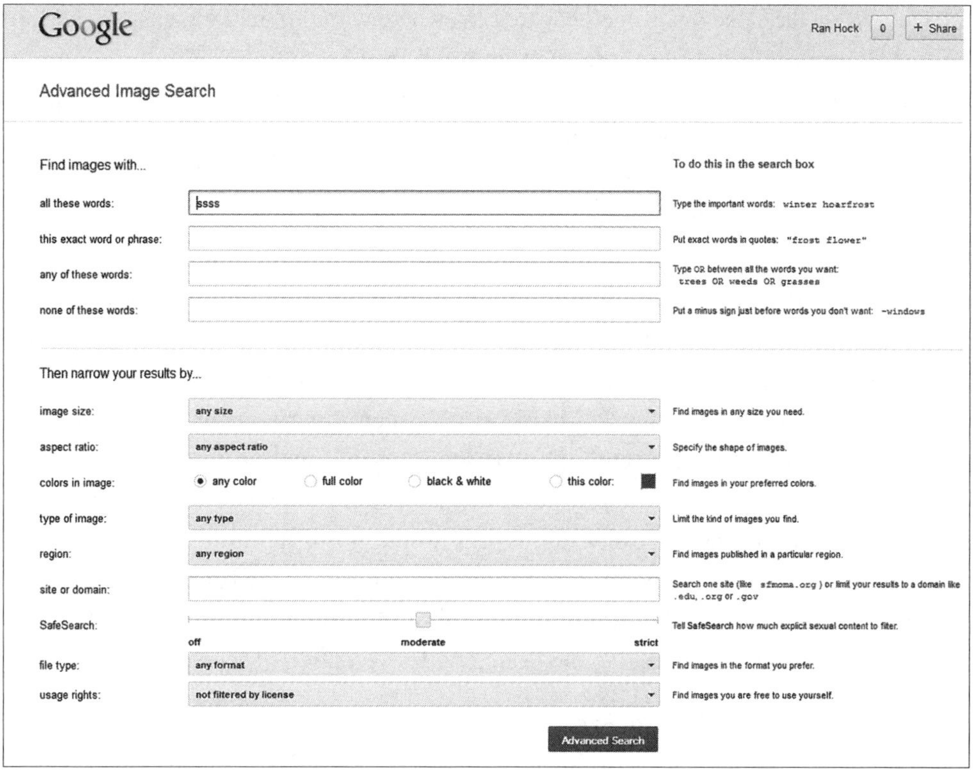

Figure 7.1   Google's advanced image search page

- Use the SafeSearch option to set adult content filtering at Off, Moderate (the default), or Strict (available only in the English version of Google).
- Specify JPG, GIF, PNG, BMP, SVG, WEBP, or ICO formats using the file types menu (default is "file type").
- Limit by usage rights (i.e., those pictures that are not filtered by license or filtered by various degrees).

Image Results Pages

As the result of a search, Google will return a page containing thumbnail images for the images retrieved. As you scroll down, additional thumbnails continually appear until all have been shown. Hold your cursor over a thumbnail to see a slightly enlarged image plus a link to the image, a link to the page on which the image is found, the dimensions in pixels, a snippet of the text around the word(s) that retrieved the image, and a link for similar images. When the same image has appeared elsewhere with different dimensions, a More Sizes link appears that shows those occurrences of the image.

Narrowing options, which differ somewhat from the options provided by the advanced search page, are shown on the left of image pages. Here you can filter by content (all, by subject, or personal), by size, by color, and by type (Face, Photo, Clip art, Line drawing). You can also choose to have the thumbnails displayed with sizes of the images (in pixels) shown on the thumbnails, and you can narrow to only those images that are new in the past 24 hours or the past week or by a date range you specify. The "by subject" choice (under the Content menu) can be tremendously useful in some situations. For example, if you search for *Madrid*, then choose the "by subject" option, results will be displayed in categories ("Madrid at night," "Madrid city," "Madrid plaza major," "Madrid map," "Real Madrid," "Madrid flag," etc.). The "personal" choice on the Content menu delivers pictures related to people to whom you are connected on Google+ or on YouTube.

When you click on an image on a results page, a screen will appear with the image (full-size) in the foreground and the page that contains the image in the background. Click on the background to see just the page. Links on the right of the screen take you to the page, to the full-size image alone, and to the Search by Image option (discussed next).

Google's Search by Image Feature

In addition to searching using words, with Google's Search by Image feature, you can search using an image itself to find similar or related images from the web. The image that you input as your search can be an image from the web or from your own computer.

To search using an image you have found on the web, enter the URL of the image into the search box and then click the camera icon now found there. (A quick way to get the URL of an image you find is to right-click on the image and, from the resulting menu, choose "copy the URL.") If you have two browser windows open, you can also just drag the image from a webpage in one window into the images search box in the other window. To search using an image found on your own computer, you can simply drag the image from your desktop or from an open folder to the search box.

Another shortcut to searching images found on the web is to install the browser extension available for either Chrome or Firefox. Having done so, when you right-click on an image, one of the options you will see is to "Search Google with this image."

Depending upon the image you use to search, results pages may include: "Pages that include matching images" and "Visually similar images." They may also include a "Best guess for this image" (with a list of pages for that subject) if Google thinks it knows what the image is. This can be useful if you have a picture of a person, object, or place that you can't identify. If Google has made a best guess among the "visually similar" images shown, you may find images that themselves are not just "visually" similar but are of the same thing. Additional best guesses may appear at the bottom of results pages.

Yahoo! and Bing's Image Searches

Yahoo! and Bing work from the same image search database, and the images retrieved and the order in which they are displayed are for all purposes the same. Each, though, does offers some features that the other doesn't. The biggest differences are that Bing provides more search options (narrowing options on results pages) and Yahoo! offers options for searching Facebook.

Bing's Image Search

Bing has a very substantial image database that competes well against the other general web search engines and has a more innovative results page than the others. You can get to it using the Images link on Bing's main page or by going to www.bing.com/images.

Image Searchability

In the main search box for Bing's images search, terms are automatically ANDed, and you can use ORs, quotation marks for phrases, a minus to exclude terms, and the *site:* prefix to narrow to a specific site. When using ORs, be sure to enclose the ORed terms in parentheses. Bing does not have an advanced image search page, but on results pages, you can refine your current results by Size (small, medium, large, wallpaper), Color (all, color only, black & white), Type (all, photograph, clipart, line drawing), Layout (all, square, wide, tall), and People (all, just faces, head & shoulders). As you see, Bing, like Google, has the "face" option, but takes it a step further and allows a head-and-shoulders option.

Image Results Pages

Bing's image search results (Figure 7.2) provide continuous scrolling—you can just keep on going until you get to the end. (Bing, under a former name, had this feature before Google did). At first, just the thumbnails alone are shown, but when you hold your cursor over the image, you get the image's file name, its dimensions and file size, and the URL of the site on which it can be found. There are links near the top of the page enabling you to filter by size, color, type, layout, and people (faces, head and shoulders), and change the SafeSearch level. When you click on a thumbnail, a window opens showing at the top, the image, and a slideshow strip for other images on the page. Beneath those is the page on which the image appeared.

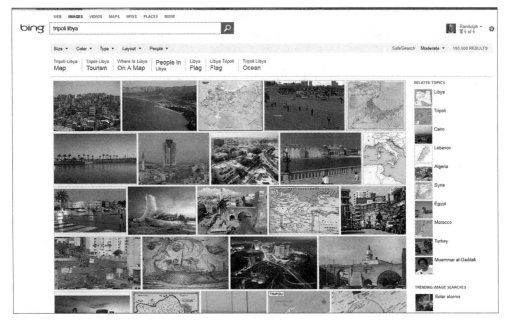

Figure 7.2 Bing image results page

Yahoo!'s Image Search

To search, either click on the Images tab on the main Yahoo! Search page and then enter your search, or click on the Images tab after doing a web or other search. The latter will automatically search your terms in the images database. You can also go directly to images.search.yahoo.com. Yahoo! Image Search pages no longer link to an advanced images search page.

Image Searchability

In the search box, you can enter one or more terms and use quotation marks for phrases. Terms are automatically ANDed. You can use the *site:* prefix to limit your results either to a specific website or to a top-level domain, such as .gov:

"space shuttle" site:gov

You cannot use the minus sign to exclude a term or use an OR.

Image Results Pages

Yahoo!'s image results pages show the number of images found and thumbnails of the first 90 or so images, with file names, dimensions in pixels, file sizes, and the addresses of the webpages on which they were found.

Click on one of the thumbnails to go to a slideshow presentation of the image.

Other Searchable Collections

There are a number of other searchable collections that contain images from webpages. The general web search engines just discussed contain the largest collections by far, but you may want to examine the three directories of image resources listed earlier to identify searchable collections in specific subject areas. The following description of Picsearch highlights one of the best-known alternative web-image search engines.

Picsearch

www.picsearch.com

Like the general web search engines, Picsearch, which only does images, gathers its image collection by crawling the web. Based on comparative searches, you can expect it to deliver fewer results than Google, Yahoo!, and Bing. The terms you enter in Picsearch's main search box are automatically ANDed, and you can use a minus sign to eliminate a term and quotation marks for phrases, but Picsearch does not allow the use of an OR. The Picsearch results pages let you limit by color (Only color, Only Black & White, Specific color), size (Small, Medium, Large, Wallpaper), orientation (Portrait, Landscape, Square), and type (Animations, Faces).

Getting Images You Can Use

If you are looking for a high-quality image for use in a publication or on a website and you don't want to worry about possibly violating copyright or tracking down an owner to ask permission, consider going to a commercial collection of images (stock image library) where you can buy the right to use an image. Corbis and Fotosearch are two examples of sites where you can do this. Other websites, such as Stock.XCHNG, provide a place where photographers display their works so others can use the images without charge. Another free option is the image collection searchable through the Creative Commons website.

Corbis Images

www.corbis.com

Drawing upon a range of collections from over 100 image partners and 30,000 photographers, Corbis collects and sells a variety of photography, fine art, illustrations, etc. The advanced search page and narrowing options offer a wide range of options as to type of picture, number of people in the picture, gender of subjects, layout, etc.

Fotosearch

www.fotosearch.com

Fotosearch lets you browse, search, and view images (for free), and then purchase usage rights for 11 million images (plus video and audio) from more than 100 image publishers.

Creative Commons

www.creativecommons.org

Creative Commons is a nonprofit organization that provides a registry of "some rights reserved" materials, including images, audio, video, text, and teaching materials. On the Creative Commons homepage, click on the Find CC-Licensed Works link. On the resulting page, you can choose from 10 sites that provide searches where you can limit to Creative Commons material.

Stock.XCHNG

www.sxc.hu

With the SXC site, you can browse or search nearly 400,000 stock photos from more than 30,000 photographers. You must be signed up to download the full-size image, but if you want to use high-quality photos for free, signing up will be worth the couple minutes it takes.

Exemplary Individual Collections

By browsing through the directories of image resources discussed earlier, users can view hundreds or perhaps thousands of sites that contain useful collections of images. The following websites are just two examples of specific collections that demonstrate the possibilities.

American Memory Project

memory.loc.gov

From the Library of Congress, this collection contains more than 9 million digital items from more than 100 historical collections at the Library of Congress. It contains

Maps, Motion Pictures, Photos & Prints, Sound Recordings, and Written Materials (Books & Other Printed Texts, Manuscripts, Sheet Music). Even though this is a government site, much of the material on the site is protected by copyright. Use the Browse button to browse by collection or topic, or use the Search page to search across collections.

WebMuseum (Paris)

www.ibiblio.org/wm

This impressive collection of artwork is a collaborative project headed by Nicolas Pioch. It is searchable by artist (about 200 of them) and by theme/period (from Gothic to the 20th century, plus Japanese art from all periods).

Websites for Storing and Sharing Your Own Photos

A number of websites let you store your own photos online for free and share them with friends, or you can use the site as a place to keep your photo files. These include Picasa, Flickr, Photobucket, SmugMug, and others. Picasa and Flickr are probably the best-known among these sites.

Picasa Web Albums

picasaweb.google.com

Picasa Web Albums, from Google, has significantly fewer publicly searchable images than does Flickr but is a good place to go for images shared by the public. Options on results pages provide for narrowing by type, (Faces, No faces), aspect ratio (All, Landscape, Portrait, Panorama), size (All, Small, Medium, Large, Extra Large), photos and videos (Photos only, Videos only), camera models, and licenses (All, Creative Commons, Commercial Use, Remix allowed), and you can sort by relevance or date. (You will find more about Picasa Web Albums in Chapter 10.)

Flickr

www.flickr.com

Flickr (owned by Yahoo!) is one of many photo sharing (and storing) sites on the web. It is among the biggest (with hundreds of millions of photos), best-known, and most fully featured. With Flickr, you can upload and save your own photos, as well as arrange them in albums, organize them, tag them and describe them as you wish, share them online, and have them printed. You can browse, search, and view your own photos, and those of others who have made their photos public. There are at least a dozen other significant features to use for either finding pictures or managing your own photo collections on Flickr. Without a paid subscription, you can load 300 MB of pictures and two videos in any month, and while the total number of photos you can store is substantial, there is a limit.

Flickr should be kept in mind not just for its storing, sharing, and organizing functions but also as a very effective image search engine because 1) it provides images you won't find in other image search engines, 2) you may be able to get much better precision for your image searches, and 3) it is a good source for images for which you can easily obtain permission to use.

Flickr Content

In contrast to image searching in engines such as Google and Yahoo!, a larger proportion of the images in Flickr are going to be more recent photos of people, places, and events, as well as images probably not found on regular webpages. You may be surprised, though, as to how many images on Flickr are of such things as drawings, antique maps, etc. In addition to images, Flickr now also contains some videos, screencasts, and other formats.

Precision Searching

Image searching with Flickr can actually be much more precise than image searching in general search engines, since those may rather liberally decide which words to associate with an image. Searches on multiple words in general search engines often yield images where the words were associated with entirely different images located elsewhere on a webpage. In Flickr, the word association is for a single particular image. The tagging of images in Flickr by users can also provide for both better precision and better recall. On Flickr, images may now also be "geotagged" by the contributors.

Search Options

The main search box provides tabs for searching Photos, Groups (Group names and descriptions or group discussions), or People (name or email addresses of Flickr members or their interests). The advanced search page provides simple Boolean and phrase searching in combination with searching of either the full text associated with the image or just tags. It also provides searching by content type (photos, videos, etc.), date (date taken or date posted), and a SafeSearch filter.

Flickr for Redistributable Images

If you need an image for a webpage, blog, newsletter, etc., and don't want to incur the cost and time spent in buying stock images, you can easily use Flickr Mail to request permission. (Flickr also provides a Creative Commons search option.)

Clip Art

While still in the category of images, clip art serves a somewhat different function and requires different sources. In the web context, the term usually refers to artwork available on the web, usually but not always free, for use on websites or printed documents. Numerous collections and directories exist for these resources, three of which are listed here. Users should read the fine print carefully. Most of the artwork is free, but you may be required to give a specific acknowledgment of the source.

Free Graphics

www.freegraphics.com

Free Graphics is a resource guide with links to collections of free clip art, graphics, photos, webpage templates, and more. The site is searchable and browsable by more than a dozen categories.

Yahoo! Directory > Graphics > Clip Art

dir.yahoo.com/Computers_and_Internet/Graphics/Clip_Art

This section of Yahoo!'s Directory provides links to more than 70 collections of clip art, arranged alphabetically and by category.

AUDIO AND VIDEO

More and more frequently used by researchers, audio and (particularly) video files have a variety of applications beyond just entertainment. In the case of video, it has, in recent years, become a first stop for some types of research. Accessing these resources is much easier than it was a few years ago, since most computers come with the necessary players, or they at least make it easy to identify and download the necessary player.

As with viewing images, hearing and viewing sound and video files is easy, but searching them has been the challenging part, mainly because of poor indexing. However, that situation is changing, with more indexing of transcripts and increased amounts of metadata.

Players

For virtually all of the sound and video file types you are likely to encounter (.wav, .au, .avi, .midi, .mp3, .mpeg, etc.), your computer probably came equipped with the software necessary to play them, including the more recent file types, such as the currently dominant, highly compressed, but high-quality sound and video file format MPEG (Moving Pictures Expert Group format, with .mpeg, .mpg, .mp2, and .mp3 file extensions). If you do encounter a file type not currently supported, there is a good chance that there will be a link on the page that leads you to an easy free download of the necessary player. Among the players that many users are likely to encounter are Windows Media Player (pre-installed with all recent Windows operating systems), RealPlayer (a free download for the basic version, with upgrades for a fee), and QuickTime (essential for Apple users but also available in a Windows version).

Audio

Historic speeches, online radio stations, and other sound resources can be valuable for many reasons, but in terms of frequency of use, the most frequently accessed audio content type on the internet is music. Unfortunately, much of the accessing that is done is illegal due to the violation of copyright. However, there is ample opportunity for legal access to music and also access to other types of useful audio content.

Since serious searchers (and their employers) who are unaware could easily become the target of copyright infringement suits, the copyright issue should be prominent in the minds of those who download audio and video from the internet. File sharing (peer-to-peer or P2P) among computer users on the internet became very popular very quickly with the advent of the Napster program. (Napster's first life was short, 1999–ca. 2000, but it has now been rehabilitated and legally reincarnated.) The Napster file sharing concept begat a number of other P2P programs, such as Kazaa, Grokster, Morpheus, and Gnutella, that have allowed listeners to continue to avoid paying for music. The intent of this book is neither to sermonize nor editorialize, but the serious searcher must be indeed aware of the copyright issue.

The next several pages list directories of audio resources, sites that help you find the audio you are looking for, and sites that focus on specific types of audio resources (music, podcasts, radio, speeches, and movie sound clips).

Digital Librarian: A Librarian's Choice of the Best of the Web—Audio
www.digital-librarian.com/audio.html

The Audio section of the Digital Librarian site features about 1,000 links—annotated and arranged alphabetically—mostly to sites containing collections of various kinds of audio.

Audio Search Engines

Other than for music searching, the number of sites that provide searches specifically of audio has actually declined in the last few years. The following search engines vary significantly in the content they cover, their searchability, and the added services they provide (such as music sales). Some cover video as well as audio.

PAV—Play Audio Video

www.playaudiovideo.com

PAV, Play Audio Video Multimedia Search, which bills itself as "The World's first Multimedia search engine," has indexed millions of audio files, videos, and images. A single search of PAV retrieves all three media in one shot. Though PAV often refers to all of its audio content as *music*, very importantly for the researcher, it actually contains a good collection of other audio, such as interviews, speeches, and lectures, both historical and current.

In PAV's homepage search box, an AND operator is implied, you can search for phrases using quotation marks, and you can NOT a term by using a minus sign immediately in front of the term. There is no advanced search link on the main page, but on results pages, you can 1) narrow your results to audio, video, or images, 2) specify that images be small, medium, or large 3) rank results by either relevance or date, and 4) filter what PAV identifies potentially as "pornography." (The PAV folks don't hide behind typical euphemisms such as "adult content.") With the latter menu, you can specify Maybe, Avoid, Put Last, or Allow.

Results pages typically show a ranked selection of audio results, followed by video results and image results. For each individual result, you will see a title, an "I" (Information) icon for which a mouseover will show a date and the site, and a home icon, which when clicked takes you to the page containing the file. Depending upon the kind of file (audio, video, image), you may see the file size and format (e.g., mp3), and icons to play a preview clip of the full file or see a cached version of the original document.

Be aware that PAV very knowingly and intentionally indexes a lot of P2P files such as "torrent" (BitTorrent) files that, by their nature, include vast quantities of copyrighted material that may have been copied illegally. The user may be legally liable for downloading such material.

FindSounds

www.findsounds.com

This site is included here as an example of a more specialized audio site. FindSounds specializes in sound effects (and similar sounds such as musical instrument samples). The main page lets you search by topic, file formats, number of channels, minimum resolution, and minimum sample rate. Click on the Types of Sounds You Can Find link for a directory of sounds (categories for animals, birds, holidays, etc.). The results pages show a waveform display, indicating not only loudness (amplitude), but also by use of color, frequency content. Here you can hear a hippo and the sounds of a siren, a sapsucker, a shotgun, a storm, a snare drum, and some singularly impressive snores.

Internet Archive—Audio Archive

www.archive.org

The Internet Archive has stored more than 1.2 million audio files, including over 100,000 legally downloadable concerts. The rest is a variety of other music and sounds including recordings from 78-rpm records, presidential speeches, lectures, Creative Commons materials, radio programs, and conference proceedings. The advanced search page can be used to search by title, creator, description, collection, date, and other specific criteria.

Audio Resources: Radio Stations (Real and Virtual)

With thousands of radio stations now providing audio archives of their programs and/or streaming audio of their current broadcasts, great possibilities are open to internet users. Besides the recreational possibilities, these radio resources not only provide another channel for news (see Chapter 8), but they can supply answers for "Who said what and when?" "Did so-and-so really say what she was quoted as having said?" and "What have people been saying about a particular topic?" Although recent interviews may not be available in transcribed form, the audio may be there, whether on a well-known source such as the BBC or on a local radio station. These radio stations can also be valuable to those who are learning a foreign language. The Radio-Locator site will be useful in locating a specific station.

In addition to real radio stations, the internet also provides virtual radio stations so you can tune in on your computer and listen to your own choice of musical genres. Some of this on-demand music is free, and some requires a subscription. If you subscribe to satellite radio for your car (or home), check with your provider for the possible added capability of accessing their services on your computer as part of your subscription.

Radio-Locator

www.radio-locator.com

Radio-Locator provides links to about 13,000 radio station sites worldwide and includes 7,000 with live, streaming audio (for continuous listening). From this site, you can search for radio stations by country, U.S. state or ZIP code, Canadian province, call letters, and station format (classical, rock, etc.). The advanced search page provides searching by multiple criteria, but it limits your results to only the U.S. or Canada.

CBS Radio

www.cbsradio.com/streaming/index.html

The CBS Radio site provides a directory of links (under the Stations tab) to streaming video from more than 120 CBS stations throughout the U.S.

Pandora

www.pandora.com

Definitely in the entertainment category but still relevant for the well-rounded researcher, Pandora is a unique and very popular virtual radio station. As well as a standard list of genre stations, through the use of Pandora's Music Genome Project technology, you can easily create your own station that automatically incorporates artists and music similar to ones that you specifically name. You can keep adding stations, and you can give a thumbs down to songs you don't like.

Spotify

www.spotify.com

Spotify, like Pandora, provides very easy delivery of music to your computer or mobile device. Music from Spotify, though, is listened to through a (quickly) downloadable program rather than through your browser. There is a heavier emphasis on the "social" aspect, with easy sharing of songs by means of Spotify's integration with Facebook accounts. The free version brings with it some ads, but the premium version will get you around that.

Podcasts

Podcasts are downloadable audio recordings (broadcasts), analogous to blog postings, that have become a source for valuable information and commentary for internet users. Podcasts are "published" using feeds (e.g., RSS) that can be downloaded via the web and transferred to an mp3 player (or to your computer) so you can listen at your convenience. There are a number of programs that will periodically check for new downloads and download them automatically, including, among others, iTunes, Juice, Doppler, and BlogMatrix Sparks.

For locating podcasts of interest, there are various tools, including the two following podcast search engines and directories. Other sites, such as blinkx, cover podcasts as well as other audio formats. Another good source for podcasts is iTunes, coming up in a few paragraphs.

For users of the podcast search and directory sites, the most important difference among them may be the categories under which the podcasts are organized and whether those particular categories match your needs.

Podcast Alley

www.podcastalley.com

Podcast Alley provides a directory of podcasts, arranged into 21 genres. Search or click on a category to see the list, and then click on a specific title to see a description plus links for more details, to subscribe, or to vote for the podcast. If you click on the Details link, you will be shown descriptions of recent episodes with a link to download the episodes. The main search box enables you to search the titles and descriptions of podcasts (but not the episodes). Terms you enter in the search box are ORed. Podcast Alley also provides a useful forum about podcasts and links to information on podcast software.

Podcastdirectory.com

www.podcastdirectory.com

Podcastdirectory.com provides a search option but emphasizes browsing by category. You can browse for podcasts by 16 main categories (and numerous subcategories), and if you look carefully, by a very useful but inexplicably tiny set of links enabling you to browse by country, language, tags, region, etc. You can also browse by using a Google map mashup that shows the location of the podcasters. A keyword search is also available on the main page. The terms you enter there are automatically ANDed, and you can use ORs, a minus in front of terms for a NOT, and quotation marks for phrases.

Browsing results usually show the podcast's logo, its name, and a brief description. Click on the name to get to a fuller description and a list of episodes, each with its own description. Search results show similar information and also provide, at the top of results pages, links to search episodes, search internet radio, and search video podcasts.

A Sampling of Other Audio Resources
The History Channel: Video

www.historychannel.com/video

A search in this section of The History Channel site will deliver links to a variety of audio and video resources on the site. On the main page, you can browse by show and by topic. Even if you are not a history buff or scholar, you are at great risk of being captivated by what this site provides.

The MovieWavs Page

www.moviewavs.com

This is a source for sound clips from more than 300 major movies as well as TV shows and cartoons, plus links to other movie sound sites.

Music Search and Sales

Some of the sites already mentioned provide a way to search for music and serve as "music stores." More and more companies have gotten into the online music sales competition, including "stores" such as Amazon. The following two sites are among the current leaders in legal music downloads; their descriptions will provide a glimpse of the possibilities.

Apple: iPod & iTunes

www.apple.com/itunes

On the iPod and iTunes website, you can download iTunes, a combination of digital jukebox, music download store, music manager, CD burner, general player for other audio files, and more. Early on, and especially because of the iPod connection, iTunes took the leadership among online music stores, allowing you to not just purchase songs legally, but also to create your own library of music and video, both by purchasing music online and by importing music and videos from your own digital music library. From there, you can organize your library, sync to your iPod, listen on your computer, create your own CDs, and do several other tasks. On the store side, you can use the iTunes software to go online and download any of more than 10 million songs, plus music videos, TV shows, audiobooks, and podcasts (the latter usually free).

When you select the iTunes Store option on iTunes, you can use the search box near the top of the window to search by keyword (artists, song, etc.). On search results pages, you will see a button where you can narrow your results by Music, Movies, TV Shows, Applications, Music Videos, Audio Books, Podcasts, or iTunes U (educational materials). The Radio option in the Library section provides access to hundreds of radio stations (both internet and "real") arranged by genre.

iTunes also provides a podcast directory (Figure 7.3). Click on Podcasts from the iTunes Library list, and toward the bottom of the resulting screen, you will see a Podcast Directory link that will take you to the Podcasts section of the Music Store. From there, you can either search or browse for podcasts of interest to download.

Figure 7.3   iTunes podcast directory

Video

Video has emphatically become a major "destination" on the web, not just for entertainment but for news, how-to's, lectures, and much more. To look for video, try the following places:

- Use the video search capabilities of YouTube, Bing, Yahoo!, or Google.
- For news video, try news services such as BBC, CNN, and MSNBC, plus local radio and TV station websites.
- Look around on subject-specific sites such as The History Channel and American Memory (discussed previously under Audio).
- Use the BUBL LINK video resource guide that follows.

Directory of Video Resources on the Internet
Digital Video Collections Guide
www.lib.umn.edu/libdata/page.phtml?page_id=4139

Produced by the Libraries at the University of Minnesota with contributions from librarians at Arizona State University and elsewhere, this page provides links to almost

100 collections of video online. The first part of the page lists proprietary databases, but the rest lists openly available collections.

Video Search Engines

Finding relevant video has become easy with the video search offerings from all of the major search engines, as well as on video sites themselves, such as YouTube. Along with the opportunities provided by the vast quantity of video available, video indexing and search technologies have expanded, including the use of enhanced RSS to provide additional meta-data that can be attached to a video or audio file, the tagging of videos by individuals, and the use of voice recognition technologies to create transcripts of news and TV shows.

As mentioned previously, all of the major web search engines provide a video search. They differ primarily in terms of the sources for the video they index and in the search features they provide. As with web search, if you want to be exhaustive or want to find something very obscure, you may want to try at least two or three of the video search sites.

Google's Video Search

video.google.com

Google claims that its video search index is the most comprehensive on the web. A large proportion of its content comes from YouTube (owned by Google), with other content obtained from the crawling of other websites across the web. In the main search box, you can do the same types of searches as with a Google Web search, including the use of ORs, a minus in front of a term for a NOT, and quotation marks for phrases. You may also want make use of the *title:* and *site:* prefixes, for example, *market OR marche intitle:montmartre site:youtube.com.*

Using the filters on video search results pages, you can narrow by duration (less than 4 minutes, 4–20 minutes, more than 20 minutes), when uploaded (past hour, 24 hours, week, month, year, or custom range), quality (any, high quality), availability of closed captioning (subtitles, as in "movie subtitles"), or source.

Yahoo!'s Video Search

video.yahoo.com

Yahoo!'s video collection contains video gathered from video sharing sites such as YouTube and video gathered directly from video publishers. It uses the same video data-base as Bing, except that some videos will appear that are exclusive to Yahoo!, because of Yahoo!'s agreements with publishers. On results pages, Exclusive Videos will appear on the first line of results. On the left of results pages, you can filter results by duration and latest, and sort results either by relevance or date.

In the search box on the Yahoo! Video Search main page, all terms you enter are automatically ANDed, you can use quotation marks for a specific phrase, and you can use OR and either NOT or a minus before a term to eliminate a term. The Advanced Video Search link, found under "Options" on the right of the search box, permits you to use simple Boolean, specify format (avi, mpeg, QuickTime, Windows Media, Real, Flash), specify duration (All Lengths, Less Than 5 minutes, 5–20 Minutes, Longer Than 20 Minutes), and site/domain (.com, .edu, .gov, .org, or a specific domain). You can also apply a SafeSearch filter.

Bing's Video Search
www.bing.com/videos

As just mentioned, except for some videos exclusive to Yahoo!, Bing and Yahoo! are searching the same video database, and the same search features are available for use in the main search box (terms you enter are automatically ANDed, you can use quotation marks for a specific phrase, and use OR and either NOT or a minus before a term to eliminate a term).

Bing's video search does not have an advanced search page, but the filtering options on results pages are slightly more extensive than Yahoo!'s results page filters (but not as extensive as the options provided on Yahoo!'s advanced video search page). With Bing's filters, you can specify video length (All Lengths, Less Than 5 minutes, 5–20 Minutes, Longer Than 20 Minutes), resolution (All, High), and source (from a list of selected video sources that appear among results). Above the video thumbnails, you will see options to sort by best match or most recent and also see a link for specifying the Safe Search level.

YouTube
www.youtube.com

YouTube, owned by Google, has become not just an entertainment site and a place to share one's own videos, but it is also becoming a significant research tool. As you have undoubtedly noticed, YouTube's popularity has grown astoundingly, as has its size (70+ hours of video is uploaded every minute). Unlike the video search engines just discussed, which index video found on other sites, all of the YouTube video is stored on the YouTube site. Individuals or organizations can upload a video in as little as a couple of minutes.

YouTube is both browsable and searchable. For browsing, the main page offers some suggestions (Recommended, Social, etc.), but for a more extensive browsing experience, click on the Browse link near the top of the page, which will take you to a list of 12 categories (Recommended for You, Autos & Vehicles, Comedy, Entertainment, Film & Animation, Gaming, Howto & Style, Nonprofits & Activism, People & Blogs, Pets &

Animals, Science & Technology, and Travel & Events). Those categories give a good sense of the variety of video available.

YouTube's powerful searching options are a bit hidden—you don't see any advanced search options until you've clicked the Search button. Once on results pages, you will find a Filter menu button. Click it and options appear (Figure 7.4) for sorting by relevance, date added, view count, or rating; by when uploaded (today, this week, this month); by type of result (channel, playlist, movie, show); and by high definition, closed caption availability, longer than 20 minutes, partner videos, Creative Commons material, and "live" (live events).

Keep YouTube in mind for how-to and other learning videos. Whether you are learning a programming language, learning to knit, or wish you could yodel, there are YouTube videos that can help. In addition to millions of how-to videos, there are almost a half-million videos indexed under "lecture."

Search Engines for Video—TV-Specific

If you are looking for video of TV news or other TV shows and want to search for it easily and effectively, take advantage of the following sites. The first one, blinkx, is free (and includes more than just TV), while the other two that follow require a fee.

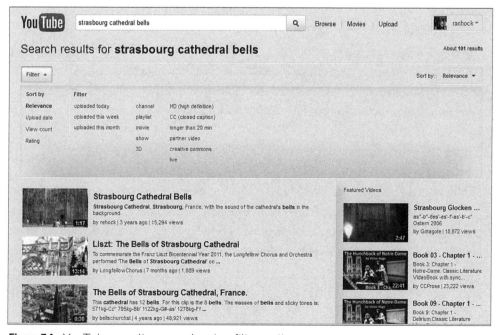

Figure 7.4   YouTube results page showing filter options

blinkx

www.blinkx.tv

At blinkx, you can get more than 35 million hours of video including lots of TV footage. With a number of major news suppliers, you will be taking advantage of full-text searching of every word spoken on the video, made possible through advanced voice recognition and speech-to-text technology, which lets blinkx automatically create transcripts of the audio and video content and index it. The search function, though, also extends to metadata beyond just the content of those transcripts. On top of that, it's free.

Click on the Partners link on the main page to see the impressive list of participants, including major TV networks, newspapers such as the *Wall Street Journal* and the *Washington Post*, plus other sources such as Forbes, PBS, the Discovery Channel, National Geographic, and Comedy Central. Search terms you enter are automatically ANDed, and you can use OR and NOT in your search statements. You can also browse videos by category.

On results pages, you will find an RSS button that will quickly set up an RSS feed for you on the topic you searched. Look around the site for a number of other features, such as Wall It, which provides a 5 x 5 "wall" of videos (on any topic) that you can put on a blog or website.

ShadowTV

www.shadowtv.com

ShadowTV is a fee-based service that monitors major networks, cable stations, and local affiliates and serves as a clipping service with automatic notification. At present, it just covers U.S. stations. It makes video available within a few minutes of when it was broadcast and also includes an archive dating back further.

TVEyes

www.tveyes.com

TVEyes is a fee-based search of radio and TV content from stations in the U.S., the U.K., the Middle East, Canada, Greece, and China. It indexes the audio feeds from these by means of voice-recognition technology and provides alerts and a searchable archive. Though it is fee-based, take a look at either the samples you can get online for free or sign up for a full demo.

CHAPTER 8

NEWS RESOURCES

Once more, the word "amazing" has to be used. To be able to read the headline stories from a newspaper 10,000 miles away, sometimes before the paper appears on local residents' doorsteps, is indeed amazing. This chapter covers the range of news resources available (news services and newswires, newspapers, news aggregation services, etc.) and how to most effectively find and use them. Importantly, this chapter emphasizes some limitations with which the researcher is faced, particularly in regard to archival and exhaustivity (comprehensiveness) issues.

TYPES OF NEWS SITES ON THE INTERNET

Understanding news resources on the web is challenging not just because there is such a broad and rich expanse of news available, but because almost every news site is designed differently from the next, with differing functions and missions. In "ancient" times, it was relatively easy to group news resources into categories such as newspapers, magazines and journals, radio, and TV. Today, it is harder to definitively categorize the types of places to go on the web for news. Although many typologies of news sources are possible, the following categories can prove to be helpful in sorting things out (while recognizing that there is considerable overlap and that many sites fit in more than one category):

- Major news networks and newswire sites: Sites that are original sources for news stories but may also gather and provide stories from other sources
- Aggregation sites: Sites that serve primarily to gather news stories from multiple sources
- Newspaper and magazine sites: Sites that serve as the online version for a printed newspaper or magazine
- Radio and TV sites

- Multisource news search engines: Sites that provide extensive search capabilities for a broad range of news sources
- Specialized news services: Sites that focus on news in a particular subject area
- Email (or RSS) alert services: Sites that provide a personalized selection of current news stories on a regular basis

Finding News—A General Strategy

A good starting point for finding news on the web is to ask the question, "What kind of news are you looking for?"

1. Are you interested in breaking news (today's headlines)?
2. Do you need older news stories?
3. Do you want to be kept up-to-date automatically on a topic?

For breaking news, you might start with virtually any of the categories listed earlier, depending upon the breadth of your interests, both with regard to subject and to the local, national, or international perspective needed. If you want to browse headlines, consider bookmarking and personalizing a general portal (such as My Yahoo!) and perhaps using it as the start page for your browser. Headlines in categories of your choice will show up every time you open your browser (or click Home). Alternatively, you might choose a news network site (BBC, MSNBC, etc.) or your favorite newspaper as your start page.

For older news stories, the choice is much more limited. If you are interested in the last few weeks, one of the general search engines may serve best. For international or high-profile news going back a few years, BBC may be a good choice because it provides searching of all stories covered on its site back to 1997. If your interest is more local, check to see if the local paper has searchable archives. To search the most retrospective collection of news on the web, take advantage of Google News' archive search, with a few sources going back to the 18th century.

If you need to keep up-to-date on a particular topic, definitely take advantage of one of the news alert services and have headlines relating to your interests delivered to you by email.

Characteristics to Look for When Accessing News Resources

For a research project or question, particularly when it is important that you know what you have and have not covered in your research, it is imperative that you be aware of exactly the kinds of items and time frames particular news sites include. You certainly do not need to know this for every search, but the following factors are among the major content variables encountered among news sources on the web:

- Time frame covered: Some sites cover only today; others go back weeks, months, or years.

- Portion of the original publication actually included: Particularly for newspapers and magazines, there is great variation as to how much of the print version is available online.

- Sources covered: Some sites may draw only from a single newswire service; others may include thousands of sources. Some go beyond the more traditional news sources and also cover blogs.

- Currency: Although old news can be tremendously valuable, news often implies *new*. Depending on the site, the stories may be only minutes old, whereas for other sites, the delay in posting stories may be considerably more.

- Searchability: Some sites only allow you to get to stories by browsing through a list or by category. Other sites allow searching by keyword, date, and other criteria. Look around on any news site for a search box.

- Availability of alert services: Although the service may not be emphasized, on many sites, if you dig around a bit, you may find that a free email alert service is available. Some sites exist specifically as alert services.

- Availability of RSS feeds: RSS as a concept is discussed near the end of the chapter. However, until you get there, RSS stands for Really Simple Syndication and, briefly, is a mechanism whereby a website, such as a news source, can code its pages so that stories are automatically distributed ("syndicated") to any website (or web user) that chooses to automatically receive those stories.

- Personalization capabilities: Some sites may allow you to personalize the site, so that when you sign in to your account, headlines in categories of your choice are displayed, along with your local news, weather, and sports.

NEWS RESOURCE GUIDES

With thousands of news sites out there, this chapter can only include a few selected sites. To find out about other sites, take advantage of one of the several good news resource guides. The guides listed here are among the more highly regarded. Each provides somewhat different options in terms of coverage and searchability or browsability. One of the most important uses of the first four sites listed here is the easy identification of newspapers and other news resources for virtually any country or large city in the world. If you need to know the website for the local newspaper in Kathmandu, these resource guides will lead you there. You will find it worthwhile to go to one of these guides, choose a country, and spend a few minutes browsing through the sites for that country. The other guides mentioned here focus on finding specific news features—political cartoons and "news in pictures" sites.

Kidon Media-Link

www.kidon.com/media-link

Kidon Media-Link is arranged to let you browse nearly 20,000 media sites by continent and country, but toward the bottom of the main page, there is a search box from which you can search by a combination of media types (newspaper, radio station, etc.) and either by city or by words in the title of the site. It will also display sites by language (English, Spanish, French, German, Italian, Portuguese, Arabic, Russian, Chinese, and Dutch). Symbols indicate whether streaming audio and video are available on the sites (Figure 8.1).

ABYZ News Links

www.abyznewslinks.com

ABYZ News Links contains mostly newspapers, but it also includes many broadcast stations, web services, magazines, and press agencies. For some countries and localities, ABYZ offers more links than Kidon Media-Link (and for some, fewer links). The search page on the site does a Google site search. You can browse by continent and country.

NewsLink

www.newslink.org

In addition to browsing newspapers worldwide by continent and country, NewsLink allows you to browse U.S. newspapers by the following categories: National Papers, Most-linked-to (state or type), Major Metros, Dailies, Non-dailies, Business, Alternative, Specialty, or Campus papers by state. It also has a collection of magazines and radio and TV stations (U.S. only). You can search for sources by city and state, and specify All, Newspaper, TV, or Radio.

NewsWealth

www.newswealth.com

NewsWealth has a respectable number of links to newspapers around the world, but its strength is in the other kinds of browsable news resource categories it provides. These

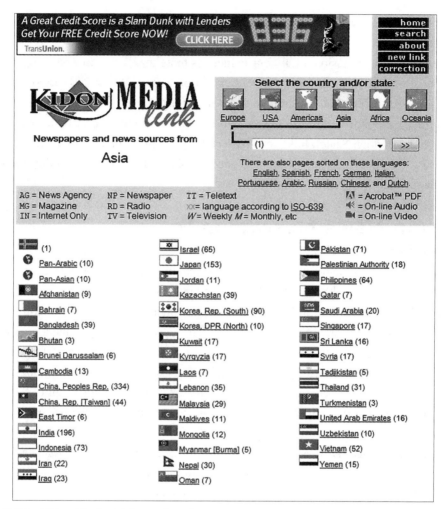

Figure 8.1   Kidon Media-Link continent page

include Magazines, Columnists, Blogs, Cartoons, Celeb Gossip, Sports, Business, Weather, Live Cams, Scanners Live, and Lotto Results.

News Resource Guides—Specialty Content
News in Pictures

www.newsinpictures.com

   News in Pictures is a collection of links to more than 100 sites that have news photo sections. Links are arranged according to the following categories: News, Sports, Disaster, Entertainment, History, Science, Miscellaneous, News in Video, USA Local News, and World News.

The Cagle Post—Cartoons & Commentary

www.cagle.com

Daryl Cagle's Professional Cartoonists Index is more than a resource guide with links to other sites; it actually contains the political cartoons from almost 200 cartoonists dating back to late-2000. You can browse and search for free, and you can purchase rights to reprint a cartoon from the site. On the homepage, you can browse by topic, and if you click on the Cartoon Search link, you can search by keyword, date, coloration, location, and artist. (Caution: You may [happily] spend considerably more time on this site than you planned on.)

MAJOR NEWS NETWORKS AND NEWSWIRES

Major news networks and newswires have sites that provide news items that they themselves have produced, although they may use and incorporate other sources as well. Sites such as BBC, CNN, and MSNBC are the choice of many web users for breaking news, because the headlines are updated continually. They also typically provide a number of other items of information beyond news headlines, such as weather. These are sites for which the "click everywhere" principle emphatically applies. By spending some time clicking around on the page, clicking through the index links at the bottom of the main page, and browsing through the site index, you can get an idea of the true richness of these sites.

Newswire services such as Reuters, UPI, Associated Press (AP), and Agence France Presse are primarily in the business of providing stories to other news outlets. Their sites contain current headlines and perhaps substantially more, but they may also be more a brochure for the service.

BBC

news.bbc.co.uk

Many experienced searchers throughout the world consider BBC (Figure 8.2) to be the best news site on the web. It is particularly noted for its international coverage. In the international section of some U.S. services, "international" seems to be defined as "news from abroad that is of particular interest to the U.S." BBC's international coverage, though, is much more truly *international*.

Among the site's strengths are its easy browsability, its search capability, and the availability of free searchable archives going back to November 1997. The BBC news site is only one small portion of what the overall BBC site offers. From the menu at the top of the main and other pages, click the More link and then choose Full A–Z. Browse through the alphabet to find content ranging from Adult Learning to Zimbabwe. (Speaking of adult learning, check out the BBC's Languages section.) Look under C at Country Profiles. On the news homepage, look at the Video and Radio sections and, at the bottom of the page, check out the News Feeds, Alerts, and E-Mail News links.

All content comes from BBC writers, although they may utilize other sources such as Reuters in writing their stories.

The search box allows searching by multiple keywords, and all the terms you enter are automatically ANDed. You can also make use of quotation marks for phrase searching. On the results pages, there will be narrowing options on the left, which will enable you to filter results by category (News, Blogs, TV & Radio, etc.), type of media (Video, Audio, Text & Images), and date. On the right side of the results pages, examples for each category for your topic are shown.

Figure 8.2 BBC News homepage

CNN

www.cnn.com

CNN.com, a Time Warner company, contains content that has appeared on CNN stations around the world. CNN has been displaying an increasingly international perspective, partly in connection with CNN's strong presence on European TV, and it has Mexico and Arabic versions as well as the U.S. and International editions. The category menu near the top of the main page makes browsing easy. Even though the search feature is "powered by Google" you are basically limited in search capabilities to the implied AND between terms and the use of quotation marks for phrases. Use the links at the bottom of pages to sign up to receive audio and video podcasts, email news alerts, RSS feeds, and mobile access.

MSNBC

www.msnbc.com

The MSNBC site, another major TV news site, on its front page provides lead stories, local weather at the top of the page, a stock market overview, video, and a search box (powered by Bing). In addition to MSNBC's own stories, you will find stories from local NBC stations, AP, *Newsweek*, and other sources. Most stories remain available online for a few weeks, some for many months. U.S. users can sign in and personalize this site by entering their ZIP code to see local news, weather, and sports headlines. At the bottom of the main page, there are links for free email and newsletters, RSS feeds, and podcasts.

Reuters

www.reuters.com

Reuters.com provides content from Reuters journalists around the world. The site lets you browse through general, financial, and investment news for the last day or so, and the search box allows retrieval of stories going back to 2006. The site is searchable by keyword, company name, or stock symbol, and you can browse current stories using 11 main news categories on the homepage. Searching by company name or ticker symbol leads to stock quotes for the company and company profiles, news, and other enterprise information. Reuters also provides RSS feeds, email newsletters, and podcasts.

Aljazeera.net

english.aljazeera.net

There is definitely some truth to Aljazeera's motto that "now when Aljazeera speaks, the world listens and 'reads'." The content on this site, which is aimed primarily at the

Arab world, is presented from an Arab perspective. The Arabic version is available at www.aljazeera.net, and it is important to note that the content there is not identical to the English version.

NEWSPAPERS

Thousands of sites for individual newspapers are available on the web. There may still be a few newspaper sites that contain an insignificant number of actual stories, but most contain at least the major stories for the current day, and most contain an archive covering a few days, a few months, or even several years. Most online versions of newspapers do not contain sections such as the classified ads (or display ads) that appear in the print version and some online versions contain things that are not in the print version, such as profiles of local companies.

Although there are many of us who are not likely to completely desert the print version of their favorite newspaper for a while to come, the online versions do provide some obvious advantages, such as searchability and archives. Some also provide greater currency, with updates during the day. Perhaps the most obvious advantage is simply their availability—the fact that newspapers from around the world are available at your fingertips almost instantly. Take advantage of the availability of distant papers particularly when doing research on issues, industries, companies, and people. For industries, take advantage of specialized coverage in newspapers dependent upon their location. For example, the *San Jose Mercury News* (online version, www.MercuryNews.com) is strong on technology because of its location in Silicon Valley, the *Washington Post* is strong on coverage of U.S. government, and Detroit papers are strong on the auto industry. In any geographic area, for local companies and people, the local paper is likely to give more coverage than larger papers.

More and more newspaper archives are available online. In some cases, you can get recent stories for free, but you have to pay for earlier stories. The price is usually quite reasonable, especially considering the cost to obtain them through alternative document-delivery channels.

Use the news resource guides mentioned earlier to find the names and websites for papers throughout the world. For availability of newspaper archives, check the site for the particular paper. Keep in mind that commercial services such as NewsLibrary, Factiva, LexisNexis, and Dialog have newspaper archives that may predate what is available on the newspaper's website. If you are not in an organization that has a library that provides access to some of these, your local public library may.

Newspapers—Front Pages

The following two sites provide a look at the actual pages of newspapers.

Today's Front Pages

www.newseum.org/todaysfrontpages

Brought to you by the Newseum, this site offers a look at the actual front pages of more than 800 newspapers from 82 countries. On the front page, under the List link, the thumbnails of the pages are listed alphabetically (by U.S. state and city, and then by other countries and cities). A link on the main page lets you choose locations on a map or regional list. Click on a thumbnail to see a larger view, and from there, you can click on a link that gives you a PDF version that can be enlarged further.

PressDisplay.com

www.pressdisplay.com

The main page of the PressDisplay.com site initially looks like many other news sites, with news headlines and images. Either the Select Title button at the top of the main page or the Titles by Country menu on the left of the page will lead you to thumbnails of the front pages of newspapers, more than 2,000 newspapers from more than 90 countries. When you click on one of the images of a newspaper front page, you will go to images of the full front page. From there you can go to images of all of the news pages of the paper, but to get beyond the front page, you may need to pay, either for a single issue or for a subscription. You are, though, once you register, allowed two free articles in every issue, every day. The window by the search box at the top of the main page permits you to search by time frame, or you can go to an advanced search page and search (within the papers) by newspaper, date, language, and author, and limit to headline.

RADIO AND TV

Sites for radio and TV stations are excellent sources for breaking news and may also contain audio (and sometimes video) archives of older programs. The next two sites make it easy to locate radio stations from around the world. The third site, NPR, is particularly valuable for its archives of National Public Radio shows.

Radio-Locator (formerly the MIT List of Radio Stations on the Internet)

www.radio-locator.com

Radio-Locator's site offers links to more than 12,000 radio station sites (and more than 7,400 audio streams) worldwide and allows you to search for radio stations by country, U.S. state or ZIP code, Canadian province, call letters, and station format (classical, rock, etc.).

RadioStationWorld

www.radiostationworld.com

RadioStationWorld is a directory of thousands of radio stations worldwide organized first by continent, then by country, and then by type of station within the country.

NPR

www.npr.org

This site provides easy access to National Public Radio programs and stations throughout the U.S., and also provides a searchable audio archive of NPR stories. Using the pull-down menu at the top of the page, you can find a list of programs ("All Things Considered," "Car Talk," etc.) and from there, schedules, summaries, and audio files for individual programs.

AGGREGATION SITES

There are a number of sites that have a main function of gathering news stories from a variety of newswires, newspapers, and other news outlets. Also, two of the largest general search engines (Google and Yahoo!) provide extensive news searches of thousands of news sources. (As for the other major search engines' news searches, Ask.com's news search is rather limited in terms of searchability, and Bing utilizes MSNBC's news database and technology, which was discussed earlier.) Among the following sites are the two search engine sites with greatest news search capability and one of the most prominent sites that focuses specifically on news aggregation. These are all good places to go to make sure you are covering a wide range of sources, and each does the job in a somewhat different way, with differing content and differing browsing and searching capabilities.

Google News

news.google.com

In 2009, Google's main news search went from covering 4,500 English-language sources (and about 3,000 sources in other languages) to covering 25,000 sources, the additional number primarily representing blogs. Google has stopped announcing how many sources it is covering, but we can probably safely assume that it is 25,000 or more. It crawls the sites continually, which means that you may be able to find some things on Google only minutes after they appear in the original source. Items are typically retained in Google's news database for 30 days, and Google provides a powerful free alert service, along with a news search in many of its country-specific news sections. You can access these by means of the pull-down menu on the main news search page. For the 72 regional (country/language) versions, Google will retrieve the same records as in the U.S. version, but the local (country/language) results will appear first on the results pages.

On Google's news page, you will find headlines arranged in 11 categories (Top Stories, World, U.S. Business, etc.) with from one to five leading stories for each (Figure 8.3). If you have a Google account, you can personalize the page by changing the order of the sections, weighting the sections and selected sources, and adding custom sections that identify stories based on keywords you choose.

Each news story record has the title, an indication of how long ago the story was indexed, a 30- to 50-word excerpt, and, for some stories, links to related stories from other sources. Sources for each story are chosen algorithmically, rather than by human editors. If the story has a photo, a thumbnail appears beside the story summary.

On the left side of the page, links for each of the news categories will take you to a full page of top stories for that category. Buttons beneath the search box enable you to change the country edition and to adjust the format of records ("Modern," Headlines, Compact, Classic).

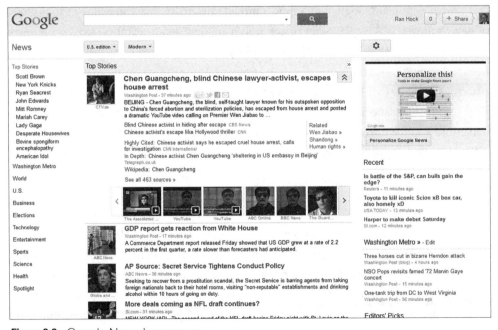

Figure 8.3   Google News homepage

In the search box, you can use prefixes such as intitle: and inurl:. (However, for narrowing down to a specific news source, the *source:* prefix will probably work best, e.g., *deficit source:"wall street journal."* Google has an advanced news search (look for its link at the bottom of results pages) that allows you to use simple Boolean, search by source, location, and date, and narrow by limiting to occurrence of your terms in the headline, the body, or the URL of the record. Search results look very similar to web search results, but you will also find sections showing local headlines, Recommended Sections, Editor's Picks, Spotlight Videos, and Most Popular.

Although news records are retained on Google for 30 days, for some sources, the article may not be there when you click, especially for newspapers that have dynamic pages that change frequently or that keep older articles in a separate archive database (mainly for fee-based access). Unlike Google web search, Google News does not offer a cached copy of news pages.

Even though the main Google News search only includes content going back 30 days, retrospectiveness does not end there. Google's news archive search allows searching of news content that goes back over 200 years. This includes content provided directly by publishers (Google "partners") and archived news content that Google has found by crawling the web. The search is free, but for most articles, you will need to pay the provider to see the full article. To get to the archive search, look under the time range choices on the left of the results page. (The news archives are a great resource for genealogists, as well as historians and other researchers.)

Yahoo! News

news.yahoo.com

For years, Yahoo! News has been a favorite place on the web for news-seekers. The content comes from news providers such as the AP, Reuters, Agence France Presse, ABC News, Business Wire, and other services, plus news found from crawling other news sites on the web. Most stories are retained for 30 days.

The main page has a menu at the top plus other tabs on the page that will display headlines for ABC News, Latest News, Slideshows, AP, and Reuters. The menu across the top of the page allows you to easily browse by the following categories (each category with a number of subcategories shown as you hold your cursor over the menu item): U.S., World, Business, Entertainment, Sports, Tech, Politics, Science, Health, Blogs, Local, and Popular (Figure 8.4). Beneath the menu is a search box.

In the search box, you can use most of the same techniques you use in a Yahoo! web search (OR, *intitle:,* etc.) plus two other prefixes, *headline:* and *author:* (*author:smith*).

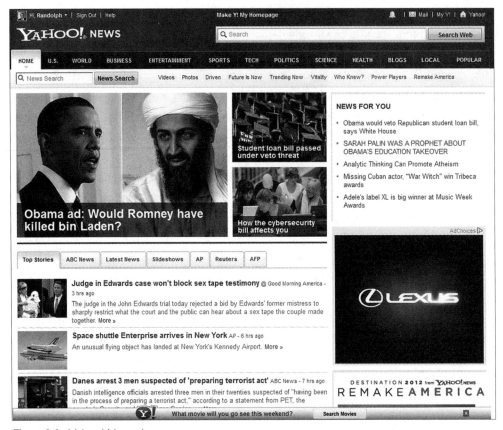

Figure 8.4 Yahoo! News homepage

On results pages, to the right of the search box is an Options link. Click on it to get to the link for Yahoo!'s advanced news search. There you can use simple Boolean; sort results by relevance or date; narrow your search by date, source, location, categories, and language; and specify the number of results to be shown on each results page.

News search results show, for each item, the story title, the place, and the first 50 or so words from the story, followed by the source, date, and time when Yahoo! indexed the story. On results pages, you will also find links to set up alerts on the topic for which you searched and to add your topic as a section on My Yahoo! or as an RSS feed elsewhere.

NewsNow

newsnow.co.uk

NewsNow is in the business of providing newsfeeds to other organizations and sites, and it was the first major news aggregation site dedicated to a U.K. audience (but actual coverage is very international). It covers more than 40,000 sources and updates from them every few minutes. From the NewsNow homepage, you can either search or browse by category. The categories are a major strength of the site, and the 11 main categories are broken down into hundreds of subcategories. Using these categories, you can quickly and easily focus in on news relevant to your specific areas of interest. In the search box, you can use multiple words (they are automatically ANDed), and you can use quotation marks for phrases.

SPECIALIZED NEWS SERVICES

Having a site for specialized news for a particular industry, area of technology, and so on can be not just useful but sometimes critical for those who need to make sure they are not missing important developments in that area. Such sites exist for a tremendous variety of subjects. In some cases, they are news-only sites, but in some cases, specialized news is just one function of the site. One very simple yet effective approach to finding a specialized news site is to use a web search engine and search for the industry or topic and the word news, for example, *paper industry news*. A good example of a more specialized news aggregator site is Silobreaker, which focuses on business and national security-type issues and presents the news in a very innovative way. Silobreaker also provides a good example of effective integration of technologies such as visualization into the delivery of news.

SiloBreaker

www.silobreaker.com

Silobreaker is a news aggregator with its initial main focus on issues related to national security. By means of relational analysis, visualization tools, and identification of entities, connections, trends, and related topics, it provides a really easy way to get to news stories, as well as better understand the context of the stories. It covers more than 10,000 news and research sources, blogs, video, and other sources.

At the top of Silobreaker's main page, you will see six browsable news categories. Above that, you will find a search box, and on the left side of the page, current major stories. The uniqueness of the site begins to be seen on the right side of the page, where you will see, among other things, snapshots of what is provided by Silobreaker's visualization tools (In Focus, Network, Hotspots, Trends). Do a search on a specific topic and you will see in the In Focus box a list of "entities" that match your term. (Hold your cursor over one and see facts about that entity, usually with a link to a more detailed, frequently updated fact sheet.) This time, the visualization displays will be specific to your topic.

Silobreaker tools include:

- In Focus: This is a list of searchable entities related to your topic.
- Network: This graphic shows connections between related topics (entities). Click on the graph for a larger, more detailed view and to reconfigure the view for emphasis on companies, organizations, persons, cities, and key phrases.
- Hot Spots: This map shows locations of current news stories.
- Trends: This graph shows the recent frequencies of stories on related entities. With the "360° Search," you will see more of an overview for your topic, including snapshots of all of the relevant graphics and other tools.

In the main search box, you can enter one or more terms connected with AND, OR, or NOT, use quotation marks for phrases, and use several search prefixes. The Advanced Search link beneath the search box enables you to narrow by content type, specific sources, and date. There's much more, including personalization of your pages, search suggestions, and creating automatic topic filters to apply to subsequent searches.

BLOGS

Fitting somewhat into the category of specialty news sites are blogs. These sites (originally known as weblogs) began to appear in very large numbers around 2001. Blogs are, according to blog pioneer Dave Winer, "often-updated sites that point to articles elsewhere on the web, often with comments, and to on-site articles." They usually focus on topics of very specialized interest and are a good way of keeping up-to-date on such specialized topics. They can range from very useful sites that gather news and provide well-informed commentary to pages of inane ramblings. In any case, they have become a significant part of the "news" content available on the web, and being able to locate either blog sites or individual blog items is now a part of news searching, as indicated by the fact that many of the news sources already discussed in this chapter include blog content. If you find a blogger whose interests closely match yours and the blogger tracks the news in that particular area, you can think of the blogger as your "agent in the field," doing the work of helping to gather your information for you.

Blog Search Engines and Directories

The popularity, usefulness, and proliferation of blogs provides web searchers with the inevitable challenge of finding useful blog sites, and, among the billions of postings, those individual postings that discuss a specific topic. Fortunately, there are a number of sites that provide some substantial search capabilities, often in addition to other blog-related functions such as readers, blog publishing services, and directories.

Be aware though that blog searching presents some unique search problems. Some blog search sites cover only blogs that provide an RSS feed (thereby leaving out some blogs), and exactly what gets indexed for a particular posting will vary, depending upon how much of the blog posting was included in the RSS feed (title, summary, full text, etc.). As with news search engines, how many sources these blog searches cover and how retrospective they are will vary greatly. You will also notice a lot of variability in what search features are provided.

Among the several blog search engines, the following are among the most popular, fully featured (for searching), and/or extensive in terms of retrospective coverage. Because of the problems mentioned, if you really don't want to miss something, use more than one of these engines.

IceRocket

www.icerocket.com

Though most results from IceRocket will be from the past 6 months, some will go back several years. IceRocket's advanced search (available from results pages) enables searching by simple Boolean, title, tag, author, site, date, posts "from" a blog site, and posts that link to a specific blog page. The following prefixes can also be used in the main search box: *title:, author:,* and *tag:*.

Technorati

www.technorati.com

Technorati indexes more than a million blogs. On its homepage, as well as the search box, you will find a blog directory with which you can browse by means of nine main categories and a number of subcategories. Note that search results will only include posts for approximately the last three weeks.

Google

www.google.com

Google now incorporates its blog search into regular web searches (although the separate blog search page is still available). To search blogs via regular web search, do your search, and then, on the left of results pages, choose Blogs. Results can be filtered by blog posts or blog homepages and by timeframe, and also sorted by date or relevance.

RSS

Depending on whom you ask, RSS stands for either Really Simple Syndication or Rich Site Summary, though the former definition seems to have considerably overshadowed the latter. RSS is a format that lets news providers (and others) easily syndicate (distribute) their content. It makes use of XML language, which is a cousin of HTML (on its mother's side). The "product" is an RSS "feed," which is basically a specially coded webpage that feeds the information to those who request it. Using RSS feeds, sites can gather the headlines from a broad range of sources and create simple links on their own pages that lead to the stories. RSS is now extensively used by a broad range of news sites, from networks such as BBC and MSNBC on down to individual newspapers. It is also used extensively by blogs, though not all blogs (nor all news sites for that matter) offer an RSS feed.

On the slightly more technical side, there are actually a number of formats that provide these kinds of feeds, and feeds may be referred to as RSS, RDF, OPML, Atom, etc. For the user, they are all essentially the same, so unless you are producing a feed yourself, don't worry about the differences.

To make use of these feeds you need an RSS reader—software, or a website, that goes out and gathers the feeds that you request. To request a feed, click on the (often orange-colored) RSS or XML button (or similar button or link) on a news site or blog. (For someone who has not yet gotten into RSS, that is where the surprise may come. Sometimes when you click on one of those buttons, what you may see is a page of code that makes little sense to the average web user. The secret: Ignore the code, look at the address bar, and copy the URL of the page.) It is the URL of that page that you need in order to sign up for an RSS feed. Take that URL to your RSS reader. Sites providing feeds have made the process easier and now more often list several readers from which you can choose and in one or two clicks you can subscribe. If, for example, you see a My Yahoo! link and you are signed up for My Yahoo!, click the link, and in another click or two, that feed will show up on your My Yahoo! page.

RSS Readers

The following tools, most of which have already been mentioned, can be used for locating RSS feeds of interest and reading them. These are just a few of many RSS readers available. Most allow you to not just add and read feeds but also to organize them into folders or groups and perform other functions.

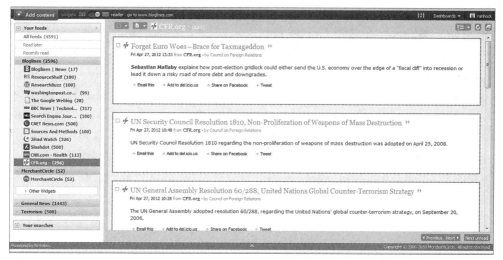

Figure 8.5 Bloglines

Bloglines

www.bloglines.com

If you click the My Feeds link in Bloglines, you will see links to RSS feeds you have already signed up for and a link to add new feeds (Figure 8.5). For the former, just click on the name of the feed to see the new items.

My Yahoo!

my.yahoo.com

Almost all of the readers are easy to use, but with a My Yahoo! account, when you see an Add to My Yahoo! link on a news site, you can have the feed appear on your My Yahoo! page with just a couple of clicks. If you find a news site with an RSS button, but no Add to My Yahoo! button, you can still add it to My Yahoo! by copying the URL. In My Yahoo!, click the Add Content link and then the Add RSS Feed link.

ALERT SERVICES

Among the most underused news offerings on the web are the numerous, valuable, and easy-to-use news alert services. These are services that automatically provide you with a listing of news stories, usually delivered by email and that are sometimes very personal- izable according to your interests. You don't have to go to the news; it comes to you.

Although the news alert concept has been around for decades, it has gone through many incarnations, ranging from mailings of 3" x 5" cards in the 1960s to the overhyped "push" services in the mid-1990s to the more typical (free) email mailings that have now stood the test of web time. If you are not familiar with the way this concept works, you find a site that provides such a service, you register and, in most cases, pick your topic, and thereafter, you will receive emails regularly that list news items on that topic. Many newspapers provide alert services, some allowing you to receive just selected categories of headlines. Some services cover a number of sources and allow you to be very specific with regard to the topic. The best way to find out about these is simply to keep an eye out as you visit sites. Several of the sites already mentioned in this chapter provide alert services. The following are two sites that epitomize the possibilities presented by this kind of service.

Google Alerts

www.google.com/alerts

Google offers a free alerting service for its 25,000 news sources. You can enter your search and then specify the delivery frequency (once a day, once a week, or as-it-happens). Multiple alerts can be established. With Google Alerts, you can choose to get news, blogs, video, discussion groups, books, or a comprehensive search including all of those.

Yahoo! Alerts

alerts.yahoo.com

From Yahoo! News pages, click the News Alerts link to set up keyword alerts on any topic you wish, using the Yahoo! Keyword Alerts option. The Yahoo! Alerts page also provides other alert options, including delivery of alerts by email, Yahoo! IM, or mobile devices.

CHAPTER 9

FINDING PRODUCTS ONLINE

Whether for their own purchase, for their organization's purchase, or for competitive analysis purposes, many searchers frequently find themselves searching for and comparing products online. The internet is a rich resource of product pages, company catalogs, product directories, evaluations, and comparisons. From the rather mundane purchase of a pair of slippers to finding vendors of programmable "servo motion" controllers, the internet can make the job quicker and easier. This chapter takes a look at where to look and how to do it efficiently and effectively. As with other chapters, the intent is not to be exhaustive, but rather to provide readers with a bit of orientation and some tips, point them in a useful direction, and provide examples of some leading sites.

CATEGORIES OF SHOPPING SITES ON THE INTERNET

A wide variety of types of shopping sites on the internet serve a wide variety of functions. Most sites could fall into one (or more) of the following categories:

- Company catalogs
- Online shopping malls
- Classifieds
- Price comparison sites
- Auction sites
- Product and merchant evaluation sites
- Consumer rights sites

Used in combination, these types of sites enable a user to find the desired product, check on the quality of both the product and the vendor, and feel confident and safe in making a purchase. ShoppingSpot.com, the first site listed here, is a good place to start if you want to explore, in an organized way, the variety of shopping resources available on the web. Many of the sites covered in this chapter serve multiple functions. They are placed in the category that seems to best fit the site's primary function.

ShoppingSpot.com

www.shoppingspot.com

ShoppingSpot.com will not only point you in a good direction as to *where* to shop, but it also has a lot of links related to *how* to shop, with review sites, price comparison sites, consumer protection sites, coupon sites, and other resources. It has an excellent directory of specialized sites, from Antiques to Travel.

LOOKING FOR PRODUCTS— A GENERAL STRATEGY

The all-purpose rule "keep it simple" works very well when looking for products online. If you already know who you want to buy from, start out with that site ("Duh!") but still maybe follow up with some comparisons. If you have in mind a specific brand, product, or set of specifications or criteria, jump into a general web search engine and get a quick (and perhaps a bit random) feel for what information is out there about the product. In the first 20 or so records, there is a good chance that you may get some links to vendors, some pages on specific models, some reviews, and often, for popular items (for example, plasma TVs), links to sites about selecting that kind of product.

Then move on to a more systematic approach. For a business-related purchase, you might next go to ThomasNet to identify vendors and specific products. For consumer products, you might go to one of the online shopping malls such as Amazon, Yahoo! Shopping, or eBay. Once you begin to focus on a likely choice, you can check out some reviews of the product itself at one of the review sites, do a search engine search on the specific model or product (ANDing the word review to your search), use one of the merchant rating sites, and look around in newsgroups to see what other buyers have said about it.

COMPANY/PRODUCT CATALOGS

If you know the name of the company you might want to buy from and don't know its web address, a simple name search should take you right to its site. If you don't know who manufactures or sells a certain product, go to one of the following company/product directories. Each will lead you to companies that produce a product, with a brief description of the company, how to contact the company, and usually a link to the company's webpage.

ThomasNet

www.thomasnet.com

ThomasNet, which was also discussed in Chapter 6, is the online replacement for the former *Thomas Register* and *Thomas Regional*—what library users and librarians in the U.S. may recognize as that shelf full of thick green books that for decades was the starting place in many libraries for identifying industrial products and manufacturers. ThomasNet contains millions of industrial product listings from 610,000 U.S. and Canadian distributors, manufacturers, and service companies, with products listed under 67,000 headings. You can either browse through the categories or make use of the search box (Figure 9.1). If you prefer to search, the Product Search link will direct your search toward Suppliers, Product Search, CAD Drawings, and Product News. Browsing is probably the best way to get a feel for what the site has to offer, and the breadth and detail of the categories. Another Thomas site, Solusource (www.solusource.com), provides information on suppliers worldwide.

Kompass

www.kompass.com

The Kompass directory includes products from 3.5 million companies in 70 countries. Products are searchable by 57,000 product/service keywords. On the Kompass main page, you can search by Products/Services, by Companies, Trade Name, or Executive Name, and by classification code, and you can search worldwide, by region, by country, or by U.S. state. The advanced search requires a subscription. The specificity of the categories and the searchability by location make it easy to precisely and thoroughly locate providers (for example, the 190 companies in Western Europe that provide velvet gloves). The site also has sections for Public Tenders (free to advertisers) and Requests for Quotations (free, but requires registration).

Kellysearch

www.kellysearch.com

From a company that goes back to 1790, Kellysearch covers products from 2 million companies around the world. From the main page, you can browse through 200,000 product headings. You will also find alphabetic indexes to companies and products. Using the advanced search page, you can search by either Product or Company and specify a country or region. A search covers product headings, trade names, and brand names.

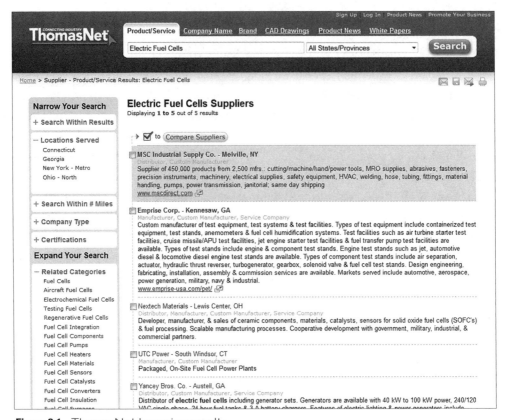

Figure 9.1 ThomasNet browsing results

SHOPPING MALLS

You don't have to look hard to find sites that enable you to purchase an item online from hundreds or thousands of online stores through a single site. Amazon and Overstock.com are among the most widely used of these online malls, but there are many, many more that serve the same function or may be specialized for a particular category of product (see ShoppingSpot.com, mentioned earlier). All the sites included in this section are ones where you can purchase items directly from the site, paying the site easily, securely, and confidently, without having to go to other merchant sites to make the purchase. This feature distinguishes online malls from the price comparison sites, where the site sends you to the websites of the individual merchants to complete your transactions. Most shopping mall sites use Shopping Cart technology, enabling you to gather multiple items and then check out all the goods at once.

Shopping mall and price comparison sites have many features in common. A third category covered in this chapter, auction sites, likewise demonstrates a lot of similarities.

Pretty obviously, they all give basic information about products (name, brand, model, price, pictures, and a brief description). All of the sites discussed here also provide a search box in which you can search multiple terms (the terms are automatically ANDed). With the exception of Google Product Search, all of the shopping sites listed here have a directory where you can browse by category and subcategories. And with the exception of Google Product Search, all of these sites allow you to perform a search in a specific category as well as across all categories.

The following descriptions focus on the ways in which these sites differ from one another.

Amazon

www.amazon.com

Initially an online bookseller, Amazon has expanded to a full shopping mall where you can buy almost anything, from rare books to sweaters and software. As well as a search box, the main page provides a detailed directory for browsing. (Hold your cursor over any of the categories to get a useful fly-out menu with subcategories.) As you browse through the subcategories, look on the left side of the pages for more detailed subcategories. When you get down to the level where you can see the actual products displayed, you will usually find a section on the left that allows you to narrow your results by category, brand, or price range, and in some cases, additional criteria related to the kinds of products.

Because of the richness of the site, both in terms of shopping breadth and shopping features, you will find it worthwhile to try the "click everywhere" approach to exploring Amazon. Among the other things you will find are: personalized recommendations based on your previous purchases; sites for Canada, the U.K., Germany, Italy, Japan, China, Spain, and France; shipment tracking; gift registries; selling options; personal lists where you can store items of interest; and the ability to "Look Inside" a book and view selected pages.

Overstock.com

www.overstock.com

Overstock.com, as hinted by its name, is an online close-out retailer, an "outlet mall" with an emphasis on discounts. Browse categories easily using the fly-out Departments menu or use the search box. (Look for the "Top Rated" and "Clearance" choices in the subcategories menus.) On search results pages, you can narrow your search by category, price, and brand, and the Community section includes user blogs, reviews, forums, and guides.

PRICE COMPARISON SITES

Basically any time you look at the same product from two different suppliers, you are doing a price comparison. In that sense, most of the sites discussed in this chapter are price comparison sites. The following sites discussed, however, put emphasis on the comparison aspect. Those that emphasize consumers' own reviews and opinions are grouped together as a separate subcategory. This division is somewhat arbitrary and reflects more a matter of emphasis of the site than a definitive distinction.

The sites that follow cover the broad range of shopping. Although the interfaces are all different, you will notice a number of commonalties. For most, expect to find the obvious product information (name of the product, make, model, a brief description, and price); name of the merchant; product and merchant ratings and reviews; links to compare prices for the same product from multiple merchants; links to do side-by-side comparisons for items that you select from the results page; and links on results pages that allow you to further narrow your selection by brand, store, price range, category, etc. Most have a directory that allows you to browse by category, and all have a search function. (Yahoo! Shopping is discussed in more detail here since its features epitomize quite well the kind of experience that these sites, overall, provide.) There are also sites on the web that do such comparisons for particular types of products or services, such as computers or travel. (For links to sites that compare travel options, see www.extreme searcher.com/travel.)

For a good list of price comparison sites, check out the Compare Prices section of ShoppingSpot.com discussed at the beginning of this chapter.

Yahoo! Shopping

shopping.yahoo.com

Yahoo! Shopping contains millions of products and provides a wide range of shopping features. Whether you get to a results page by browsing or searching, on that page, for most products you will see the price range, a button to compare prices, and a link to the page for that single product. On the left of the page will be several options to narrow results by price range, brand, stores, and so on and often several narrowing options that relate to the specific kind of product (for coffeemakers, for example, functions, color, and capacity).

For each product listed, you will see a link to the product's page, a picture, a brief description, and sometimes a star rating and link to reviews. On results pages, you will also see a link to Show Grid View that shows the products in a grid rather than a list (Figure 9.2). For each item, there will also be either a Compare Prices button or a link that takes you to the supplier's (e.g., Amazon) own page for that product. In case you are just interested in a few of the items shown on the results page, there is a checkbox for each item that allows you to compare just selected items. The Compare Prices button directs you to a page that will show details and prices for the stores carrying the product.

From results pages, if you click on the name of one of the products, you are (usually) taken to either the Yahoo! Shopping page for that product or to the supplier's page for the product. The Yahoo! product page will typically give you extensive information about the specific product, including description, specification, user reviews, list of suppliers and their prices, and more. In Yahoo! Shopping and most other shopping comparison sites, a

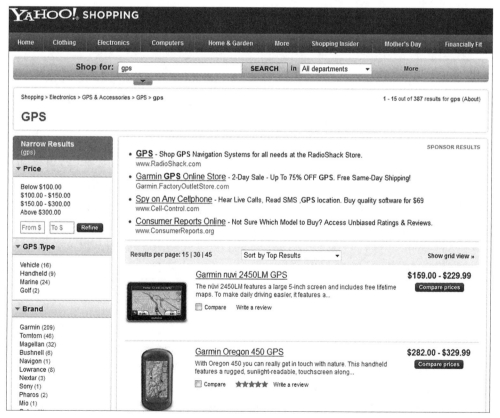

Figure 9.2 Yahoo! Shopping product page

wide range of navigation and viewing options are presented. Spending a bit of time exploring the options that work best for you will, in the end make your shopping experience more efficient and easier.

mySimon
www.mysimon.com

mySimon, one of the earliest comparison shopping sites, gathers price and product information from thousands of merchants. On the homepage and results pages, take advantage of the Consumer Reports and Shopping Guides sections for advice on a range of popular products. To get to what mySimon can tell you about specific products, use the category tabs or the search box near the top of the page. When searching, use the categories menu on results pages to narrow to a specific category. The Several Offers button for a product will give you a list that provides a price comparison chart for the various stores that sell that item, and on that page, you can sort results by best matches, total price, store name, or store rating.

PriceGrabber
www.pricegrabber.com

PriceGrabber has a very clean, easily navigable interface, with an emphasis on its search function and its 26 product categories, each of which is further divided into additional levels of categories. (Use the Shop by Department menu next to the search box to see categories.) Product pages are likewise easy to use, but rich in functionality (Figure 9.3). On the left is a panel where you can narrow your results by brand, price range, and so on often with a wide range of additional criteria depending on the product (for laptops, there are 20 criteria). Whether you get there by searching or browsing, you can sort results lists by price, popularity, or "Power Score" rating. With the Compare Now button, for an individual product, you can see prices and other comparisons for the stores that sell the product. See the Buying Guides links on the tops of pages for a rather extensive list of guides for categories of products.

Shopping.com
www.shopping.com

Shopping.com, owned by eBay, has websites in the U.S., the U.K., Australia, France, and Germany. Get to a product listing either by browsing the categories on the homepage or by using the search box. Once on a product page, you will find options to further narrow your results by category, price range, brand, keyword, and often a wide range of

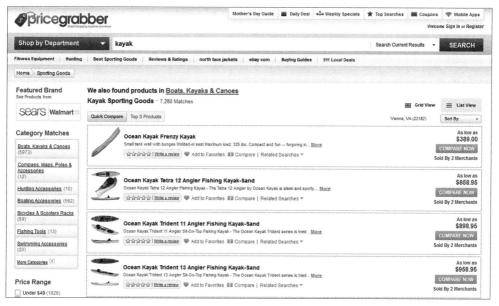

Figure 9.3 PriceGrabber product page

other product-specific criteria. As with both Yahoo! Shopping and PriceGrabber.com, you will find buttons to get charts comparing selected products from the list, or prices for a particular product from different merchants.

Shopzilla

www.shopzilla.com

Shopzilla provides information on more than 100 million products from tens of thousands of stores. Either Shopzilla's search box or its categories will lead you to a product page where you can narrow your search by price range, brand, and other criteria. Results can be sorted by popularity, or price (high–low or low–high). On the pages for individual products, you can sort by price, store, or store rating.

Become.com

www.become.com

Become.com has features similar to most comparison sites (browsing, searching, etc.) but also has some that are unique and/or particularly useful. Try the Research option next to the search box to find articles, news, reviews, product guides, and more relating to your product that Become.com has identified by crawling the web. Buttons on the Research results pages will filter those results by research category (product reviews, buying guides, etc.).

Google Shopping

www.google.com/products

Google Product Search (formerly Froogle, a much more clever name) includes content that 1) is the result of Google's crawling of the web to identify product sites, or 2) was submitted by merchants (but Google accepts no payment for this). On the homepage, you will mainly find a search box and links to currently featured deals. Perform a search for a product and Google will display results by most popular, plus an additional section of results, below that, showing what "people also considered." Interestingly, Google does not provide a browsable directory of product categories, but on results pages, you will find a Related Categories section.

On results pages, as with results pages for most shopping comparison sites, there will be options shown on the left for narrowing your results by price, brand, and other criteria. Click on any of the items shown on the results list and Google will deliver a page for that particular product, with a description, link to reviews, and a table listing sellers, seller ratings, condition, tax and shipping fees, total price, and base price. Scroll down and you will find a Google map of nearby stores for the sellers listed, other products from the same maker, similar products from other makers, and reviews.

The advanced search page allows you to search by simple Boolean and price range, and limit your search to product name or description. On the search results pages, you can choose to view results in a list or grid, and sort results by relevance, price, product rating, or seller rating. Though some searches will take you to a results list that will individually show products from each separate store, most searches will take you to a listing by product (as available from multiple stores). There, beside each result, look for a Compare Prices button and links to reviews that Google has found by crawling the web. Also on the search results page, you can add items to your Shopping List. Clicking either on the product name or the Compare Prices button will take you to the page for the specific product, where you will see pricing details from the various stores where the product is available and links or tabs for details on seller ratings, reviews, technical specifications, and related items.

Items cannot be purchased through Google, but for some sellers, you can take advantage of Google Checkout for easy payment.

Auctions

Auction sites on the web have a lot in common with the shopping malls and price comparison sites, but differ, of course, in the "bidding" approach. The best-known auction site is eBay, though there are a number of others and some shopping sites, such as Overstock.com, that have an auctions option.

eBay

www.ebay.com

Although many people think of eBay as an auction site where almost anything but body parts are auctioned off, it is also a shopping mall where you can buy things outright, avoiding either the fun or effort (however you see it) of having to go through the auction process. With the Buy It Now option, you can do just that. eBay has one of the most sophisticated sets of search features of any of the shopping sites. Look for the Advanced Search links on the main page and other pages. eBay's advanced search allows you to search by simple Boolean ("All words, any order," "Any words, any order," "Exact words, exact order," "Exact words, any order") and by category, title and description words, price range, buying formats (Auction, Buy It Now, Classifieds), location, seller, etc.

On search results or browsing pages (Figure 9.4), you will find a section that contains links to categories that match your search terms and a number of narrowing criteria such as price and condition, as well as criteria that relate particularly to the auction side of eBay, such as location of the seller. Also on the results pages, you will find suggested related searches and options to sort your results by auction times (Newly Listed, Ending Soonest, etc.), price, and distance. Click on the name of an item to find full details about the item, the seller, and the auction status. If you are new to auctions, the Customer Support section is an excellent place to find out how it all works.

Classifieds

Most of the shopping sites just discussed are designed to lead to a transaction between a purchaser and a merchant. eBay, in addition to connecting a potential purchaser with "stores," makes it possible for anyone to become a "store" and sell items. What about people who only have one or two things to sell or who don't want to sell things on an ongoing basis? Just as with newspapers, this is where "classifieds" come in. Classifieds make it possible for individuals to sell to individuals and to buy and sell "locally." craigslist is by far the best-known site for classifieds.

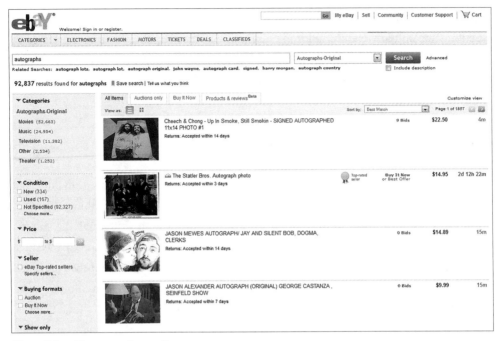

Figure 9.4 eBay search results page

craigslist

www.craigslist.org

craigslist has a very plain-looking homepage, but one that indeed gets the job done—providing easy-to-use and primarily free classified listings for localities around the world. Except for job postings, some apartment rental postings, and therapeutic services, all ads are posted for free. The main page is arranged geographically (county/continent, state, city), and after choosing a locality, you can browse through or search the classified sections. On most pages, you will find a search box with an attached menu by which you can narrow your search to "For Sale," Community, Events, Gigs, Housing, Jobs, Personals, Resumes, or Services and any of about 100 categories for type of things being sold. Whether searching or browsing, the listings to which you are led are shown most-recent-first order. craigslist makes both buying and selling a really easy experience, attested to by the fact that it serves up more than 30 billion page views a month.

PRODUCT AND MERCHANT EVALUATIONS

Some of the sites just discussed may build both product and merchant reviews into their results. Other sites on the internet specialize in reviews and evaluations, including consumer opinion sites and merchant rating sites. Among these are Angie's List, Bizrate, Epinions, Consumer Reports, and ConsumerSearch.

In addition to using these sites, you can use web search engines effectively to find reviews and evaluations by simply doing a search on the name of the product (e.g., *Nikon D60*) or the type of product (e.g., *digital cameras*), in combination with the term *evaluations* or *reviews*:

> *"digital cameras" (reviews OR evaluations)*

Going one step further, especially if you are tracking your own or competitors' products, you can take advantage of the frequent comments regarding products that appear in newsgroups. Look at Google Groups (groups.google.com), Yahoo! Groups (groups.yahoo.com), and other group sites discussed in Chapter 5.

Angie's List

www.angieslist.com

Unlike the vast majority of sites covered in this book, Angie's List is not free, but it is rather inexpensive with a monthly fee that's fairly close to the cost of a gallon of milk (plus a start-up fee). With Angie's List, you get reviews for local businesses and services. Expect the quality of reviews to be higher than on many sites since reviews cannot be anonymous and providers are prevented from posting reviews about themselves. In addition, though, providers *can* respond to reports, thereby enabling readers to get a fuller picture. Angie's List also provides live call center support and a Complaint Resolution Team.

Bizrate

www.bizrate.com

Bizrate was created with the purpose of providing customers' ratings of online store experience. It rather quickly evolved into a combination of that and a product search-and-comparison site. Bizrate's product search features are very similar to those you will have found in the previously discussed product search sites. You can browse using 18 main categories or do a search. Resulting pages that list matching products have narrowing features on the left side of pages. For products available from more than one store, there will be a Compare Prices button that yields a page showing comparative prices.

The greatest strength of this site is probably under the "smileys" you will see next to store names. Click there to get to consumer reviews for that store. You will find comments, plus for each comment, a rating for Overall, Would Shop Here Again, On Time Delivery, and Customer Support. The page will show a summary of those, plus detailed ratings for 11 other criteria.

Epinions

www.epinions.com

On the surface, Epinions looks much like other shopping sites, with a search box and browsable categories that include millions of products and services. What differs is that the emphasis in Epinions is on the reviews. For each product, you will find links to further details about the product and to reviews written by Epinions users. To provide reliable reviews, even the reviewers can be reviewed through Epinions' "Web of Trust" system. For various products, you will also find advanced search options, buyer's guides, and store ratings.

Consumer Reports

www.consumerreports.org

Consumer Reports, the publisher of the well-known product review journal, has its evaluations available online but only to paid subscribers. There are some parts, such as buying guides, that you can read (or view videos) without a subscription.

ConsumerSearch

www.consumersearch.com

ConsumerSearch takes a different approach to providing reviews by having its editors "scour the Internet and print publications for comparative reviews and other information sources relevant to the topic." The reviews on the site are based on those sources and a set of criteria that ConsumerSearch developed.

BUYING SAFELY

Although many internet users quickly began to take advantage of the benefits of online purchasing, some users are still quite shy about giving up their credit card numbers to a machine. Having a healthy skepticism is indeed a reasonable approach. Knowing where caution ends and paranoia begins is the problem. In general, following a few basic rules should keep the online purchaser fairly safe. There are few guarantees, but there are also few guarantees that the waiter to whom you gave your credit card in the restaurant did not do something illegal with it. If the following precautions are kept in mind, online purchasers should feel reasonably secure:

1. Consider who the seller is. If it is a well-known company, there is some security in that. (Yes, we *do* remember Enron.) If you don't recognize the seller, do you know the site? Sites such as Amazon and Barnes & Noble are respected and want to protect their reputations. If you are buying through an intermediary such as eBay, it likewise has a reputation to protect and builds in some protections, such as providing access to feedback about sellers from other customers. On some merchant sites, you will see symbols displayed that indicate the merchant is registered with organizations that are in the business of assuring that member merchants meet high standards. The best known of these organizations is BBBOnline (from the Better Business Bureau, www.bbbonline.org). On its site, you can search to see if a company is a member. For various legitimate reasons, even large and reputable sites may not necessarily participate in programs such as these, so the lack of a seal of approval alone should certainly not keep you from buying.

2. When you get to the point of putting in payment information, check to see that the site is secure. Look for the closed padlock icon on the status bar at the bottom of your browser, or the *https:* (instead of *http:*) at the beginning of the URL in the address bar of the browser.

3. As with traditional purchases, read the fine print. Look for information on the payment methods, terms, and return policy. Also look around for seller contact points, such as phone number and address.

4. Print and keep a copy of the purchase confirmation message you receive when you complete the purchase.

5. When possible, pay by credit card to be able to take advantage of the protections the card issuer provides regarding unauthorized billings. Some sites, such as eBay, will also provide services that help protect your payments. These services charge the seller a fee and may cause a slight delay but hold the money until the product is received. Payment services such as PayPal also build in some safeguards.

If you encounter problems with an online purchase, you may want to consult the Online Shopping & E-Payments page of the Federal Trade Commission's site (www.ftc.gov/bcp/menus/consumer/tech/online.shtm). For cross-border complaints, consult eConsumer.gov (www.econsumer.gov).

CHAPTER 10

YOUR OWN PLACE ON THE WEB: PARTICIPATING AND PUBLISHING

The internet is, obviously, a two-way street. So far, this book has primarily discussed using the internet to *find* information. The other direction is providing information to be found. Creating and participating in groups (discussion groups, etc.), which were discussed in Chapter 5, are ways of contributing to the content on the internet, but there are numerous other ways of participating, providing information to others, and having your own presence on the web—something that hundreds of millions of web users are already doing. Achieving a presence on the web can be as simple as sending a Twitter message or as intensive as maintaining a full-fledged website with many pages and a broad range of features.

Indeed, the major change in the nature of the web in the last several years is the phenomenon that is often referred to as Web 2.0. The term refers not to an actual "version" of the web but to the fact that by the middle of the first decade of the 21st century, the web had changed from being primarily a place to go to find information to being a place that was much more personalized and interactive, with collaboration, sharing, desktop-type programs, and social networking. Chances are that, perhaps not even realizing it, most readers of this book are themselves already a part of the Web 2.0 phenomenon.

A "PLACE" ON THE WEB

There are numerous ways to be a part of this, to make a place for yourself on the web, ways that provide varying levels of simplicity, exposure, and impact. One way already mentioned in Chapter 5 is participation in groups and forums, but there are a lot more ways. These include "social networking" at a general level and such things as collaborative web-based software, personal networking sites, "sharing" sites, microblogs, blogs, podcasts, and full-fledged websites. As with the rest of this book, the sites that follow are just a sampling, but they are leading sites in their category and/or are representative of their type.

WEB-BASED SOFTWARE

"The web as platform," meaning making use of software that resides on the web rather than on your own computer, is often cited as one of the manifestations of the new web. Web-based applications provide an easy way to be a "producer" of web-based content as well as a user. Like many other things that are part of recent trends, web-based software is not a new concept. Many people have been using web-based email programs such as Yahoo! Mail and Hotmail for well over a decade. Some newer examples, though, not only reside on the web but by doing so, they provide a very useful means of sharing and collaboration. Among the best examples of these are Google Drive and PBworks, and the sites in the later section here on "sharing" can also be considered web-based software.

Google Drive

drive.google.com

Google Drive is a combination of word processor, spreadsheet, presentations program (very similar to PowerPoint), drawing tool, and HTML forms processor. With it, you can create, import, export, work with, and share these kinds of documents online. It is the sharing and collaborative aspect that is most powerful. For example, a number of people can be working with the same report at the same time and see changes made by others almost instantaneously. You can allow the world at large to see it or only those to whom you have given permission. Likewise, you can choose for an individual to see it but not be able to edit it. Documents can be imported from or saved in a variety of formats, making them compatible with a variety of software (e.g., a word processing document can be downloaded in Word, HTML, RTF, text, Open Office, or PDF, and spreadsheet documents can be saved in Excel format and make use of documents that were created in Excel).

PBworks

www.pbworks.com

PBworks allows anyone, without programming experience, to set up either a private or public wiki, for free. (In case you've forgotten, a wiki is a site created and maintained as a collaborative project of internet users that allows fast and easy input and online editing by users. To see an example, look at Wikipedia.) PBworks, whose name derives from its slogan that it is as easy to make as a peanut butter sandwich, can be used for just about any situation where multiple people need to have collaborative access to a document or documents. As with Google Drive, reading, writing, and editing permissions can be selective. Like in many other situations, there is both a free version of PBwiki and a more-robust version available for a fee.

SOCIAL NETWORKING SITES

Social networking sites are one of the easiest ways to make yourself known on the web, to allow people to find you and connect with you, and to keep in touch with others in your "network." The more "social" sites such as Facebook and Myspace have expanded rapidly and now include a much broader demographic. They include not just people, but organizations, causes, etc. Professionally oriented networking sites, such as LinkedIn, allow for similar connections but with a professional, workplace slant.

Facebook

www.facebook.com

Facebook started in 2004 as a social networking site with its membership limited to those associated with particular colleges and universities. But once it opened up its membership to anyone, the site took off and quickly began to overtake the then-current leader, Myspace. By 2009, Facebook had more than 300 million users. It rather quickly surpassed Myspace in terms of popularity and, by 2012, was already well on its way to the 1 billion user mark. Facebook presents a user-friendly interface that very effectively accomplishes what social networking is all about: sharing and gathering information (and photos, and music, and apps and games, and more) with friends. Since the early days of the web, individuals have had the desire and need for personal webpages but frequently found "traditional" website approaches cumbersome to establish and maintain. Facebook and other social networking sites make it easy.

Myspace

www.myspace.com

Myspace, one of the first very successful social networking sites, was—in the beginning at least—primarily populated with teens, 20-somethings, bands, and celebrities (or, more likely, their publicists). It introduced a format that allowed easy networking, but factors such as a growing prevalence of spam presented challenges that put it at a competitive disadvantage.

LinkedIn

www.linkedin.com

LinkedIn provides networking with an emphasis on business connections. Content is primarily business-oriented (with members' profiles often resembling resumes), and communications and network connections usually have a business purpose. LinkedIn, like the other social networking sites, can also serve as a research tool. If your research involves identifying individuals and finding more about them, LinkedIn is a good resource, since its pages contain useful information and also have a search function. LinkedIn particularly has become a site of interest to researchers who are doing company intelligence, since people often post information that provides clues as to what their companies are up to.

SHARING SITES

Sharing tends to be a very human trait, and the internet provides ample opportunities and platforms where things can be shared. There are a variety of sites where such sharing is the essence of the site, including sites for sharing photos, videos, slideshows, bookmarks, news, opinions, and much more. As with the social networking sites, because of the kind of content on these sharing sites, they are also of interest for searching purposes. Among the most popular sites are those that enable sharing of photos and videos. YouTube, the best-known video sharing site, was discussed in Chapter 7. Two of the best-known image sharing sites, Flickr and Picasa Web Albums, and Delicious, a site for sharing bookmarks, are discussed in this section.

Flickr
www.flickr.com

Flickr was discussed in Chapter 7, primarily in terms of its usefulness as a search engine for images. Its initial intent, however, is a photo sharing site where users can share with family and friends the photos (and videos) they have taken. On Flickr, images can be edited, tagged, organized, stored, and viewed as groups and as a slideshow. A photo, a group of photos, or all of your photos can be shared with everyone, or you can choose to restrict access to friends or family. As well as tagging your pictures with words and phrases, you can geo-tag photos and access them by location from a map. You can even get statistics as to which photos are being viewed and where the people viewing them are coming from. Flickr allows you to upload up to 3 MB of photos and two videos per month for free, but for a quarterly or annual fee, you can have unlimited storage. The next time you are planning a trip, check out photos of the place that other people have shared through Flickr.

Picasa Web Albums
www.picasaweb.google.com

Picasa is a free downloadable photo editing and organizing program from Google that provides a site on the web where you can store and share your photos. The Picasa program is nicely integrated with the online Picasa Web Albums (also discussed in Chapter 7), enabling a large number of images to be uploaded at once. Images you have stored can be arranged and viewed by album or in a slideshow, and you can tag them, email them, order prints, and do lots more. If you sync your Picasa program with Picasa Web Albums, most changes you make locally (on Picasa) will be reflected in Picasa Web Albums. Your Picasa Web Albums are also closely integrated with Google+, and if you are signed up for Google+, photos that you upload to Picasa Web Albums that you make public will also appear as photos on your Google+ pages.

You can upload as many images as you wish if you use the uploaded image size recommended by Picasa, and you can designate their visibility as "Only You," "Your Circles," "Extended Circles," "Limited, anyone with the link," or "Public." As well as adding regular tags (captions), you can geo-tag the images and place them on a map.

Delicious
www.delicious.com

Delicious is a social bookmarking site on which you can store your bookmarks, share them with others (if you wish), and see other's bookmarks (if they wish). Keep Delicious in mind because it allows you to 1) have access to your bookmarks from any internet-connected computer anywhere, 2) add bookmarks regardless of where you are, 3) easily organize your bookmarks by the tags you apply to them, 4) search for bookmarks by tags you assign or for bookmarks from others who have used that tag; and 5) see bookmarks of people who have similar interests. You can also see those users who have linked to one of your saved sites and what other sites those users have bookmarked. One of the best ways to get a feel for the possibilities that Delicious offers is to do a search on a term of interest, and then from that results list, explore the tags associated with the sites and the users who have bookmarked the sites (links to both the user names and the tags are shown next to each bookmark on your search results list). Sign up and practice adding some sites to your own list.

MICROBLOGS

Working our way generally from the simpler to the more complicated tools, we should talk about microblogs before we talk about blogs (weblogs). Blogs, as you will recall, are frequently updated pages that provide commentary, news, etc.—usually, though not always, from individuals. Microblogs are simpler, consisting just of very brief messages, updating "followers" with news, comments, etc. from the microblogger. They can actually be thought of as a hybrid of blog, email, mailing list, and newsfeed—but very simple and very short. Though there are a number of sites that provide a microblogging capability (including Facebook and Myspace), the site that made microblogging famous is Twitter.

Twitter

www.twitter.com

Twitter, one of those websites whose name we suddenly began seeing numerous times every day, provides a quick and easy way to send very short messages to everyone who has chosen to "follow" you. It is a way of staying connected and letting family, friends, and colleagues know where you are and what you are up to, but it is also a way to send short messages to a TV commentator, to share ideas with colleagues, and to ask for and get advice.

Posts (Twitter updates) are called tweets and are limited to 140 characters (including spaces). When you post them, they appear on your page of the Twitter site, but more importantly, they are sent to followers (people who have signed up to receive your tweets automatically on their Twitter pages, or for that matter, on their mobile devices). Tweets can be searched using the search box on Twitter pages. On search results pages, click the gear icon next to the search box to get to the advanced search page, where you can search for tweets by words, language, people, places, and attitudes (positive or negative or those containing a question).

BLOGS

If you have something you wish to say and/or information that you feel should be shared not just with friends and Twitter followers, there is really no easier way to make a place for yourself on the web than to get yourself a blog. Blogging has found much favor and publicity over the last decade and getting started requires little effort. Discussed earlier in Chapter 8 from the news content perspective, blogs provide an easy means to gather and distribute news, commentary, advice, and so forth. The main intent of blogs is to provide a place for short and frequently updated postings. Although blogs may lack the fancier graphics and other capabilities of a website, their ease of use has been a major factor in their popularity.

Software and Sites for Creating Blogs

There are a number of sites and software programs (blogging tools) that allow you to create blogs, some that you can use through your browser, and some that you download and install on your server. Those that allow you to do your blogging online, through your browser, typically will also host your blog on their sites. The following are some of the more well-known places where you can go to create a blog.

Blogger

www.blogger.com

Blogger is a free blogging tool and hosting service. It is one of the best known and is both simple to use and powerful. On the Blogger site, you can create your blog, and Blogger will host the site for you on its hosting site, blogspot.com. Indeed, in the five minutes or less that Blogger advertises, you really can get your blog created and up on the web. You can choose from several templates for your page or, with some HTML skills, you can modify one as you wish. Posts can be made from the Blogger site (using a WYSIWYG interface), by email, or from your mobile device (Figure 10.1). Among the other features that Blogger provides, you can moderate and otherwise control visitor comments, block spam robots, post photos from your computer or your camera phone, display webcam views, post video, share posts to your Google+ page, and easily create a newsfeed.

WordPress.com

www.wordpress.com

WordPress.com provides a free, quite full-featured, easy-to-use web-based interface for creating and hosting blogs, and you can get a blog set up in minutes. With the features WordPress.com offers, you can categorize posts, you can automatically set up RSS feeds for both your posts and for comments, you can create a site index and have multiple pages, you can import posts you have posted on another blog service, you can automatically get statistics (volume, referrers, and top posts, for both the blog and feeds), you can control spam with your own list of spam words and your own blacklist, and you can conduct polls. WordPress.com in general gives you quite good control both over how posts are displayed and over comments. Posting images, audio, and video is quite easy.

Blogs created on WordPress.com can be hosted elsewhere, as well as on the WordPress.com site, and if you wish, you can download the program to your own server. The basic WordPress.com service is free, but for advanced services such as extra storage and domain hosting, there is a fee. WordPress.com can get a beginner going quickly, easily, and free, yet it allows users to take advantage of features that should keep even experienced bloggers happy.

Figure 10.1   Page to compose a post on Blogger

Movable Type

www.movabletype.com

Movable Type, a pioneer in blogging software, is client software that you download to your own computer or server (rather than using online software such as Blogger). It is very full-featured, and because of that, it is the favorite of many professional bloggers, even though it is less easy to use than Blogger and some other programs. It is designed to allow management of many blogs from many people. There is a free downloadable version, but for a supported version, you must pay. Movable Type does not itself provide hosting of blogs. The installation of the program is best handled by someone with some technical expertise.

LiveJournal

www.livejournal.com

LiveJournal is a community-focused blogging tool. When you are signed up with LiveJournal, you can create a journal and you can join its Communities, which are interest-specific or region-specific. LiveJournal has two levels of free service and a paid version. By allowing ads, you get access to more features. The paid version gives you additional control over the style of your journal, more room for pictures, polling capabilities, and more.

PODCASTS

Podcasts, which were discussed in Chapter 8 from the perspective of finding them, are also a way for anyone to publish on the internet. For messages that are best conveyed aurally, for genres such as storytelling, or as an avenue for reaching a sight-impaired audience, podcasts present a very viable publishing option.

To create a podcast of your own, you need the following, some of which should be pretty obvious: 1) something to say, 2) a microphone, 3) a computer with an internet connection, 4) sound recording software, 5) an mp3 encoder to convert what you record into mp3 format, and 6) a place on the web to host your podcast. For hosting, a blog or other personal website can work fine. For more detail, visit the following site.

Podcasting Tools

www.podcasting-tools.com

Podcasting Tools contains all the information you need to know to get started podcasting: tutorials for getting started, directories of podcasting software and places where you can host podcasts online, and a variety of other resources.

CROWDSOURCING

As well as contributing information on the web as "an individual," people can also contribute as part of something bigger, indeed sometimes "for the greater good." Individuals can contribute ideas and data to jointly, and often on a very large scale, address or solve a problem in a context where thousands of heads are better than one. At a broad level, this activity is often referred to as *crowdsourcing*, a general term that can apply to activities taking place outside of the internet as well as on the internet. There are also narrower segments of this phenomenon, particularly what is referred to as "citizen science." An entire chapter here could have been devoted to crowdsourcing on the web, but space does not permit that, and it is indeed a topic that perhaps only a small portion of readers may find of interest. However, to help make all readers aware of the existence of, and potential for, this kind of activity, one example, eBird, will be given.

eBird

www.ebird.org

A prime example of citizen science, eBird is a project from the Cornell Lab of Ornithology and the National Audubon Society. Its goal is "to maximize the utility and accessibility of the vast numbers of bird observations made each year by recreational and professional bird watchers." In a single month in 2012 alone, more than 3 million observations across North America were contributed by participants. Even if you couldn't care less about birds and don't know the difference between a robin and a raven, go to this site and check out the Explore Data section. You will hopefully be impressed by the magnitude of data that can be gathered when enough people put their heads together.

YOUR OWN FULL-FLEDGED WEBSITE

Beyond the ways of achieving a web presence that were already discussed, for the full experience and the greatest level of exposure, versatility, variety, and communications power (plus self-esteem and social standing), you can set up an actual website of your own, with, as you wish, your own domain name, design, photos, links, images, audio, video, and much more.

As for why you would wish to do any of this, there are many reasons to consider publishing a website: You may wish to provide a fully "personal" space for yourself, or a space for an organization to which you belong, a course you teach, a "cause," your own business, etc. To varying degrees, social networking sites such as Facebook may also provide what you need for those situations. However, especially for your own business, anything less than a "real" website may not convey the level of seriousness that you might want to present.

Whatever your reasons, as you move into website publishing, keep two words in mind: *content* and *style*. It is a truism that on the web "Content is king." You must have useful content to make visitors to your place feel it was worth the trip and to make them come back. Have something to say! What you say may be as simple as family news, family photos, your resume, or a syllabus for a course. As for style, the term in this context has two aspects: personal style and presentation style. For the first, don't put yourself on the web unless you can do so with "style." You don't need to come across as suave, sophisticated, sexy, or debonair, but what you put on your website should reflect the best you have to offer.

The other aspect of style is your writing style and the design of your page. You want the look of your place to convey neatness, thoughtfulness, and organization. If you are going the blog route or are creating a website using a template, the style of the page will pretty much take care of itself. As for what you write, do it correctly. Poor grammar and other writing problems definitely communicate something, but not what you want. (Think about your own reaction when you encounter a page with multiple spelling errors.) Though it is written primarily for people building webpages, the following site can be useful for most people who want to have any form of effective web presence.

Web Style Guide

www.webstyleguide.com

Written for people who are creating websites, the well-known Web Style Guide presents, in an easy-to-read, nontechnical way, the basic principles of design that should be considered for any website. Even for those who are using templates, or who are just involved in some way in the management of a website, this time-tested guide is worthwhile and interesting reading. (Though the Web Style Guide website is great, the inexpensive, beautifully presented book version is slicker and perhaps more convenient to read. Sometimes "books are better.")

On "Personal" Web Places

We are all our own "company," even if we work for someone else. As Tom Peters said, "To be in business today, our most important job is to be head marketer for the brand called You" (www.fastcompany.com/magazine/10/brandyou.html). This is true not just for executives and aspiring executives, but very true for academics, artists, writers, entrepreneurs, and others. Having a personal place on the web, where you can send people or where people can find you, is both easy and (for many but not all people) important. If you choose to have a personal website, do it with style. Make sure it conveys the degree of professionalism you want it to convey. Then advertise it. Submit it to search engines. Put the URL in your automatic email signatures. Put it on your business cards.

WEBSITES

In addition to the reasons previously mentioned, having a website of your own is also useful for another reason. For those who are involved in contributing input to their organization's site or to someone else's site, having done your own website can provide a healthy perspective. It can, on one hand, take away a lot of the mystique (you will no longer be unnecessarily awed by some of the cute little things you see), and on the other hand, you will have a better appreciation for the more sophisticated things you see. Also, if your time and inclinations permit such, building your own site can be enjoyable and fulfilling.

What follows is not intended to teach you how to build a website, but rather to provide an overview of what is involved in order to help answer the questions: Can I do it (build my own website)? What is involved? What will it cost?

If you go for a website, you have a range of options and levels of sophistication. You can have, or not have, your own domain name; you can use templates or a webpage editor, or if you are (or want to be) in the techie category, you can build pages from scratch by writing HTML.

What's Needed

The main tools needed for building a website of your own are a purpose, time, software, skills, and a place to publish. Depending on what you want to produce, each of these components can either be minimal or extensive.

Purpose

The introductory paragraphs to this chapter mentioned some of the reasons for creating your own place on the web. Before you start with a website, though, it is advisable to give a fair amount of consideration to why you are doing it and what you want to accomplish. Though those things may seem very obvious, a focus on those two considerations is important for all website designers, from beginner to the most experienced. Your aims may change continually, but the more direction you have established to begin with, the less you may have to go back and change later. Write down your purpose. The main purpose of almost any page is "communication." What do you want to communicate and why?

Tied in closely to your statement of purpose will be an analysis of your intended audience. Whom are you addressing? What background are they likely to have in connection with your topic? What age level are you addressing? How skilled are they likely to be in using and navigating through webpages? What is their level of interest? If your site is for a course you are teaching, users have a high level of interest in that they may be required to use the site. If you are selling something, you need to design a page that will do a good job of attracting and keeping the readers' attention.

Time

Most hosting services (discussion coming up) provide templates that can present a very professional appearance and, if you already know what information you want to put on the site, the templates can allow you to have a website created and available for use in an hour or so. If you want to create your own layout, the time required to build and maintain a site goes up from there, depending upon how fancy you want to get, how much content you want to include, and how much maintenance the site will require (updating, etc.).

Software

If you are building a site using templates, you can get by with no software other than your browser. Templates provide what you need to make a basic but at the same time very attractive site, with room for lots of content and many pages. Beyond that, unless you decide to learn how to write HTML (HyperText Markup Language) code, you will need a webpage editing program such as Dreamweaver or KompoZer (there are many, many more). These are basically word-processor-like programs that convert what you enter, and the features you choose, into HTML code.

The cost of these programs ranges from free (e.g., KompoZer) to several hundred dollars. If you are using the editor for educational purposes, you may be able to find an educator's rate for some programs that is substantially less than the full price.

KompoZer provides the basics of what you need to build a webpage. Parts of the program can be a bit clunky, and it does not provide the more sophisticated features, such as image maps capability and integration of various web developer languages. It does, however, provide what most beginners need, and the fact that it is free is significant.

If you think you are going to want a more sophisticated site, have many pages on your site, and make it interactive, you may want to start with a sophisticated but still relatively easy-to-use program such as Dreamweaver (Figure 10.2).

Uploading your finished pages to a web server will require file transfer software. HTML editors usually build in this feature.

Graphics Software

It is likely that you will want some images on your site, and unlikely that you will want to put them on your page without making some modifications to the images, such as

Figure 10.2 Example of page built in Dreamweaver

cropping and some other easy changes that can improve the image. Programs such as Picasa provide some, maybe all, of the photo editing capabilities you may need. If you want to move up a step, consider Adobe PhotoShop Elements, a program that does the vast majority of things that the well-known and more expensive PhotoShop does.

Skills

To build a website using the minimalist approach (with templates) requires only the ability to follow step-by-step instructions. Beyond that, the ability to use (or learn how to use) an HTML editor will be necessary, and the ability to work with graphics will be useful. Gaining a basic understanding of CSS (Cascading Style Sheets) would be the next step beyond that. Be aware that the use of graphics software can be addictive—as well as using it for your website, you may find yourself up at 3 AM fixing the cracks and tears in that photo of your great-grandfather and adding feathered edges, drop-shadows, and other special effects to your pictures.

If you are new to using web editors and graphics software, there are a number of ways to learn. Your choice will probably depend upon your own learning style. Most programs you purchase will have a built-in tutorial, and if you commit an hour or so, you can be on your way. If you are willing to commit several hours, you will probably find yourself in quite good control of the program. There are also tutorials available on the web for most popular programs, and they sometimes provide a more simplified, yet effective, approach to page editing and graphics software. Do a web search for the name of your program and the word tutorial, and you will probably find several. YouTube is an excellent place to find video tutorials. (It has thousands of Dreamweaver-related tutorials.) There are also numerous books and classes available for the more popular programs.

The alternative to using an HTML editor is to learn to write all the HTML code yourself. Most people would probably consider this the hard way, but it can actually be fun. (Then again, some people also consider jumping into an icy river on New Year's Day fun.) For most, starting with a webpage editing program makes the most sense, but as you get more heavily into webpage building, you eventually will want to learn the basics of HTML because of the added control it can give you. (In the interest of full disclosure, the author admits to having had fun writing HTML code.) Knowing some HTML code can make the use of an editor such as Dreamweaver easier, quicker, and more flexible.

Domain Names

Though there are still some free website hosting services that also provide you with a web address for your site, you most likely will want to make use of a paid hosting service. If you do not already have a domain name, the hosting service will also help you get one.

For someone who has a company and/or needs to make the most professional impression, having one's own domain name is the way to go. The cost of purchasing (registering) a domain name is now very low and when you sign up for a web-hosting service, the service will usually bundle the process and cost of getting the name of your choice registered into the hosting.

Related to that last point is the issue of whether you would prefer to sign up through a domain registration service and then, separately, choose a host; or whether you want to just have your chosen hosting service do the registration process for you. The latter is easier, but if you decide later to switch hosts, some extra steps will be involved.

Even if you aren't ready to build a site, you may want to get a domain name for your own name (*yourname.com*) or reserve a name for the company you dream of having. (This is called "domain parking" and is a way of protecting some of your "intellectual property.") Some domain name registration services will not only register and "park" your name for you, but they will throw in an email service so you can use your domain name for your email even if you do not yet have a website. These services can be very inexpensive (less than $15 per year). Regarding the email service, as long as you keep your name registered, your address will always be there. If you change jobs, you will still have your personal email address, and it also provides that backup email address you can use when you don't want to use (or shouldn't be using) your employer's email system. (For that purpose, you can, of course, just use a free email service such as Yahoo! Mail or Gmail, but an address from a free webmail provider does not convey the same "importance" as an address from your own domain name.) The following is one example of a registration service that specializes in providing these added services. (For an excellent book that addresses what's involved in getting and implementing a domain name, see *I've Got a Domain Name—Now What???* by Jean Bedord, HappyAbout.info, Silicon Valley, CA, 2008.)

Dotster
www.dotster.com

Dotster provides registration services for more than 50 top-level domains, including the usual general domains (.com, .net, etc.), plus several country domains such as .us, .uk, and .de. In addition to domain registration, Dotster includes, among other services, design templates, email services, and a number of other features that are useful for expanding the sophistication of a website.

Publishing Your Website Using a Web-Hosting Service

Once you have decided that you want to have a website of your own with your own domain name, you will need to choose a web-hosting company (service) where your webpages will reside.

Though there are some "free" hosting sites still functioning, most have gone away and, if you are serious about a website, you will want to avail yourself of a paid web-hosting service. (Google is still in the free website game with Google Sites, sites.google.com, which offers extensive storage and easy incorporation of other Google services such as the Google Calendar, Google Drive, and more. With Google Sites, you cannot, however, upload pages created elsewhere.)

Web-hosting companies can easily be located through their ads in computer magazines, a yellow pages directory, or a web search. There are numerous directories specifically of web-hosting services. To locate these directories, you can use the following Open Directory (www.dmoz.org) category:

Computers > Internet > Web Design and Development > Hosting > Directories

Web-host services will host your site for as little as $5 per month or even less for basic service and will also guide you through the process of getting your own domain name. One of the big advantages of these services is that they handle most of the paperwork of the domain name registration. Compare their ads, call their toll-free numbers, and talk to two or three of them, partly to get a feel for their degree of customer service orientation.

As you explore these, you will get a feel for the various levels of service provided and be able to decide which you need. (If, for example, you aren't selling a product, it is unlikely that you will need a Shopping Cart service as part of your hosting contract.) Be sure to check the reviews of web-hosting services. The following site will help.

Upperhost

www.upperhost.com

Upperhost is an independent web-host reviewing service. It provides up-to-date benchmarking and reviews, done by webmasters, on a very wide range of web-hosting companies. You will also find user comments and a useful collection of articles on web hosting.

Putting Your Site on Your Organization's Server

If you are in an academic institution, there is a good chance that your institution will provide some free web space for you. For other organizations, there may be similar possibilities, depending on your purpose and the nature of the organization. Do not be surprised if you are presented with a list of criteria that must be met, with regard to both content and format. If you are a faculty member at a university, you may easily be assigned web space with minimal restrictions and permission to upload your pages when and as you like. At the K–12 level, there is a very good chance that there will be cooperation and enthusiasm for teachers or others to create school and classroom sites (or, at least, pages). In other situations, it may not be as easy, and there are situations where you will encounter institutional web administrators who impose requirements that make little sense. Fortunately, a larger proportion of those in charge of organizational sites are realistic and helpful.

Sites to Help You Build Your Websites

There are thousands of websites that provide help in building webpages, ranging from the tutorials already mentioned to sites that provide specific features you can place on your pages (such as graphics and JavaScript scripts) to sites that bring together a large collection of a variety of tools. The following representative site, Webmonkey, is one that the beginner may want to explore, particularly to get a feel for the kind of help that is out there.

Webmonkey
www.webmonkey.com

Webmonkey is especially strong on tutorials for a variety of things you might want to place on your page (Figure 10.3). Webmonkey's content is presented and arranged in such a way that you can, at your own speed, build up your webmaster skills one step at a time.

Though it wasn't emphasized in the discussion of reasons for creating blogs and websites, if you are the kind of person who is inclined to try out the publishing side of the web, an added benefit that will almost undoubtedly accrue is that you will have some fun—probably a lot of fun—doing it!

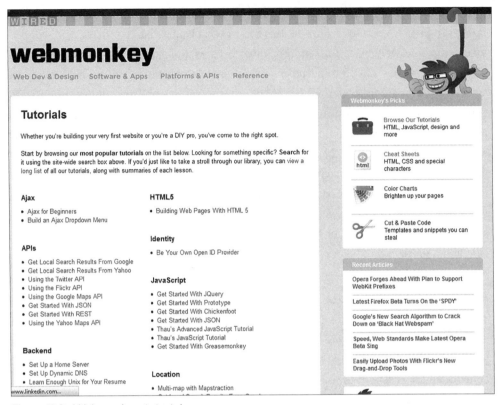

Figure 10.3 Webmonkey tutorials menu

CONCLUSION

It is hoped that the preceding chapters have provided some new and useful ideas, information, and sites, even for the very experienced internet user. My final bit of advice is: "Explore!" As you use the sites I've mentioned, or any site, take a few extra seconds to look around. Poke into the corners of a site, and if it looks very promising, "click everywhere."

—*Ran Hock*

GLOSSARY

The following words are defined in the context of the internet and are not necessarily intended to be applied generally.

Ajax. Asynchronous JavaScript And XML. A technique for creating interactive web applications. It increases the interactivity of a page by making it unnecessary to reload the entire page when only a portion of the page needs to be changed.

algorithm. A step-by-step procedure for solving a problem or achieving a task. In the context of search engines, this is the part of the service's program that performs a task, such as identifying which pages should be retrieved or ranking retrieved pages.

ALT attribute. Text associated with an image, in the HTML code of a page, that can be used to identify the content of the image or for other purposes. Standing for "alternate text," the ALT initially provided a description while waiting for the image to load, but it is now used more for other purposes, such as providing a description of the image that can be read by screen readers for sight-impaired users. In some browsers, you will see the ALT text pop up when you hold your cursor over an image.

AND. The Boolean operator (or connector) that specifies the "intersection" of sets. When used between words in a search engine query, it specifies that only those records are to be retrieved that contain both words (the words preceding and following the "AND"). For example, stomach AND growling would only retrieve records containing both of those words. For major search engines, you do not actually type AND since it is implied (automatically applied). (See **Boolean.**)

API. Application Program Interface. An interface that one program provides to allow requests for services or interchange of data from another program.

applet. A small Java program used on a webpage to perform certain display, computational, or other functions. The origin of the term refers to "small applications programs."

blog. Originally called weblogs, websites, or pages, most typically created by individuals that are updated frequently and usually provide commentary, news, links to news items elsewhere on the web, etc., usually on a specific topic.

bookmark. A feature in web browsers, analogous to bookmarks in a book, that remembers the location of a particular webpage and adds it to a list so a user can return to the page easily. Firefox and others refer to these as bookmarks, while Internet Explorer uses the term favorites.

Boolean. Mathematical system of notation created by 19th-century mathematician George Boole that symbolically represents relationships between sets (entities). For information retrieval, it uses AND, OR, and NOT (or their equivalents) to identify those records that meet the criteria of having both of two terms within the same record (AND), having either of two terms within the records (OR), or will eliminate records that contain a particular term (NOT).

breadcrumbs. A set of links found on some webpages and some search results that shows the current page's position in the hierarchy of the site. Clicking on one of the links will take you to that level of the site.

broadband. High-speed data transmission capability. In the home or office context, it usually refers to DSL (Digital Subscriber Line), cable, high-speed fiber-optic access, or T1 (or higher) internet access.

browser. Software that enables display of webpages by interpreting HTML code, translating it, and performing related tasks. The first widely used browser was Mosaic, which evolved into Netscape. Internet Explorer is the browser developed by Microsoft. Among the several others are Firefox, Opera, and Safari.

browsing. Examining the contents of a database or website by scanning lists or categories and subcategories. When a site provides this capability, it is referred to as having browsability.

case-sensitivity. The ability to recognize the difference between upper- and lowercase letters in text. In information retrieval, it means the difference between being able to recognize White as a name versus white as a color, or AIDS as the disease versus aids as something that provides assistance.

classification. Arrangement of items (such as websites) by subject area, often using a hierarchical scheme with several levels of categories and subcategories. In some cases, alphanumeric codes are used instead of words (for example, the Library of Congress or Dewey Decimal classifications).

concept-based retrieval. Retrieval based on finding records that contain words related to the concept searched for, not necessarily the specific word(s).

co-occurrence. Occurrence of specific other terms in the same records. Analyzing the frequency of co-occurrence is one technique used to find records that are similar to a selected record.

cookies. Small files of information generated by a web server and stored on the user's computer, used for personalization of sites, etc.

crawler. See **spiders.**

crowdsourcing. The process of a group of people working together, usually unpaid, to address and/or solve a problem.

Deep Web. Those pages that are not indexed by web search engines and therefore cannot be retrieved by means of a search on those engines. (Also referred to as the "Invisible Web" and the "Hidden Web.")

diacritical marks. Marks such as accents that are applied to a letter to indicate a different phonetic value.

directory (web). Collection of webpage records classified by subject to allow easy browsing of the collection.

domain name. The part of a URL (web address) that usually specifies the organization (computer) and type of organization where the webpage is located (e.g., in www.microsoft.com, "microsoft.com" is the domain name). Domain names always have at least two parts: The first part usually identifies the organization or specific machine; the second part (e.g., ".com") identifies the kind of organization. In some cases, there will be a two-letter code indicating the country of origin. All domain names have a corresponding numeric address, such as 207.158.227.228.

domain name server. A computer that converts the URL you enter into the numeric address of a domain and identifies the location of the requested computer.

field. A specific portion of a record or webpage, such as title, metatags, URL, etc.

file extension. In a file name, such as *letter.doc* or *house.gif*, the part of the file name that follows the period, usually indicating the type of file.

folksonomy. A process whereby users of a site, such as one that contains photos, can "tag" items with their own choice of descriptive terms. Theoretically, this is an aid to help other users locate items of interest.

FTP. File Transfer Protocol. Computer protocol (set of instructions) for uploading and downloading files.

gopher. A menu-based directory that allows access to files from a remote computer. Gophers were supplanted in the mid-1990s by web tools such as directories and search engines.

Hidden Web. See **Deep Web.**

homepage. The main page of a website. It also refers to the page designated by a user to automatically display when the user's browser is loaded.

HTML. HyperText Markup Language. The coding language used to create webpages. It tells a browser how to display a record, including specifications for fonts, colors, location of images, identification of hypertext links, etc.

internet. Worldwide network of networks based on the TCP/IP protocol.

Invisible Web. See **Deep Web.**

Java. A programming language designed for use on networks, particularly the internet, which allows programs to be downloaded and run on a variety of platforms. Java is incorporated into webpages with small applications programs called applets that provide features such as animation, calculators, games, etc.

JavaScript. A computer language used to write "scripts" for use in web browsers to allow creation of features such as scrolling marquees, navigation buttons that change appearance when you hold your mouse over them, etc.

mashup. In the web context, a product (web application, webpage, etc.) that combines data from two or more sources, such as map data provided by a source such as Google or Yahoo! and descriptive information provided by a user or other party.

metadata. Data about data. Words, phrases, etc. that describe the content and nature of information resources such as books, articles, webpages, images, videos, etc.

metasearch engines. Search services that search several individual search engines and then combine the results.

metasites. See **resource guides.**

metatags. The portion (field) of the HTML coding for a webpage that allows the person creating the page to enter text describing the content of the page (see **metadata**). The content of metatags is not shown on the page itself when the page is viewed in a browser window.

NEAR. A "proximity" connector that is used between two words in a search query to specify that a page should be retrieved only when those words are near each other in the page. (See **proximity**.)

nesting. The use of parentheses to specify the way terms in a Boolean expression should be grouped (i.e., the order of the operations). For example, *landmines (detection OR disarming)*.

newsgroup. An online discussion group. A group of people and the messages they communicate on a specific topic of interest. The term also refers more narrowly to such a discussion group on Usenet.

NOT. The Boolean operator (connector) that when used with a term eliminates the records containing that term. (See **Boolean**.)

OR. The Boolean operator (connector) that is used between two terms to retrieve all those records that contain either term. (See **Boolean**.)

podcasts. Downloadable audio recordings (broadcasts), analogous to blog postings. Podcasts are usually published using feeds (e.g., RSS) that can be downloaded via the web and transferred to an mp3 player (or to a CD) so the user can listen to the broadcast at his or her convenience.

portal. A site that serves as a gateway or starting point for a collection of web resources. Portals typically have a variety of tools (such as a search engine, directory, news, etc.) on a single page, so users can use that page as the start page for their browsers. Portals are often personalizable for content, layout, etc.

precision. In information retrieval, the degree to which a group of retrieved records actually match the searcher's needs. More technically, precision is the ratio of the number of retrieved relevant items to the total number of retrieved items (multiplied by 100 percent to express the ratio as a percentage). For example, if a query produced 10 records and six of them were judged relevant, the precision would be 60 percent. Precision is sometimes referred to as *relevance*.

proximity. The nearness of two terms. Some search engines provide proximity operators, such as NEAR, which allow a user to specify how close two terms must be for a record containing those terms to be retrieved.

QR Code. Quick Response Code. A bar code image that can be scanned by software installed on a mobile or other device and provides text, data, or URLs. Typically, one scans the code using a mobile device, which then opens the contained URL in the device's web browser.

ranking. The process for determining in what order records retrieved by a search engine should be displayed. Search engines use algorithms that evaluate records to assign a score that is meant to indicate the relative "relevance" of each record. The retrieved records can then be ranked and listed on the basis of those scores.

recall. In information retrieval, the degree to which a search has actually managed to find all the relevant records in the database. More technically, it is the ratio of the number of relevant records that were retrieved to the total number of relevant records in the database (multiplied by 100 percent to express the ratio as a percentage). For example, if a query retrieved four relevant records, but there were 10 relevant records in the database, the recall for that search would be 40 percent. Recall is usually difficult to measure since the number of relevant records in a database is often subjective and difficult to determine.

record. The unit of information in a database that contains items of related data. In an address book database, for example, each single record might be the collection of information about an individual person, such as name, address, ZIP code, phone number, etc. In the databases of web search engines, each record is the collection of information that describes a single webpage.

relevance. The degree to which a record matches the user's query (or the user's needs as expressed in a query). Search engines may assign relevance scores to each retrieved record, with the scores representing an estimate of the relevance of that record.

resource guides. Small, specialized web directories that provide a collection of related links on a specific topic. Also known as metasites, cyberguides, resource guides, specialized directories, webliographies, etc.

RSS. Acronym for Really Simple Syndication or Rich Site Summary. This is an HTML format by which news providers (and others sources such as blogs) can easily syndicate (distribute) their content over the internet.

screencast. A recording of a series of steps or events that take place on a computer screen, often used for providing instruction as to how to perform a certain task.

search engines. Programs that accept a user's query, search a database, and return to the user those records matching the query. The term is often used more broadly to refer not just to the information retrieval program itself, but also to the interface and associated features, programs, and services.

social networking sites. Websites designed to provide a place where individuals can connect with, interact with, and share things with ("network" with) other individuals with similar interests. For some such sites, groups (companies, organizations, etc.) may also participate,

social software. Though definitions vary depending upon the context, in relation to general usage of the internet, social software encompasses those web-based programs that allow people to easily interact with one another, network, share, and collaborate.

spiders. Programs that search the World Wide Web to identify new (or changed) pages for the purpose of adding those pages to a search service's (search engine's) database. Also known as *crawlers*.

start page. The page that loads automatically when you open your browser, sometimes called your homepage. You select what you want your start page to be by using the "Edit > Preferences" or "Tools > Internet Options" choices on your browser's menu.

stopwords. Small or frequently occurring words that an information retrieval program does not bother to index (ostensibly because the words are "insignificant," but more likely because the indexing of those words would take up too much storage space or require too much processing).

submitted URLs. URLs (internet addresses) that a person directly submits to a search engine service to have that address and its associated webpage added to the service's database.

syntax. The specific order of elements, notations, etc., by which instructions must be submitted to a computer system.

tagging. The process of attaching descriptive terms by users to pictures and other items found on the web. In its most typical application, tagging refers to the capability of any user of a site to add their own terms to help other users search for items on a particular topic.

TCP/IP. Transfer Control Protocol/Internet Protocol. The collection of data transfer protocols (set of instructions) used on the internet.

telnet. A program that lets a user log on to and access a remote computer using a text-based interface.

thesaurus. Listing of terms usually displaying the relationship between the terms, such as whether one term is narrower or broader than another. Thesauri are used in information retrieval to identify related terms to be searched.

thread. Within a group (newsgroup, discussion group, etc.), a series of messages on a specific topic, consisting of the original message, replies to that message, replies to those replies, etc.

timeout. The amount of time a system will work on a task or wait for results before either stopping the task or the waiting.

truncation. Feature in information retrieval systems that lets a user search with the stem or root of a word and automatically retrieve records with all terms that begin with that string of characters. Truncation is usually specified using a symbol such as an asterisk. For example, in some search engines, *town** would retrieve town, towns, township, etc.

URL. Uniform Resource Locator. The address by which a webpage can be located on the World Wide Web. URLs consist of several parts separated by periods and sometimes slashes. URLs may have various parts such as the domain name, subdomains, paths (directories), and file names.

Usenet. The world's largest system of internet discussion groups (newsgroups).

videotext. Systems, developed beginning in the 1970s, that allow for interactive delivery of text and images on television or computer screens. One of the first applications was the delivery of newspaper content.

web (World Wide Web, WWW). That portion of the internet that uses http (HyperText Transfer Protocol) and its variations to transmit files. The files involved are typically written in some version of HTML (HyperText Markup Language), thereby viewable using browser software, allowing a GUI (Graphical User Interface), incorporation of hypertext point-and-click navigation of text, and extensive incorporation of images and other types of media and formats.

Web 2.0. A term for a "second generation" of the web that provides a much greater focus on, and use of, desktop applications on the web, and collaboration and sharing by users.

Forerunners of this include wikis, blogs, RSS, and podcasts. Though there is no precise definition, some people also define Web 2.0 in terms of the programs used, including APIs (Application Programming Interfaces), social software, and Ajax.

wiki (or WikiWiki). A site created and maintained as a collaborative project of internet users that allows fast and easy input and online editing by multiple users.

WYSIWYG. What You See Is What You Get. Refers to interfaces, such as in word processors, where the way something looks as you input the content is basically what it will look like when it is displayed in its final form (e.g., on a printer, website, or blog).

URL List

Links to all of the sites covered in this book can be found at www.extreme searcher.com.

CHAPTER 1

On the Internet: A Brief History of the Internet, Part I
www.isoc.org/oti/articles/0597/leiner.html

Internet History and Growth
www.isoc.org/internet/history/2002_0918_Internet_History_and_Growth.ppt

Hobbes' Internet Timeline
www.zakon.org/robert/internet/timeline

Internet World Stats
www.internetworldstats.com/stats.htm

Virtual Chase: Information Quality
www.virtualchase.justia.com/other-resources/information-quality

Evaluating the Quality of WWW Resources
library.valpo.edu/user/evaluation.html

Wayback Machine—Internet Archive
www.archive.org

CompletePlanet
www.completeplanet.com

U.S. Copyright Office
www.copyright.gov

[U.K.] Intellectual Property Office—Copyright

www.ipo.gov.uk/copy

Canadian Intellectual Property Office—A Guide to Copyrights

www.cipo.ic.gc.ca/eic/site/cipointernet-internetopic.nsf/eng/h_wr02281.html

Copyright Website

www.benedict.com

Copyright and Fair Use in the UMUC Online or Face-to-Face Classroom

www.umuc.edu/library/libhow/copyright.cfm

Know Which Style to Use: Citation Styles

subjectguides.library.american.edu/citation

Citation Styles, Style Guides, and Avoiding Plagiarism: Citing Your Sources

www.lib.berkeley.edu/instruct/guides/citations.html

ResourceShelf by FreePint

www.resourceshelf.com

FreePint

www.freepint.com

ResearchBuzz

www.researchbuzz.me

Internet Scout Project

www.scout.wisc.edu

CHAPTER 2

Yahoo! Directory

dir.yahoo.com

Open Directory Project

www.dmoz.org

ipl^2: Information You Can Trust

www.ipl.org

The WWW Virtual Library

www.vlib.org

Search Engine Guide—Search Engines Directory

www.searchengineguide.com/searchengines.html

Refdesk

www.refdesk.com

INFOMINE

infomine.ucr.edu

Library of Congress Gateway to Library Catalogs

lcweb.loc.gov/z3950/gateway.html

Best of History Web Sites

www.besthistorysites.net

Virtual Religion Index

www.virtualreligion.net/vri

Selected Internet Resources in Science and Technology

www.loc.gov/rr/scitech/resources.html

healthfinder

www.healthfinder.gov

MedlinePlus

www.nlm.nih.gov/medlineplus

New York Times > Business > A Web Guide: Business Navigator

www.nytimes.com/ref/business/business-navigator.html

CEOExpress

www.ceoexpress.com

globalEDGE: Global Resource Directory

globaledge.msu.edu/Global-Resources

Resources for Economists on the Internet

www.rfe.org

Governments on the WWW

www.gksoft.com/govt

eRepublic.org

www.erepublic.org

USA.gov

www.usa.gov

Directgov: Website of the U.K. Government

www.direct.gov.uk

Government of Canada Official Website

www.canada.gc.ca

Political Resources on the Net

www.politicalresources.net

FindLaw

www.findlaw.com

GlobaLex

www.nyulawglobal.org/globalex

Kathy Schrock's Guide for Educators

school.discoveryeducation.com/schrockguide

Education World

www.educationworld.com

Education Atlas

www.educationatlas.com

Kidon Media-Link

www.kidon.com/media-link

Cyndi's List

www.cyndislist.com

Traveler's Web

www.extremesearcher.com/travel

Traffick: Frequently Asked Questions about Portals

www.traffick.com/article.asp?aID=9#what

CHAPTER 3

Open Directory

www.dmoz.org

CHAPTER 4

Google
www.google.com

Bing
www.bing.com

Yahoo!
www.yahoo.com

Ask.com
www.ask.com

Blekko
www.blekko.com

TouchGraph
www.touchgraph.com

Quintura
www.quintura.com

Zuula
www.zuula.com

TurboScout
www.turboscout.com

CHAPTER 5

Omgili
www.omgili.com

BoardReader
www.boardreader.com

Google Groups
groups.google.com

Yahoo! Groups
groups.yahoo.com

Delphi Forums

www.delphiforums.com

Yuku

www.yuku.com

Big Boards

www.big-boards.com

Topica Email List Directory

lists.topica.com

L-Soft CataList, the Official Catalog of LISTSERV Lists

www.lsoft.com/lists/listref.html

CHAPTER 6

Encyclopedia.com

www.encyclopedia.com

Encyclopaedia Britannica Online

www.britannica.com

Wikipedia

www.wikipedia.org

HowStuffWorks

www.howstuffworks.com

YourDictionary

www.yourdictionary.com

Merriam-Webster Online

www.merriam-webster.com

Collins

www.collinsdictionary.com/dictionary/english

Diccionarios.com

www.diccionarios.com

LEO Deutsch-Englisches Wörterbuch

dict.leo.org

Answers.com
www.answers.com

InfoPlease
www.infoplease.com

Infobel
www.infobel.com

Wayp International White and Yellow Pages
www.wayp.com

Yahoo! People Search
people.yahoo.com

AnyWho
www.anywho.com

WhitePages
www.whitepages.com and www.whitepages.ca

The Quotations Page
www.quotationspage.com

Bartleby.com
www.bartleby.com

Yahoo! Finance—Currency Converter
finance.yahoo.com/currency-converter

Weather Underground
www.wunderground.com

Perry-Castañeda Library Map Collection
www.lib.utexas.edu/maps

David Rumsey Historical Map Collection
www.davidrumsey.com

Global Gazetteer
www.fallingrain.com/world

World Gazetteer
www.world-gazetteer.com

U.S. Postal Service ZIP Code Lookup

www.usps.com/zip4

Yahoo! Finance

finance.yahoo.com

BEOnline—Statistics

www.loc.gov/rr/business/beonline/subjects.php?%20SubjectID=56

OFFSTATS

www.offstats.auckland.ac.nz

USA Statistics in Brief

www.census.gov/compendia/statab/brief.html

FedStats

www.fedstats.gov

Amazon

www.amazon.com

Barnes & Noble

www.barnesandnoble.com

Library of Congress Online Catalog

catalog.loc.gov

The British Library

blpc.bl.uk

Google Book Search

books.google.com

Gallica

gallica.bnf.fr

The Online Books Page

digital.library.upenn.edu/books

Project Gutenberg

www.gutenberg.org

Bartleby.com

www.bartleby.com

EuroDocs: Online Sources for European History
eudocs.lib.byu.edu

A Chronology of U.S. Historical Documents
www.law.ou.edu/hist

Governments on the WWW
www.gksoft.com/govt

CIA World Factbook
https://www.cia.gov/library/publications/the-world-factbook/index.html

U.K. Foreign & Commonwealth Office—Country Profiles
www.fco.gov.uk/en/travel-and-living-abroad/travel-advice-by-country/country-profile

USA.gov
www.usa.gov

U.S. Government Printing Office—FDsys
www.gpo.gov/fdsys

THOMAS: Legislative Information on the Internet
thomas.loc.gov

Open CRS
www.opencrs.com

Library of Congress—State and Local Governments
www.loc.gov/rr/news/stategov/stategov.html

Directgov—Website of the U.K. Government
www.direct.gov.uk

CorporateInformation
www.corporateinformation.com

Hoover's
www.hoovers.com

ThomasNet
www.thomasnet.com

American Society of Association Executives Gateway to Associations
www.asaecenter.org/Community/Directories/AssociationSearch.cfm

AMA DoctorFinder
extapps.ama-assn.org/doctorfinder

Lawyers.com
www.lawyers.com

Pipl
www.pipl.com

Facebook
www.facebook.com

LinkedIn
www.linkedin.com

Google+
plus.google.com

Twitter
www.twitter.com

ingentaconnect
www.ingentaconnect.com

HighBeam Research
www.highbeam.com

Google Scholar
scholar.google.com

Peterson's
www.petersons.com

College Board
www.collegeboard.com

Snopes
www.snopes.com

FactCheck.org
www.factcheck.org

PolitiFact
www.politifact.com

The Traveler's Web

www.extremesearcher.com/travel

Fodor's

www.fodors.com

Lonely Planet

www.lonelyplanet.com

Travelocity

www.travelocity.com

Expedia

www.expedia.com

Orbitz

www.orbitz.com

Internet Movie Database (IMDb)

www.imdb.com

CHAPTER 7

Digital Librarian: A Librarian's Choice of the Best of the Web—Images

www.digital-librarian.com/images.html

Image Collections Guides

www.lib.umn.edu/media/imageguide

Google's Image Search

images.google.com

Bing's Image Search

www.bing.com/images

Yahoo!'s Image Search

images.search.yahoo.com

Picsearch

www.picsearch.com

Corbis Images

www.corbis.com

Fotosearch
www.fotosearch.com

Creative Commons
www.creativecommons.org

Stock.XCHNG
www.sxc.hu

American Memory Project
memory.loc.gov

WebMuseum (Paris)
www.ibiblio.org/wm

Picasa Web Albums
picasaweb.google.com

Flickr
www.flickr.com

Free Graphics
www.freegraphics.com

Yahoo! Directory > Graphics > Clip Art
dir.yahoo.com/Computers_and_Internet/Graphics/Clip_Art

Digital Librarian: A Librarian's Choice of the Best of the Web—Audio
www.digital-librarian.com/audio.html

PAV—Play Audio Video
www.playaudiovideo.com

FindSounds
www.findsounds.com

Internet Archive—Audio Archive
www.archive.org

Radio-Locator
www.radio-locator.com

CBS Radio
www.cbsradio.com/streaming/index.html

Pandora

www.pandora.com

Spotify

www.spotify.com

Podcast Alley

www.podcastalley.com

Podcastdirectory.com

www.podcastdirectory.com

The History Channel: Video

www.historychannel.com/video

The MovieWavs Page

www.moviewavs.com

Apple: iPod & iTunes

www.apple.com/itunes

Digital Video Collections Guide

www.lib.umn.edu/libdata/page.phtml?page_id=4139

Google's Video Search

video.google.com

Yahoo!'s Video Search

video.yahoo.com

Bing's Video Search

www.bing.com/videos

YouTube

www.youtube.com

blinkx

www.blinkx.tv

ShadowTV

www.shadowtv.com

TVEyes

www.tveyes.com

CHAPTER 8

Kidon Media-Link

www.kidon.com/media-link

ABYZ News Links

www.abyznewslinks.com

NewsLink

www.newslink.org

NewsWealth

www.newswealth.com

News in Pictures

www.newsinpictures.com

The Cagle Post—Cartoons & Commentary

www.cagle.com

BBC

news.bbc.co.uk

CNN

www.cnn.com

MSNBC

www.msnbc.com

Reuters

www.reuters.com

Aljazeera.net

english.aljazeera.net

Today's Front Pages

www.newseum.org/todaysfrontpages

PressDisplay.com

www.pressdisplay.com

Radio-Locator (formerly the MIT List of Radio Stations on the Internet)

www.radio-locator.com

RadioStationWorld

www.radiostationworld.com

NPR

www.npr.org

Google News

news.google.com

Yahoo! News

news.yahoo.com

NewsNow

newsnow.co.uk

SiloBreaker

www.silobreaker.com

IceRocket

www.icerocket.com

Technorati

www.technorati.com

Google

www.google.com

Bloglines

www.bloglines.com

My Yahoo!

my.yahoo.com

Google Alerts

www.google.com/alerts

Yahoo! Alerts

alerts.yahoo.com

CHAPTER 9

ShoppingSpot.com

www.shoppingspot.com

ThomasNet

www.thomasnet.com

Kompass
www.kompass.com

Kellysearch
www.kellysearch.com

Amazon
www.amazon.com

Overstock.com
www.overstock.com

Yahoo! Shopping
shopping.yahoo.com

mySimon
www.mysimon.com

PriceGrabber
www.pricegrabber.com

Shopping.com
www.shopping.com

Shopzilla
www.shopzilla.com

Become.com
www.become.com

Google Shopping
www.google.com/products

eBay
www.ebay.com

craigslist
www.craigslist.org

Angie's List
www.angieslist.com

Bizrate
www.bizrate.com

Epinions

www.epinions.com

Consumer Reports

www.consumerreports.org

ConsumerSearch

www.consumersearch.com

Federal Trade Commission—Online Shopping & E-Payments

www.ftc.gov/bcp/menus/consumer/tech/online.shtm

eConsumer.gov

www.econsumer.gov

CHAPTER 10

Google Drive

drive.google.com

PBworks

www.pbworks.com

Facebook

www.facebook.com

Myspace

www.myspace.com

LinkedIn

www.linkedin.com

Flickr

www.flickr.com

Picasa Web Albums

www.picasaweb.google.com

Delicious

www.delicious.com

Twitter

www.twitter.com

Blogger
www.blogger.com

WordPress.com
www.wordpress.com

Movable Type
www.movabletype.com

LiveJournal
www.livejournal.com

Podcasting Tools
www.podcasting-tools.com

eBird
www.ebird.org

Web Style Guide
www.webstyleguide.com

Dotster.com
www.dotster.com

Open Directory
www.dmoz.org

Upperhost
www.upperhost.com

Webmonkey
www.webmonkey.com

About the Author

Randolph Hock, Ph.D.

Ran Hock divides his work time between writing and teaching. On the teaching side, he specializes in customized courses teaching people how to use the internet effectively (through his one-person company, Online Strategies). His courses have been offered—in the U.S. and in 11 other countries—to companies, government agencies, nongovernmental organizations, schools, universities, and associations. On the writing side, in addition to this book, he has written *The Extreme Searcher's Guide to Web Search Engines* (CyberAge Books, 1999, 2001), *Yahoo! to the Max* (CyberAge Books, 2005), and *The Traveler's Web* (CyberAge Books, 2007). He has also been a chemistry teacher and a librarian at two universities, as well as having held training and management positions with DIALOG Information Services and Knight-Ridder Information. He lives in Vienna, Virginia, with his wife, Pamela; they have two sons, Matthew and Stephen, and one daughter, Elizabeth. One of Ran's passions is travel, and he hopes to someday have time to return to his hobby of genealogy.

INDEX

Italicized page numbers refer to figures. Italicized page numbers followed by "t" refer to tables.

A

ABYZ News Links, 216
academic reference tools, 46–47, *47,* 77, 93
add-ons, 96
address books, 117
addresses
  ip, 104
  street, 91, 116, 117, 156–157, 176
Adobe Acrobat files (PDFs), 24, 67, 82, 90
Adobe Photoshop Elements, 189, 262
adult content filters, 79, 90, 101, 110, 122,
  200, 203
Advanced Research Projects Agency (ARPA),
  3
advanced search pages
  Bing, 101
  BoardReader, 136
  Flickr, 200
  Google, 78–80, *79,* 94
  Google Image Search, 192–193, *193*
  INFOMINE, 46–47, *47*
  Omgili, 136
  Open Directory, 40
  as search engine component, 62
  as search tool option, 17, 66
  Silobreaker, 228
  Yahoo!, 108–110, *109*
advertising, 70–71, 147
aerial views, 91–92, 94–96, *95,* 106
aggregation news sites, 213, 223–227, *224, 226*
Ajax (Asynchronous JavaScript And XML), 7
alert services, 28, 37, 97, 214, 215, 231–232
Aljazeera.net, 220–221
allinanchor:, 83
allintitle:, 81, 94
allinurl:, 81
AllTheWeb, 125

almanacs, 155–156
AltaVista, 125
AMA DoctorFinder, 177
Amazon
  book information, 166
  music information and sales, 207
  people searches using, 178
  personalization of results options, 7
  shopping, 237
  visualization engines using, 126
American Economic Association, 50
American Memory Project, 198–199
American Society of Association Executives
  (ASAE), 176–177
American University, 28
AND operations
  search engine comparisons, *70t, 123t*
  as search strategy, 16, 40, 42, *67,* 67–69, 80
Android, 116–117
Angie's List, 245
Answers.com, 155
AnyWho, 157
AOL (America Online), 5, 55, 58, 75, 147
AOL Instant Messenger, 147
AOL Search, 75
APIs (Application Program Interfaces), 5, 7
Apple, 207, *208*
apps, 116–117
Arabic news, 220–221
archives, 22, 132, 134, 145, 147, 214, 221. *See
  also* retrospective content
arithmetic calculations, 86, 106–107, 112–113
ARPA (Advanced Research Projects Agency),
  3
ARPANET, 3, 4
ASAE (American Society of Association
  Executives), 176–177

Ask.com (*formerly* Ask Jeeves), *70t,* 118–122, *119, 123t*
AskEraser, 122
associations, 134, 135, 176–177
asterisk (*), 42, 84
Asynchronous JavaScript And XML (Ajax), 7
attorney directories, 177
auctions, 243
audio
    copyright issues, 187–188, 202, 203
    developmental history of, 5
    directories for, 202–204
    historical resources, 206
    indexing capabilities, 24, 201
    movie sound clips, 207
    player software for accessing, 202
    podcasts, 205–206
    radio stations, 204–205
    as search tool, 9
    sound effects, 203–204
author:, 225, 229
author identifications, and content quality, 19,
    27–28
autos, 118

B

Baidu, 72
Barnes & Noble, 166
Bartleby.com, 20, 151, 157–160, *159,* 169, 170
BBBOnline, 247
BBC, 214, 218–219, *219*
BBN, 4
Because It's Time Network (BITNET), 4
Become.com, 241–242
Bedord, Jean, 263
Bellovin, Steve, 3, 133
BEOnline—Statistics, 164
Berners-Lee, Tim, 2, 4, 44
Best of History Web Sites, 47–48
bibliographic databases, 166–169
Big Boards, 135, 143
Bing
    advanced search pages, 101
    Boolean syntax for, 69, *70t,* 101
    databases in, 104–106, 210
    entertainment, 106
    history and overview, 100
    homepage, *100,* 100–101

image collections, 104–105, 189, 195–196,
    196
other features and content, 106–107, *123t,*
    223
results pages, 104, *105*
as search engine service provider, 107, 125
search features of, 102–104, *123t*
shortcuts, 73
BITNET (Because It's Time Network), 4
BitTorrent, 203
Bizrate, 245–246
Blekko, 122, 123–125, *125*
blinkx, 122, 127, 136, 205–206, 212
Blogger (Google), 98, 255, 256
Bloglines, 231, *231*
blogs (weblogs)
    creating personal, 98, 254–256, *256*
    Google search, 77, 93–94, 229
    groups compared to, 132
    history of, 5, 7
    microblogs compared to, 253
    as news sites, 228–229
    searches using, 124
blogurl:, 93
BoardReader, 134, 136
bookmarks, 98, 117, 253
books, 21, 77, 93, 165–170, *167*
bookstores, 166
Boolean operations
    Ask.com, 120
    Bing, 100, 101, 195
    Flickr, 200
    Google, 78, 80, 168, 192
    ipl², 42
    Open Directory, 40
    PAV—Play Audio Video, 203
    search engine comparisons, *70t, 123t*
    as search strategy, 16, 40, 42, *67,* 67–69, *69*
    Yahoo!, 108, 110–111, 226
breadcrumbs, 37
The British Library, 167–168
browsers
    Google, 57, 96, 98, 99
    history of, 5
    image displays and, 188, 194
    starter page selection for, 57
    toolbar options for, 96
businesses
    company information references, 173–176,
    175

company/product catalogs, 234–236, *236*
engine search options for, 92, 116, 122
news sites focusing on, 227
specialized directories for, 49–50, *50*
Business Navigator Web Guide, 49

C

cache:, 83
cached options, 22, 76, 83, 89, 113
The Cagle Post, 218
calculators, 86, 106–107, 112–113
calendars, 57, 77, 78, 98, 118
Calishain, Tara, 29
Canadian Intellectual Property Office—A Guide
    to Copyrights, 27
capitalization, 86
cartoons, political, 218
CBS Radio, 205
census data, 164, *165*
Central Intelligence Agency (CIA), 161, 171
CEOExpress, 49, 50
Cerf, Vinton G., 3, 6
CERN (Conseil Européen pour la Recherche
    Nucléaire), 2, 4
chat rooms, 147
A Chronology of U.S. Historical Documents, 170
CIA (Central Intelligence Agency), 161, 171
CIA World Factbook, 171
citations, 19, 26–27, 27–28
Citation Styles, Style Guides, and Avoiding
    Plagiarism, 28
CiteSeer, 181
cities, 92, 104, 106, 116, 162
citizen science, 257–258
Clark, David D., 6
classifieds, 243, 244
clip art, 201
clouds, concept, 127, *127*
clubs, 134
CNN, 220
College Board, 182
colleges, 182
Collins, 154
company information. *See* businesses
company/product catalogs, 234–236, *236*
competitive intelligence, 131, 146
CompletePlanet, 25–26
CompuServe, 5

computer-aided design (CAD) programs, 99
Computer Science Network (CSNET), 4
concepts, organization of, 13–14, 127, *127*
Congressional Research Service (CRS), 172
Conseil Européen pour la Recherche Nucléaire
    (CERN), 2, 4
Consumer Reports, 246
consumer rights and safety, 246–247
ConsumerSearch, 246
contains:, 103
content
    citations and using, 27–28
    copyright issues, 26–27
    of general web directories, 32
    international search engines restrictions, 72
    invisible/unindexed, 23–26
    of news resources, 215
    for personal websites, 258–259
    quality assessments of, 18–21
    of question and answer results, 121
    retrospective coverage of, 21–23, *23*
conversions
    currency, 160
    metric, 86, 112
copyright
    audio materials, 187–188, 202
    books and, 169
    Creative Commons options, 80, 197, 198, 201
    images, 187–188, 197
    overview, 26–27
    retrospective materials and, 21
Copyright and Fair Use in the UMUC Online or
    Face-to-Face Classroom, 27
Copyright Website, 27
Corbis Images, 189, 197, 198
CorporateInformation, 174
countries
    government information, 50–51
    people searches, 117
    political parties in, 52
    resource guides for, 162, 171
    searching by, 112, 117
    specialized directories for, 53
craigslist, 244
crawlers, 62
Creative Commons, 80, 197, 198, 201
cross-references (@), 33–34, 37, 39
crowdsourcing, 257–258
CRS (Congressional Research Service), 172
CSNET (Computer Science Network), 4

currency (timeliness), 19–20, 215, 221
currency conversions, 160
cyberguides, 11
Cyndi's List, 54

D

Daniel, Steve, 133
databases
    Ask.com, 121–122
    bibliographic, 166–169
    Bing, 104–106, 105
    Blekko, 124–125, *125*
    commercial services development, 3
    directories for, 25–26
    film, 136, 185
    of general directories, 32
    Google, 77, 90–96, *92, 95,* 242
    indexing of information on, 25
    literature, 180–182
    search engine comparisons, *123t*
    Yahoo!, 115–117, 238–240, *239*
date:, 168
date searching, 66, 82, 88, 123, 168
David Rumsey Historical Map Collection, 162
Deep Web, 23–26, 104
define, 85–86, 107
definitions, 85–86, 107
Deja News, 133–134
Delicious, 178, 253
Delphi Forums, 134, 135, 143
destination guides, 184
Dialog, 3
Diccionarios.com, 155
dictionaries, 153–155, *154*
digest-delivered messages, 145
Digital Librarian: A Librarian's Choice of the
    Best of the Web, 191, 202
The Digital Scriptorium, 189
Directgov: Website of the U.K. Government, 51,
    173
directories
    address/phone, 156–157
    audio resources, 202–204
    blog, 228–229
    company, 174–176, *175*
    image resource, 190–191
    mail list, 145–147, *146*
    podcast, 206, 207, *208*

professional, 177
shopping, 234
slashtag, 124
video resource, 208–209
web, 38, 42, 61, 116 (*see also* general web
    directories; specialized web directories)
web-hosting service, 264
discussion groups, 99, 132. *See also* groups
doctor directories, 177
documents
    government, 83
    historical, 21, 170
    web-based software creating, 77, 96, 99, 250
Dogpile, 72
domain names
    content quality and ownership identification,
        18–19
    history of, 5
    for personal websites, 262–263
    searches using, 65, 81, 103, 108, 111, 120
domain parking, 263
DomainTools, 18
Dotster, 263
Dreamweaver, 260–261, *261*
driving directions, 91–92, 106
Duke University, 133

E

eBay, 243, *244,* 247
eBird, 257–258
economics directories, 50
eConsumer.gov, 247
Education Atlas, 53–54
education directories, 53–54
EducationWorld, 53
Ellis, Jim, 3, 133
email
    alert services, 28, 37, 97, 214, 215, 220,
        231–232
    Ask.com notifications, 122
    domain name, 263
    Google, 77, 96, 98, 263
    history of, 2
    mailing lists, 132, 139, 141, 143–147, *146,*
        147–148
    Yahoo!, 57, 108, 117, 118, 263
emoticons, 3
employment databases, 115

Encyclopedia Britannica Online, 151–152
Encyclopedia.com, 150, 151, *152*
encyclopedias, 151–153, *152*
entertainment, 106, 118
Epinions, 246
eRepublic, 51
EuroDocs: Online Sources for European History, 170
Evaluating the Quality of WWW Resources, 21
Excel (Microsoft) files, 24, 67, 83, 90
Excite, 55, 58
Expedia, 185

F

Facebook
    history, 5, 6, 7, 8, 251
    instant messaging formats, 147
    music sharing, 205
    people searches using, 178, 179
    personal account creation, 251
    search engine links to, 101
    visualization engines using, 126
FactCheck.org, 183
facts, verification of, 20, 183–184
FareChase (Bing), 106
Federal Trade Commission (FTC), 247
FedStats, 165
feed:, 104
feeds. *See* RSS (Really Simple Syndication) feeds
File Transfer Protocol (FTP), 2
filetype:, 83, 96, 103, 112
file types
    for audio materials, 202
    for digital images, 188, 189
    peer-to-peer programs, 212, 213
    search engine options, 67, 80, 82–83, 90, 96, 103, 110, 112, *123t*
films, 24, 118, 136, 185, 207. *See also* video
finances, 77, 98, 101, 118, 160
FindLaw, 52–53
FindSounds, 203–204
Firefox, 57, 96, 98
flame wars, 148
Flickr, 7, 178, 189, 190, 199–201, 252
Fodor's, 184
folksonomies, 7
foreign exchange rates, 160

forums. *See* groups
forwarding messages, 148
Fotosearch, 197, 198
Free Graphics, 201
free material, 21
FreePint, 29
Froogle. *See* Google Product Search
FTC (Federal Trade Commission), 247
FTP (File Transfer Protocol), 2

G

Gallica, 21, 168–169
gateway sites. *See* portals
Gateway to Associations (ASAE), 177
Gateway to Library Catalogs (Library of Congress), 47, 169
gazetteers, 162
GBookmarks, 98
genealogy directories, 54
general web directories
    for children, 38
    database sizes of, 34
    examples of, 35–42, *36, 39, 41*
    finding, 42
    regional-specific, 40, 42
    role of, 9–10
    searchability of, 34
    search engines compared to, 9, 10, 11, 32, 34
    as search tool, overview, 9–10, *10,* 31, 32–33
    site classifications in, 33–34
    specialized directories compared to, 59
    strengths and weaknesses, 33
    usage situations, 10, 11, 34–35, 59
German language dictionaries, 155
GIF (Graphics Interchange Format), 188
globalEDGE, 49
GlobaLex, 53
Global Gazetteer, 162
Gmail (Google), 77, 96, 98, 263
Gnutella, 202
Goff, Bill, 50
Google
    advanced search pages, *12,* 78–80, *79*
    aerial/satellite views, 83, 92, 94–96, *95*
    alert services, 97, 232
    blogs by, 98, 255, 256
    blog searches, 77, 93–94, 229
    books, 21, 93, 168

Google (*cont.*)
Boolean syntax for, 69, *70t*
browsers of, 57, 96, 98, 99
databases in, 90–96, *92, 95*
database size, 76
email services, 77, 96, 98, 263
groups databases, 77, 91, 133, 134, 136–140, *138*
history and overview, 5, 75–76
homepage, *76,* 76–78
image collections, 91, 189, 190, 191–195, *193*
literature, 181–182
maps, 77, 91–93, *92*
menu search options, 63, *63*
news collections, 91, 223–225, *224*
other features and content, 97–99, *123t*
personalization of results options, 7
privacy settings, 78
results pages, *87,* 87–90, *89*
search engine services, 61
search features of, 80–86, *85, 123t*
shopping features and databases, 77, 91, 242
shortcuts, 73
social networking sites of, 77, 78, 89, 97, 179–180
toolbars, 96–97
usage and prominence, 75
Usenet archives on, 134
video search indexes, 209
video sites of, 77, 98, 178, 209, 210–211, *211*
visualization engines using, 126
web-based software of, 7, 96, 99, 250
web-hosting services, 99, 264
Google+, 77, 78, 89, 97, 179–180
Google Alerts, 232
Google Blog Search, 93–94, 229
Google Books, 21
Google Book Search, 93, 168
Google Chrome, 57, 96, 98, 99
Google Drive (*formerly* Google Docs), 7, 96, 99, 250
Google Earth, 83, 92, 94–96, *95*
Google Earth Pro, 95
Google eBooks, 168
Google Groups, 91, 134, 136–138, *138*
Google Hangouts, 98
Google Image Search, 191–195, *193*
Google Instant, 85, 90

Google Latitude, 99
Google Maps, 77, 91–93, *92*
Google Maps Mania, 93
Google Mobile, 98
Google Moderator, 99
Google News, 214, 223–225, *224*
Google Patent Search, 94
Google Product Search (*formerly* Froogle), 91, 242
Google Reader, 99
Google Scholar, 21, 93, 181–182
Google Sites, 99, 264
Google Toolbar, 96–97
Google Wallet, 99
gophers, 2, 4
government information, 50–52, *52,* 83, 165, 170–173
Government of Canada Official Website, 51–52
Governments on the WWW, 51, 171
Graphical User Interface (GUI), 2
Graphics Interchange Format (GIF), 188
graphics software, 260–262, *261*
Grokster, 202
groups (forums, message boards)
blogs compared to, 132
collections of, 133–134
communication methods of, 132
functions and benefits of, 131
Google as source of, 77, 91, 99, 134, 136–140, *138*
instant messaging, 147
locating and using, 134–135
mailing lists, 132, 143–147, *146*
message format, 132–133
moderated *vs.* unmoderated, 132
netiquette for, 147–148
other sources of, 142–143
search engines for, 135–136
as search tool, 9
specialized, 134
terminology used for, 132
Yahoo! as source of, 117, 135, 140–142, *141*
GUI (Graphical User Interface), 2

H

Hann, William, 29
harmful websites, 110
hasfeed:, 104

headline:, 225
healthfinder, 48
health information, 48, 115, 118
Hidden Web, 23–26
HighBeam Research, 181
historical documents, 21, 170
The History Channel: Video, 206
history-related directories, 47–48
Hobbes' Internet Timeline, 6
homepages
 Ask.com, 119, *119*
 Bartleby.com, *159*
 BBC News, 219, *219*
 Blekko, 124
 Google, *76,* 76–78
 Google News, 223–225, *224*
 linking to, 17
 of search engines, overview, 62
 Yahoo!, 108
 Yahoo! News, 225–226, *226*
Hoover's, 174–175, *175*
HotBot, 125
hot spots, 101, *102*
HowStuffWorks, 153
HTML (Hyper Text Markup Language), 62, 90,
 259, 260, 262
https:, 247
humanities directories, 47–48
hypertext (term origin), 3

I

IceRocket, 229
Image Collections Guides, 191
images
 Ask.com options, 121
 Bing collections, 104–105, 195–196, *196*
 clip art, 201
 collection types, 189
 commercial collections of, 197–198
 copyright issues, 187–188, 197
 directories for, 190
 file types for, 188
 Google collections, 77, 88, 91, 92, 98,
 191–195, *193*
 graphics software for personal websites,
 260–262, *261*
 "hot spots" for information on, 101, *102*
 individual collections, 198–199

 multimedia engines with, 203
 news resource guides, 217
 other collections for, 197
 searchability of, 190
 as search tool, 9
 storage and sharing sites for, 7, 98, 178, 189,
 190, 199–201, 252–253
 street views, 92
 technical information on, 188–189
 visualization engine searches, 127
 Yahoo! collections, 115, 196–197
IMDb (Internet Movie Database), 136, 185
I'm Feeling Lucky (Google), 76, *76*
inanchor:, 83, 103
inassignee:, 94
inauthor:, 168
inblogtitle:, 93
inbody:, 103
indexing and indexing programs, 24–25, 62
info:, 83
Infobel, 156
INFOMINE, 46–47, *47*
InfoPlease, 155–156
ingentaconnect, 21, 181
ininventor:, 94
inpostauthor:, 93
inposttitle:, 93
inpublisher:, 168
inreply:, 136
instant answers, 85, 90, 107
instant messaging, 118, 147
Intellius, 157, 178
International Network Working Group (INWG),
 3
internet, history and overview, 1–6
Internet Archive, 22, 204
Internet Assigned Numbers Authority, 18
Internet Explorer (Microsoft), 5, 57, 96, 98
Internet History and Growth, 6
Internet Movie Database (IMDb), 136, 185
Internet Protocol (IP), 3, 4, 5
Internet Public Library, 41
Internet Scout Project, 29
Internet Service Providers (ISPs), 133
Internet World Stats, 6
intitle:, 63, 76, 81, 93, 94, 102, 111, 120, 136,
 168, 225
intlpclass:, 94
intopic:, 136

inurl:, 64, 81, 120
Invisible Web, 23–26
The Invisible Web (Sherman and Price), 25
INWG (International Network Working Group),
      3
IP (Internet Protocol), 3, 4, 5
ip:, 104
iPhone, 116
ipl², 41–42
iPod, 207
isbn:, 168
ISPs (Internet Service Providers), 133
iTunes, 205, 206, 207
I've Got a Domain Name—Now What???
      (Bedord), 263
Ixquick, 72

J

journals, 21–22, 44, 167, 180–182
JPEG or JPG (Joint Photographic Experts
      Group), 188
Justia.com, 20–21

K

Kahn, Robert E. (Bob), 3, 6
Kathy Schrock's Guide for Educators, 53
Kazaa, 202
Kellysearch, 176, 235
Kidon Media-Link, 54, *55, 216, 217*
Kleinrock, Leonard, 6
Know Which Style to Use: Citation Styles, 28
Kompass, 176, 235
KompoZer, 260–261

L

language:, 103, 112
languages
      dictionary references for, 153–155
      news searches by, 216, 224, 226
      search engines in, 72
      search features using, 66, 82, 103, 110,
            111–112, *123t,* 136
      translation options, 71, 77, 90, 97
Lawyers.com, 177
learning videos, 189, 211, 262, 265, *266*
lectures, 203, 204, 211

legal directories, 52–53
Leiner, Barry M., 6
LEO Deutsch-Englisches Wörterbuch, 155
LexisNexis, 3, 221
Librarians' Internet Index, 41
library catalogs and directories, 47, 167, *167,*
      169
Library of Congress
      federal government resources, 172
      image collections, 198–199
      online library catalogs, 47, 167, *167,* 169
      science and technology directories, 48
      state and local government resources,
            172–173
      statistics collections, 164
Licklider, J. C. R., 3
link:, 82, 93
LinkedIn, 178, 179, 251–252
links
      content quality and, 20
      home page access and, 15
      popularity based on, 75
      as search option, *123t*
      search strategies using, 66, 82, 89–90, 93,
            101, 103, 108
LISTSERV, 144, 146–147
liszt.com. *See* Topica
literature databases, 180–182
LiveJournal, 256
loc: or *location:,* 103
local information, 116, 122, 172, 243
locations, default, 99, 103, 116
logos, 17
Lonely Planet, 184
L-Soft CataList, 146–147
lurking, 147
Lycos, 125
Lynch, Daniel C., 6

M

magazines, 21–22, 213, 216
mailing lists, 132, 135, 143–147, *146,* 147–148
mapping, *126,* 126–127, *127*
maps
      online reference tools for, *161,* 161–162
      search engine options, 77, 91–93, *92,* 106,
            116, 118
mashup maps, 93, 106

McKenzie, Kevin, 3
media, *123t. See also* images; news; video
Medline Plus, 48–49
merchant evaluations, 244–246
Merriam-Webster Online, 154, *154*
message boards. *See* groups
MetaCrawler, 72
metasearch engines, 72–73
metasites, 11, 42, 72
metatags, 62
metric-imperial conversions, 86, 112
Michigan State University, 49
microblogs, 136, 147, 253–254. *See also* Twitter
Microsoft Internet Explorer, 5, 57, 96, 98
minus (-) signs, 34, 76, 80, 102, 110, 120, 140
mobile services, 98, 116, 118
Monster, 115
Morpheus, 202
Mosaic, 5
motivation, and content quality, 19
Movable Type, 256
movies, 24, 118, 136, 185, 207. *See also* video
The MovieWavs Page, 207
MPEG (Moving Pictures Expert Group), 202
MSN, 58. *See also* Bing
MSNBC, 220, 223
music, 118, 170, 202–205, 207, *208*
musical instrument sounds, 203–204
My Maps (Google), 93
My Places (Bing), 106
mySimon, 240
My Space, 251
My Yahoo!
    news alerts, 214, 232
    as personalized portal, 9, 56–57, 58, *58*, 107
    RSS readers, 37, 230, 231
    stock quotes, 163
    weather, 160

N

Napster, 202
narcissistic web, 7
narrowing techniques
    group searches, 136
    image searches, 200
    search engine searches, 87–88, 104–105, 113, 122–124
    strategies, overview, 14–15, 16

video searches, 209
NASCAR, 119
National Institutes of Health, 48
National Library of Medicine, 48
National Public Radio (NPR), 223
National Science Foundation (NSF), 4
National Science Foundation Network (NSFNET), 4
national security, 227–228
Nelson, Ted, 3
nesting, 106–107, 113
netiquette, 147–148
Netscape Navigator, 5
networking sites. *See* social networking sites
Network Solutions, 18
news
    aggregation sites for, 223–227, *224, 226*
    alert services, 214, 231–232
    blogs, 228–229
    content variable factors, 214–215
    directories for, 54, *55*
    networks and newswires, 218–221, *219*
    newspapers, 22, 213, 221–222
    radio stations for, 222–223
    resource guides for, 215–218, *217*
    RSS feeds and readers, 230–231, *231*
    on search engines, 77, 87, 88, 91, 106, 116, 121
    search strategies, 214
    site types, 213–214
    specialized services, 227–228
    TV-specific videos for, 211–212
newsgroups, 2, 132, 133–134
News in Pictures, 217
NewsLink, 216
NewsNow, 226–227
newspapers, 22, 213, 216–217, 221–222
newsreaders, 133
NewsWealth, 216–217
newswires, 218–221, *219*
New York Times, 49
The New York Times Databank, 3
NOT operations
    search engine comparisons, *70t, 123t*
    as search strategy, 16, 42, 67, *67,* 67–69, 135
NPR (National Public Radio), 223
NSF (National Science Foundation), 4
NSFNET (National Science Foundation Network), 4, 5

numeric ranges, 83–84, *123t*
numrange:, 83–84

O

Ockerbloom, John Mark, 169
OFFSTATS, 164
OMG! (Yahoo!), 118
Omgili, 134, 135–136
Online Searcher (journal), 44
The Online Books Page, 21, 169
On the Internet (Leiner, Cerf, et al.), 6
Open CRS, 172
Open Directory (Open Directory Project)
    for international portal searches, 58
    overview, 9, *10,* 11, 38–40, *39, 41*
    searchability of, 34
    specialty search engine category in, 72
    web-hosting directories, 264
    Yahoo! Directory compared to, 34, 35, 38, 39
Orbitz, 185
OR operations
    search engine comparisons, *70t, 123t*
    as search strategy, 16, 40, 42, 67, *67,* 67–69
Overstock.com, 236, 237–238

P

Pandora, 205
Panoramio, 115
parentheses operations, 68, 69, 102, 106–107,
    108, 110, 113
passwords, 25
patent:, 94
patents, 94
PAV—Play Audio Video, 203
Paypal, 247
PBworks, 250
PDFs (Portable Document Formats), 24, 67, 82,
    90
peer-to-peer (P2P) programs, 202, 203
PeopleFinders, 178
people searches, 117, 157, 177–178
Perry-Castañeda Library Map Collection, 161,
    161
personalizability, 56–57, 78, 97, 104, 215
Peters, Tom, 259
Peterson's, 182
phone numbers, 91, 116, 117, 156–157, 176

photographs. *See* images
phrase searching, 16, 40, 64, *69,* 84, 108, 192
physical science directories, 48–49
Picasa Web Albums, 77, 98, 178, 189, 199,
    252–253
Picsearch, 197
Pioch, Nicolas, 199
Pipl, 178
pixels, 188
Pixlr, 189
players, 202
plus signs (+), 97, 102, 110
PNG (Portable Network Graphics), 188
Podcast Alley, 206
Podcastdirectory.com, 206
Podcasting Tools, 257
podcasts, 7, 205–206, 207, *208,* 257
political cartoons, 218
political fact-checking, 183–184
political parties directories, 52
Political Resources on the Net, 52
PolitiFact, 184
Polly, Jean Armour, 5
Portable Document Formats (PDFs), 24, 67, 82,
    90
Portable Network Graphics (PNG), 188
portals (gateway sites). *See also* My Yahoo!
    definition, 9
    for news alerts, 214, 232
    reference information provided by, 160, 163
    as search tool, overview, 31, *48,* 54–59
    for specialized directories, 45
Postel, Jon, 6
Powell, Colin, 46
Powerpoint (Microsoft) files, 67, 83, 90
precision, 14–15. *See also* narrowing techniques
prefer:, 104
prefixes (qualifying a term). *See also* prefix
    examples
    aerial/satellite view searches, 96
    Ask.com, 120
    Bing options, 102–104
    blog searches, 229
    book searches, 168
    Google options, 76, 81–84, 93, 94, 96
    image searches, 192
    news searches, 225
    Omgili options, 136
    patent searches, 94

as search engine strategy, 63, *63,* 64, 65
video searches, 209
Yahoo! options, 111–112
prefix examples
allinanchor:, 83
allintitle:, 81, 94
allinurl:, 81
author:, 225, 229
blogurl:, 93
cache:, 83
contains:, 103
date:, 168
define, 85–86, 107
feed:, 104
filetype:, 83, 96, 103, 112
hasfeed:, 104
headline:, 225
inanchor:, 83, 103
inassignee:, 94
inauthor:, 168
inblogtitle:, 93
inbody:, 103
info:, 83
ininventor:, 94
inpostauthor:, 93
inposttitle:, 93
inpublisher:, 168
inreply:, 136
intitle:, 63, 76, 81, 93, 94, 102, 111, 120, 136, 168, 225
intlpclass:, 94
intopic:, 136
inurl:, 64, 81, 120
ip:, 104
isbn:, 168
language:, 103, 112
link:, 82, 93
loc: or *location:,* 103
numrange:, 83–84
patent:, 94
prefer:, 104
related:, 83
site:, 65, 81, 82, 93, 103, 111, 120, 192, 209
source:, 225
stocks:, 83
tag:, 229
title:, 209, 229
url:, 103, 111, 120
uspclass:, 94

PressDisplay.com, 222
Price, Gary, 25, 29
price comparisons, 238–242, *239, 241*
PriceGrabber, 240, *241*
privacy, 8, 78, 148
Prodigy, 5
product catalogs, 234–236, *236*
product evaluations, 244–246
products. *See* shopping
professional directories, 177
Project Gutenberg, 21, 169–170
"A Protocol for Packet Network Interconnection" (Cerf and Kahn), 3
P2P (peer-to-peer) programs, 202, 203
PubMed, 181
punctuation, 86. *See also specific operational symbols*
Purdue University, 4

Q

quality assessments, 18–21, 121
questions and answers (Q&A), 118, 119, *119,* 121, 155
QuickTime, 202
Quintura, 127, *127*
quotation marks, 16, 40, 64, 73, 76, 85, 110, 135, 156
quotations, 157–160, *159*
The Quotations Page, 157

R

Radio-Locator, 204–205, 222–223
radio stations, 204–205, 207, 213, 216, 222–223
RadioStationWorld, 223
rail timetables, 185
Rand Corporation, 3, 4
rankings. *See* relevance ranking
RealAudio, 5
Really Simple Syndication. *See* RSS
RealPlayer, 202
recall, 14–15, 64
Refdesk, 46
reference tools
academic/scholarly, 46–47, *47,* 77, 93
address/phone, 91–92, *92,* 156–157
almanacs, 155–156
associations, 176–177

reference tools (*cont.*)
    books, 21, 77, 93, 165–170, *167*
    colleges and universities, 182
    combined, 155–156
    company information, 173–176, *175*
    dictionaries, 153–155, *154*
    encyclopedias, 151–153, *152*
    fact-checking, 183–184
    film, 185
    foreign exchange rates/currency converters,
        160
    gazetteers, 162
    governments and countries, 170–173
    historical documents, 170
    literature, 180–182
    maps, *161,* 161–162
    people information, 177–180
    questions and answers, 118, 119, *119,* 121,
        122
    quotations, 157–160, *159*
    selection criteria, 150
    specialized directories for, 46–47, *47*
    statistics, 163–165, *165*
    stock quotes, 163
    travel, 184–185
    usage tricks, 150
    usefulness assessments, 150–151
    weather, 160
    ZIP codes, 162
related:, 83
related (similar) pages, 83, 113, *123t*
relevance ranking
    directories *vs.* search engines, 9, 33
    prefix searches for, 104
    results pages featuring, 71, 88, 104
    as search engine feature, 62
    search strategies using, 15–16, 104–105
    visualization engines with, 127
religion directories, 48
ResearchBuzz, 29
reservations, travel, 185
resources
    archives and retrospective content, 22
    citation, 28
    content quality, 20–21
    copyright, 27
    databases and specialty search programs,
        25–26
    domain ownership, 18

    general regional directories, 42
    internet history, 6
    for keeping up-to-date on internet, 28–29
    portals, 59
Resources for Economists on the Internet, 50
ResourceShelf, 29
results pages
    Ask.com, 121
    Bing, 104, *105,* 195, *196*
    Blekko, 124, *125*
    Google, *87,* 87–90, *89*
    Google Groups, 138, *138*
    Google Image Search, *193,* 193–194
    Omgili, 135–136
    Quintura, 127, *127*
    of search engines, overview, 70–71, *123t*
    Touch Graph, *126,* 126–127
    visualization engines, *126,* 126–127, *127*
    Yahoo!, 113–115, *114,* 197
    You Tube, 211, *211*
    Zuula, *128*
retrospective content
    cached options, 22, 76, 83, 89, 113
    group message archives, 132, 147
    mailing list messages, 145
    news resources, 214, 221, 225
    types of documents with, 21–23, *23*
Reuters, 220
reverse phone number search, 157
Roberts, Larry G., 6
robots.txt files, 24
Royal Radar Establishment, 3
RSS (Really Simple Syndication) feeds
    blog searching and, 229
    definition, 37
    for news, 215, 220, 230–231, *231*
    podcast publishing using, 205
    for portals, 58–59
    prefix searches for, 104
    readers for, 77, 99, 230–231, *231*
    for TV-specific videos, 212
    as Web 2.0 forerunner, 7
    Yahoo! Directory alert services using, 37

S

Safari, 57
SafeSearch, 79, 90, 101, 110
satellite views, 91–92, 94–96, *95,* 106

scholarly directories and references, 46–47, *47,* 93, 180–182
Scholastic Aptitude Tests (SATs), 182
science directories, 48–49
Scirus, 181
Scout Report, 29
SDC Orbit, 3
search boxes
    Bing, 100, *100*
    of directories, 34, 37, 38, 42
    Google, 76, *76,* 78, 81, 86
    information not indexed due to, 25
    of search engines, overview, 61, 62, 63, *63*
    Yahoo!, 108
Search.com, 72
Search Engine Colossus, 42
Search Engine Guide, 44
search engine programs, 62
search engines. *See also* Ask.com; Bing; Google; Yahoo!
    accounts for, 71
    audio, 203–204
    blog searches, 228–229
    Boolean syntax comparisons, *70t*
    browsing *vs.,* 31
    comparison searches, *128,* 128–129
    components of, 61–62
    definition, 61
    defunct, 125
    directories compared to, 9, 10, 11, 32, 34, 61
    features of major, *123t*
    for groups, 135–136
    for historical quotations, 160
    history of, 5
    image collections in, 191–197, *193, 196*
    information not indexed in, 24–25
    keeping up-to-date on, 28–29
    metasearch (multiple engine searches), 72–73
    news aggregation, 223–227
    overlap, 69–70
    for people searches, 117, 157, 178
    presentation of, 63, *63*
    results pages, 70–71
    retrospective content searches in, 22
    role of, 11
    search options for, 64–69, *67, 69, 70t*
    as search tool, 11, *12*
    shortcuts for, 72
    with slashtag features, 122, 123–125, *125*
    specialty, 71–72
    for statistics, 163–164
    visualization, *126,* 126–127, *127*
search history, deletion of, 122
searching, overview
    citation of resources, 27–28
    content and, 18–26
    copyright and, 26–27
    resources for, 28–29
    strategies for, 13–18, *17*
    tools for, 8–12
    up-to-date resources, 28–29
SearchScan, 110
Selected Internet Resources in Science and Technology, 48
series discussions, 99
ShadowTV, 212
sharing sites, 199–201, 252–253. *See also* YouTube
sheet music, 170
Sherman, Chris, 25
Shockwave Flash, 83
shopping
    auctions, 243, *244*
    categories of, 233–234
    classifieds, 243, 244
    company/product catalogs, 234–236, *236*
    consumer rights and safety, 246–247
    price comparison sites, 238–242, *239, 241*
    product and merchant evaluations, 244–246
    search engine features and databases, 77, 91, 105, 115, 238–240, *239,* 242
    search strategies, 234
    shopping mall sites, 236–238
Shopping.com, 240–241
shopping malls, 236–238
ShoppingSpot.com, 234
Shopzilla, 241
shortcuts, 72, 73
SiloBreaker, 227–228
similar (related) pages, 83, 113, *123t*
site:, 65, 81, 82, 93, 103, 111, 120, 192, 209
sitelinks, 89–90
sites
    indexes for, 25
    search boxes for, 25
    searches using, 65, 81–82, 103, 111, 120, 124
    search features comparisons, *123t*
Sketchup (Google), 99

slashtags, 122–123, 124
Slater, William F., III, 6
Snopes.com, 183
social bookmarking sites, 253
social networking sites. *See also* Facebook
  benefits of, 8
  creating personal, 251–252
  Google options, 77, 78, 89, 97
  history, 7–8
  instant messaging of, 147
  privacy issues, 8
  as research tools, 178–180
social sciences directories, 47–48
Solusource, 235
sound clips, 207
sound effects, 203–204
source:, 225
sources, 18–19, 20, 26–27, 215
spam, 5, 62, 71, 147–148
Spanish language dictionaries, 155
specialized web directories
  academic/reference examples, 46–47, *47*
  business/economics examples, 49–50, *50*
  categories of, 11–12
  education examples, 53–54
  finding, 43–45
  genealogy examples, 54
  general directories compared to, 59
  government/governments examples, 50–52,
    52
  legal examples, 52–53
  news examples, 54, *55*
  physical/life science and technology exam-
    ples, 48–49
  role of, 12
  as search tool, overview, 11–12, 31, 42–43
  selection factors, 45
  shopping, 234–236, *236*
  social sciences/humanities examples, 47–48
  strengths and weaknesses, 43
  travel examples, 54
  for unindexed information, 25
  usage situations, 59
speeches, 203, 204
spelling, 70, 88, 97, 114–115
spiders, 62
Sponsor Links/Results, 70
Spotify, 205
Sputnik, influence of, 3

start pages, 54–55, 56, 57
statistics, 163–165, *165*
stemming, *123t*
stocks, 96, 98, 106, 113, 162–163
stocks:, 83
Stock.XCHNG, 198
stopwords, 110
streaming, 5, 204, 205, 216
streets, 92
suggestions feature, 85, *85,* 115
"surfing" (term origin), 5
synonyms, 84–85

T

tag:, 229
tags, 7, 98, 190, 200, 229, 253
TCP (Transmission Control Protocol), 3, 4
technology directories, 48
Technorati, 229
Telenet, 3, 4
telephone numbers, 91, 116, 117, 146–157, 176
television, 211–212, 213, 216
terms
  frequency of occurrence graphs, 136
  qualifying, 63 (*see also* prefixes; prefix
    examples)
  relevance ranking and, as search strategy,
    15–16, *17*
  selection of, as search strategy, 14
  visualization engines and concept clouds of,
    127, *127*
  word order, 86
THOMAS: Legislative Information on the
    Internet, 172
ThomasNet, 175–176, 235, *236*
Thorn Tree Forum, 184
threads, 132–133
tilde characters (~), 19, 84–85
timeliness, 19–20, 215, 221
title:, 209, 229
title searching, 15, 65, 81, 102, 111, 120, *123t*
Today's Front Pages, 222
toolbars, 96–97, 117
Topica (*formerly* liszt.com), 145–146, *146*
top-level domains, 19, 65, 103, 108, 111, 120,
    263
torrent files, 203
TouchGraph, *126,* 126–127

Traffick: Frequently Asked Questions About Portals, 59
translations, 71, 77, 90, 96
Transmission Control Protocol (TCP), 3, 4
travel
    country profiles, 162, 171
    destination guides, 184
    foreign exchange rates/currency converters, 160
    overview, 184
    reservation sites, 106, 185
    as search engine feature, 106, 107, 118
    specialized directories for, 54
    weather, 160
The Traveler's Web, 54
Travelocity, 185
trending, 114
truncation, 84, 140
Truscott, Tom, 3, 133
TurboScout, 129
tutorials, 189, 211, 262, 265, *266*
TVEyes, 212
Twitter, 5–8, 136, 147, 180, 254
Tyburski, Genie, 20–21
Tymnet, 3

U

U.K. Foreign & Commonwealth Office—Country Profiles, 171
U.K. government information, 51, 173
U.K. Intellectual Property Office—A Guide to Copyrights, 27
universities, 182
University College of London, 3
University of Auckland Library, 164
University of California, 46
University of Maryland, 27
University of Minnesota, 191
University of North Carolina, 133
University of Texas, 161
University of Washington, 4
Upperhost, 264
up-to-date content, 19–20
up-to-date resources, 28–29
url:, 103, 111, 120
URLs
    citations of, 28
    consumer safety indications, 247

content quality assessments, 18–19
information not indexed, 24
search engine submission and usage, 62
searches using, 65, 66, 80, 81, 83, 103, 111, 120, 136
search features comparisons, *123t*
U.S. Census Bureau, 164, *165*
U.S. Copyright Office, 27
U.S. Department of Health and Human Services, 48
U.S. government information, 51, *52,* 94, 165, 171–173
U.S. Government Printing Office—FDsys, 172
U.S. historical documents, 170
U.S. Patent and Trademark Office (USPTO), 94
U.S. state resources, 172–173
USA.gov, 51, 171
USA Statistics in Brief, 164, *165*
Usenet, 2, 7, 133–134, 137
uspclass:, 94

V

Valparaiso University, 21
video
    Ask.com, 122
    Bing collections, 105, 210
    copyright issues and, 187–188
    directories for, 208–209
    Google collections, 209
    Google sites, 77, 98, 178, 209, 210–211, *211*
    indexing capabilities, 24, 201
    multimedia engines with, 203
    player software for accessing, 202
    search engines for, 209–211
    search options for, 208
    TV-specific search engines, 211–212
    visualization engine searches, 127
    Yahoo! collections, 115, 118, 209–110
videoconferencing, 98
Virtual Chase: Information Quality, 20–21
Virtual Earth (MSN), 106
Virtual Religion Index, 48
visualization search engines, *126,* 126–127, *127*
voice recognition, 209, 212
voice search, 99
Voila!, 55

W

Wall It, 212
Wayback Machine, 22, *23*
Wayp International White and Yellow Pages, 156
weather, 92, 160
Weather Underground, 160
Web 2.0, 5, 7–8, 132, 249
"the web" (term usage), 1–2
web-based software, 7, 96, 99, 250
WebCrawler, 5
web-hosting services, 260, 262–263, 264–265
webliographies, 11, 42
weblogs. *See* blogs
Webmonkey, 265, *266*
WebMuseum, 199
web presence options. *See also* websites, personal
  blogs, 254–256, *256*
  crowdsourcing, 257–258
  microblogs, 253–254
  participation methods, 249
  podcasts, 257
  sharing sites, 252–253
  social networking sites, 251–252
  web-based software to create, 250
website-building software, 260–262, *261*
websites, personal
  building-assistance sites, 265–266, *266*
  prerequisites for, 260–263, *261*
  publishing methods for, 264–265
  purpose of, 258–259
  search engine options for, 99
WELL (Whole Earth 'Lectronic Link), 4
WhitePages, 157
white pages, 117, 156–157
WHOIS Search, 18
Wikipedia, 122, 152–153, 250
wikis, 7, 152, 250
wildcard words and characters, 84
Windows Media Player (Microsoft), 202
Winer, Dave, 228
Wolff, Stephen, 6
Word (Microsoft) files, 24, 67, 83, 90
WordPress.com, 255
World Gazetteer, 162
World Wide Web ("the web"), history, 1–2, 4
Wright Investors' Service, 174
writing quality and style, 19, 258

writings, ancient, 21
WWW Virtual Library, 44

X

XML, 7, 230

Y

Yahoo!
  advanced search pages, 108–110, *109*
  alert services, 214, 232
  Boolean syntax for, 69, *69, 70t*
  currency conversion, 160
  databases in, 115–117
  defunct search engines owned by, 125
  email services, 57, 108, 117, 118, 263
  entertainment, 118
  finances, 118, 163
  general web directories of (*see* Yahoo! Directory)
  groups, 117, 135, 140–142, *141*
  history and overview, 107
  homepage, 108
  image collections, 115, 196–197
  instant messaging, 147
  menu search options, 63, *63*
  news, 225–226, *226*
  other features and content, 117–118
  people search, 117, 157
  photograph storing and sharing (*see* Flickr)
  portal pages, 57 (*see also* My Yahoo!)
  preferences pages, 110, 113
  relevance ranking examples, *14*
  results page, 113–115, *114*
  RSS reader features, 37, 230, 231
  search engine services, 61, 107
  search features, 110–113, *123t*
  search page, 107, *107*
  shopping features and databases, 115, 238–240, *239*
  shortcuts, 73
  stock quotes, 163
  toolbars, 117
  videos, 209–210
  visualization engines using, 127
  weather, 160
Yahoo! Apps, 116–117
Yahoo! Directory
  clip art, 201

Yahoo! Directory (*cont.*)
    description and overview, 9, 11, 35–38, *36,*
      116
    Open Directory compared to, 34, 35, 38, 39
    searchability of, 34
    usage and prominence, 9, 33
Yahoo! Finance, 163
Yahoo! Finance—Currency Converter, 160
Yahoo! for Kids, 127
Yahoo! Groups, 117, 135, 140–142, *141*
Yahoo! Kids, 38
Yahoo! Local, 116
Yahoo! Mail, 57, 108, 117, 118, 263
Yahoo! News, 225–226, *226*
Yahoo! People Search, 117, 157

Yahoo! Search, 107, 108
Yahoo! Shopping, 115, 238–240, *239*
Yahoo! Video Search, 209–210
Yandex, 72, 127
yellow pages, 106, 116, 156–157
Yippy, 72, 73
YourDictionary, 153
YouTube, 77, 98, 178, 209, 210–211, *211*
Yuku, 134, 135, 143

Z

ZIP codes, 162
Zuula, 128, *128*

More Great Books from Information Today, Inc.

Web of Deceit
Misinformation and Manipulation in the Age of Social Media

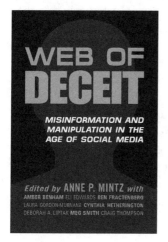

Edited by Anne P. Mintz

For all its amazing benefits, the worldwide social media phenomenon has provided manipulative people and organizations with the tools (and human targets) that allow hoaxes and con games to be perpetrated on a vast scale. In this eye-opening follow-up to her popular 2002 book, *Web of Deception*, Anne P. Mintz brings together a team of experts to explain how misinformation is intentionally spread and to illuminate the dangers in a range of critical areas. *Web of Deceit* is a must-read for any internet user who wants to avoid being victimized.

224 pp/softbound/ISBN 978-0-910965-91-0 $29.95

True Crime Online
Shocking Stories of Scamming, Stalking, Murder, and Mayhem

By J. A. Hitchcock

This new book by a top cybercrime expert and victim's advocate explores horrific real-life crimes with roots in cyberspace. Author J. A. Hitchcock (*Net Crimes & Misdemeanors*) is celebrated for her work to pass tough cybercrime legislation, train law enforcement personnel, and help victims fight back. In *True Crime Online*, she journeys into the darkest recesses of the internet to document the most depraved criminals imaginable, from bullies and stalkers to scam artists, sexual predators, and serial killers.

True Crime Online is a must-read for true crime aficionados and fans of such television fare as *48 Hours Mystery*, *Forensic Files*, and the Investigation Discovery channel. You'll never think about your online "friends" the same way again!

176 pp/softbound/ISBN 978-1-937290-00-9 $14.95

Face2Face
Using Facebook, Twitter, and Other Social Media Tools to Create Great Customer Connections

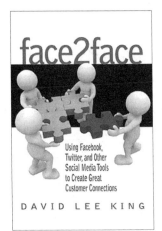

By David Lee King

Consumer-centric organizations know that social media can be used to engage with customers, leading to increased satisfaction and the acquisition of new customers through the power of viral marketing—yet relatively few firms are doing it well. With *Face2Face*, David Lee King (*Designing the Digital Experience*) presents a practical guide for any organization that aspires to create deep, direct, and rewarding relationships with patrons and prospects.

Going far beyond Facebook and Twitter, King demonstrates how a range of Web 2.0 tools and techniques can be used to start and sustain conversations and humanize the organization in the eyes of those it seeks to serve. He uses real-world examples to illustrate the do's and don'ts of responding to criticism, and explains why and how listening, tone, human-centered site design, and measuring results are all critical components of any customer engagement strategy.

216 pp/softbound/ISBN 978-0-910965-99-6 $24.95

Research on Main Street
Using the Web to Find Local Business and Market Information

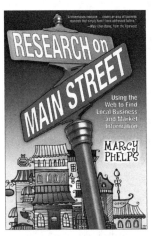

By Marcy Phelps

Even in a global economy, businesses need targeted, localized information about customers, companies, and industries. But as skilled searchers know, adding the element of geography to any research project creates new challenges. With *Research on Main Street*, Marcy Phelps presents a unique and useful guide to finding business and market information about places—including counties, cities, census blocks, and other sub-state areas—using free and low-cost online resources. You'll learn expert techniques and strategies for approaching location-specific research, including advice on how to tap local sources for in-depth information about business and economic conditions, issues, and outlooks. Don't miss the author's companion website at www.ResearchOnMainStreet.com!

280 pp/softbound/ISBN 978-0-910965-88-0 $29.95

Teach Beyond Your Reach, 2nd Edition

An Instructor's Guide to Developing and Running Successful Distance Learning Classes, Workshops, Training Sessions, and More

By Robin Neidorf

In this expanded new edition, Robin Neidorf takes a practical, curriculum-focused approach designed to help distance educators develop and deliver courses and training sessions. She shares best practices, surveys the tools of the trade, and covers such key issues as instructional design, course craft, adult learning styles, student-teacher interaction, and learning communities.

224 pp/softbound/ISBN 978-1-937290-01-6 $29.95

Dancing With Digital Natives

Staying in Step With the Generation That's Transforming the Way Business Is Done

Edited by Michelle Manafy and Heidi Gautschi

Generational differences have always influenced how business is done, but in the case of digital natives—those immersed in digital technology from birth—we are witnessing a tectonic shift. As an always connected, socially networked generation increasingly dominates business and society, organizations can ignore the implications only at the risk of irrelevance. In this fascinating book, Michelle Manafy, Heidi Gautschi, and a stellar assemblage of experts from business and academia provide vital insights into the characteristics of this transformative generation. Here is an in-depth look at how digital natives work, shop, play and learn, along with practical advice geared to help managers, marketers, coworkers, and educators maximize their interactions and create environments where everyone wins.

408 pp/hardbound/ISBN 978-0-910965-87-3 $27.95

The Internet Book of Life
Use the Web to Grow Richer, Smarter, Healthier, and Happier

By Irene E. McDermott

No matter what you want to accomplish in life, there are quality, free online resources available to help—if you only had the time to find and evaluate them all! Now, noted author, columnist, reference librarian, and working mom Irene McDermott rides to the rescue with *The Internet Book of Life*—a handy guide to websites, blogs, online tools, and mobile apps. From matters of personal finance to parenting, relationships, health and medicine, careers, travel, hobbies, pets, home improvement, and more, *The Internet Book of Life*—along with its supporting blog addresses real-life goals, dilemmas, and solutions.

320 pp/softbound/ISBN 978-0-910965-89-7 $19.95

Building & Running a Successful Research Business, 2nd Edition
A Guide for the Independent Information Professional

By Mary Ellen Bates

This is the handbook every aspiring independent information professional needs to launch, manage, and build a research business. Organized into four sections, the book walks you through every step of the process. Author and long-time independent researcher Mary Ellen Bates covers everything from "is this right for you?" to closing the sale, managing clients, promoting your business, and tapping into powerful information sources.

488 pp/softbound/ISBN 978-0-910965-85-9 $34.95